Study Guide

for

Cole and Smith's

Criminal Justice in America

Fourth Edition

Scott P. Johnson, Ph.D.
Frostburg State University

THOMSON

WADSWORTH

Australia • Canada • Mexico • Singapore • Spain • United Kingdom • United States

Printed in the United States of America
1 2 3 4 5 6 7 07 06 05 04

Printer: Thomson West

0-534-62968-7

For more information about our products,
contact us at:
Thomson Learning Academic Resource Center
1-800-423-0563

For permission to use material from this text or
product, submit a request online at
http://www.thomsonrights.com
Any additional questions about permissions can be
submitted at
thomsonrights@thomson.com

Thomson Wadsworth
10 Davis Drive
Belmont, CA 94002-3098
USA

Asia
Thomson Learning
5 Shenton Way #01-01
UIC Building
Singapore 068808

Australia/New Zealand
Thomson Learning
102 Dodds Street
Southbank, Victoria 3006
Australia

Canada
Nelson
1120 Birchmount Road
Toronto, Ontario M1K 5G4
Canada

Europe/Middle East/South Africa
Thomson Learning
High Holborn House
50/51 Bedford Row
London WC1R 4LR
United Kingdom

Latin America
Thomson Learning
Seneca, 53
Colonia Polanco
11560 Mexico D.F.
Mexico

Spain/Portugal
Paraninfo
Calle/Magallanes, 25
28015 Madrid, Spain

TABLE OF CONTENTS

Introduction

1	The Criminal Justice System	1
2	Crime and Justice in America	18
3	Criminal Justice and The Rule of Law	35
4	Police	53
5	Police Officers and Law Enforcement Operations	68
6	Police and Constitutional Law	82
7	Policing: Issues and Trends	94
8	Courts and Adjudication	108
9	Pretrial Procedures, Plea Bargaining, and the Criminal Trial	126
10	Punishment and Sentencing	146
11	Corrections	163
12	Community Corrections: Probation and Intermediate Sanctions	183
13	Incarceration and Prison Society	199
14	Reentry into the Community	221
15	The Juvenile Justice	234
	ANSWER KEY	250

INTRODUCTION

By using this study guide, you can learn and review the material in the textbook. The summaries and outlines for each chapter highlight the important topics covered in the text. In addition, the review questions will reinforce the key terms and people from each chapter. By reviewing the study guide as you complete each chapter and prior to each exam, you should be able to put forth your best effort on exams and, more importantly, you should be able to absorb, understand, and retain more ideas and information from the course. Each chapter also includes Multiple Choice questions, True and False questions and "Worksheet" assignments. If your instructor does not assign them to you, you may want to do them on your own to expand your knowledge.

This study guide is not the only resource available to support your study of criminal justice. In conjunction with your textbook, you can find a wealth of information about criminal justice on the World Wide Web. By exploring and utilizing web sites, you can study materials from your textbook while obtaining a wealth of additional information. Wadsworth Publishing's criminal justice web site (**http://cj.wadsworth.com**) provides a valuable resource, including links to hundreds of web sites containing information about criminal justice. Use this web site as your starting point to undertake research, explore career options, or simply keep up to date with developments in criminal justice. Contemporary criminal justice is being shaped by new technologies and instant access to world-wide sources of information. Here is your chance to step into the twenty-first century by gaining valuable knowledge and skills involving computers and new information technologies.

Practical Advice for Students

A study guide is a useful tool for improving one's academic performance. However, a study guide cannot "rescue" those who have neglected their assignments and failed to make a solid effort to succeed throughout the entire semester. You can best achieve your academic goals by approaching this course -- and every other course -- with a few important principles in mind. These principles, if taken to heart, can help any student achieve better grades and gain greater benefits from his or her education.

1. Complete all reading assignments **before** the materials are covered in class.

You will have a much better understanding of lectures and class discussions if you have become familiar with assigned topics beforehand. Although today's students lead busy lives with jobs, family responsibilities, active social lives, and community involvement, it is possible for nearly any student to fulfill class reading assignments merely by making such assignments a regular part of his or her weekly schedule. If you set aside specific hours each week for reading and studying criminal justice materials, just as you may set aside certain hours each week for friends or favorite television shows, you will automatically become well-prepared for class as part of your regular weekly routine.

2. Take notes as you read just as you would during a lecture.

You will gain much greater understanding of the material in the textbook if you merely spend the extra time that it takes to write notes as you read. The process of writing notes forces you to organize material and it reinforces in your memory the important points from the reading assignments. In addition, when it is time to study for exams, you will have additional notes to assist your reviewing process.

3. Be active in class. Even if you do not think you have important comments to contribute, think of questions to ask that will expand your knowledge about the material in the textbook.

The greatest regret of many former students is that they did not take a more active role in their own education. It can be very easy to be passive in the classroom, especially in large classes. However, students who make an effort to participate actively in class discussions gain huge benefits. By asking questions or volunteering to participate in discussions, you keep your mind actively involved in exploring the topics of the course. Passive students merely receive and record information, while active students gain analytical insights by questioning and exploring ideas. In addition, you will have an easier time learning and remembering concepts in any course if you are actively involved in discussing them.

Moreover, as a practical matter, active students attract the attention of instructors. This attention can provide many additional benefits. Such students are most likely to develop relationships with instructors that enable them to meet and discuss freely the course material, career planning, and other useful subjects. Instructors often formally or informally give extra credit toward high grades to students who make regular contributions to class discussions. Active students also will inevitably receive better letters of recommendation if they ever need to use a professor as a reference for a job or graduate school application.

It is very easy to be active in class, even if you are struggling to understand or to generate your own interest in specific course topics. As you do the reading for each assignment, think of three or four comments and questions to take to class. Write them down and raise them at appropriate times during class discussions. Even students who do not feel confident about their abilities to contribute significantly to class discussions can become actively involved by planning their comments and questions before they arrive at class. After consciously preparing comments and questions for a few classes, most students find that they start to think of additional questions and gain new insights as they participate in each class. Eventually students feel so "connected" to the lectures and discussions that their interest and enthusiasm generate questions and comments during each class whether or not they formally prepared specific comments beforehand.

4. Push yourself to go above and beyond the minimum expectations for the course.

You will learn much more and get better grades if you push yourself to go beyond the minimum expectations for the course. When you encounter a topic that interests you in the textbook, go to the library and read more about the subject by using the sources listed at the end of each textbook chapter. If you receive a writing assignment, after checking with the instructor to make sure that there is no *maximum page limit*, write a longer paper than required for the assignment. Pushing yourself to do extra work will add to your knowledge and interest, give you more information and understanding to exhibit in the exams, and impress the instructor with your enthusiasm and effort. Many students throughout the country who are not naturally "gifted" consistently receive higher grades than so-called "smarter" students simply by out-working them. Virtually every college instructor has had students who achieved 'A's through determination, willpower, and consistent effort, while naturally gifted students may receive lower grades by choosing to coast through their courses rather than apply themselves. You never know how well you can do in your studies until you really make the effort to do your best work. Many students will surprise themselves and find that they are "smarter" than they thought when they get high grades from making the effort to go above and beyond minimum course requirements. Even if you do not receive an 'A' after putting forth maximum effort, at least you can rest easy knowing that you gave your best effort. This is a much better feeling than receiving a 'B-' and always wondering whether or not you could have done better if you had tried harder.

5. Take pride in your work.

Do not hand in sloppy work. Proofread your papers. Have friends or family members read your work to check for silly errors in spelling, typing, and grammar. Everyone makes mistakes, especially in their formal writing assignments. The strong students are often separated from the weak students by taking the extra time to double-check for errors. As you check for errors, you will often notice ways in which you can add additional material or otherwise make your writing stronger. The development of good work habits will carry over into your professional career. When you write a memo for your boss in a law enforcement agency, business, or government agency, you will be judged by your presentation as well as by the content of your analysis. Take the extra step necessary to present your best work to your instructors.

6. Talk to your classmates.

Even if your instructor wants you to complete all assignments on your own, you can still gain great benefits by talking to your classmates about interesting topics that emerge from the textbook and lectures. As many former students look back on their college experiences, they recognize that some of the most valuable and educational moments during college came while discussing, debating, and analyzing issues with their classmates. The process of interacting with others forces us to reexamine and clarify our own thoughts. This process helps to reinforce concepts and provides a stronger basis for good performances on exams, papers, and other academic assignments.

7. Go to see your instructor during his or her office hours.

Students gain many benefits from seeking one-on-one contacts with their instructors. You can ask additional questions about the course material. You can clarify expectations about class assignments. More importantly, personal contacts with instructors can make the instructor better able to understand how well students understand the course material. Such contacts can provide feedback to enable the instructor to review material or reinforce specific topics. In addition, personal contact with instructors also permits instructors to provide advice about careers and graduate school possibilities when instructors become personally acquainted with their students.

8. Try to connect the course material to your own life.

Spend time thinking about the implications of the topics covered in the textbook. Do not file the course away in one section of your mind for the limited purpose of passing exams and earning a grade. Criminal justice subjects are important to all of us. As citizens and voters, we must choose the legislators, governors, judges, and presidents who will shape criminal justice policy. Someday *you* might be a leader who will make decisions about criminal justice. Thus, it is especially important that you read newspapers, read news magazines, watch television news, and keep yourself informed about what is happening in the world. As you view the news, think about how contemporary events fit with the topics and analysis contained in the textbook. The material that you learn in this course should enable you to gain a better understanding of developments in American society and help you to evaluate the campaign promises and policy proposals of politicians who present themselves to you during each election season.

If you are interested in a criminal justice career, use the textbook and course material to analyze your own interests and aspirations. For example, many students want to be FBI agents or police officers. They frequently focus on the most "exciting" aspects of those jobs, such as apprehending dangerous lawbreakers through fascinating investigations. However, you must get beyond the *image* of law enforcement officers in order to make good choices about careers. Just as the television show "Law and Order" does not provide an accurate presentation of the daily lives of lawyers, most television images of law enforcement officers, prosecutors, and other criminal justice actors provide incomplete if not inaccurate images.

To choose a career, you must first examine *yourself*. How do you want to spend eight to ten hours each working day for (potentially) thirty or more years? What kinds of tasks are of interest to you? Do you want to work with people? Do you want to work in an office? What kind of organization do you want to work for? As you examine yourself, think about the daily lives of professionals in the criminal justice system. Remember, for example, police officers can spend significant amounts of time directing traffic, getting cats out of trees, or just watching activity on several city blocks. Every job has its "boring" aspects and those aspects must be recognized in order to make a wise choice about careers. Some students also use the material in this course to think about different kinds of jobs that are less visible than those of police officers and prosecutors. For example, how many students have really examined opportunities for becoming parole officers, court administrators, or counselors in a correctional setting? By applying the course topics to yourself, you can use the textbook to help shape your own life if you have an interest in a criminal justice career.

If you begin to identify jobs that may be of interest to you, think about how you can learn more about those jobs. You could make an appointment with a local criminal justice professional to ask him or her about how to begin a career as, for example, a probation officer. Although students may initially feel too shy to seek appointments with prosecutors or police chiefs or other justice professionals, they soon discover that these professionals often enjoy talking about their careers, backgrounds, and life experiences. Remember, all of these people were once students who had to think about what careers to pursue. They remember how difficult it can be to gain enough understanding about various careers in order to make wise choices about which directions to pursue.

<u>9. Enjoy your studies</u>.

College can be a very burdensome time of life, as students juggle classes, jobs, and family responsibilities while trying to make ends meet. College is, however, one of the few moments in life when people have the opportunity to focus their attention on *ideas*. College courses force you to learn about ideas, but it is up to you to think deeply about these ideas. This is your moment to question the things that you have always taken for granted. This is your moment to clarify your values, beliefs, and goals. College will not shape you into a certain kind of person. It merely provides the opportunity for you to explore, to wonder, to debate, and to discuss as you learn relevant concepts and theories about specific subjects. When you stop attending college classes and undertaking reading assignments, it is more difficult to take the time to encounter new ideas and to analyze your place in the world. Seize the opportunity that college presents for you to expand your mind. Although you may ultimately conclude that your beliefs, values, and world-view suit you just fine, you can have greater confidence in that conclusion by recognizing and seizing the opportunity that college presents for exploring ideas with the assistance of your instructors and classmates. Even if you feel burdened at this moment by seemingly impossible workloads and financial strains, do not lose sight of the *opportunity for education* that you are experiencing. Make the most of it. Enjoy it. For most people, the same opportunity may not present itself again at another stage in life.

CHAPTER 1

THE CRIMINAL JUSTICE SYSTEM

LEARNING OBJECTIVES

After covering the material in this chapter, students should understand:

1.   the goals of criminal justice include doing justice, controlling crime and preventing crime;

2.   the existence, organization, and jurisdiction of national and state criminal justice systems, including the dual court system;

3.   criminal justice as a "system," with specific characteristics: discretion, resource dependence, sequential tasks, and filtering;

4.   the primary agencies of criminal justice, and the prevalence of local agencies and institutions;

5.   the flow of decision making in the criminal justice system, including the thirteen steps in the decision making process;

6.   the criminal justice wedding cake.

7.   the comparison and reality of Packer's Crime Control Model and Due Process Model.

8.   crime and justice in a multicultural society

CHAPTER SUMMARY

The three goals of criminal justice are doing justice, controlling crime, and preventing crime. The dual court system contains a national system and state systems of criminal justice that enforce laws, try cases, and punish offenders. Criminal justice is a system made up of a number of parts or subsystems--police, courts, corrections. Exchange is a key concept for the analysis of criminal justice processes. The four major characteristics of the criminal justice system are discretion, resource dependence, sequential tasks, and filtering. The processing of cases in the criminal justice system involves a series of decisions by police officers, prosecutors, judges, probation officers, wardens, and parole board members. The criminal justice system consists of thirteen steps that cover the stages of law enforcement, adjudication, and corrections. The four-layered criminal justice wedding cake model indicates that not all cases are treated equally. The existence of unequal treatment of people within the criminal justice system would clash with the American values of equality, fairness, and due process. Racial disparities in criminal justice are explained in one of three ways: minorities commit more crimes; the criminal justice system is racist; the criminal justice system expresses the racism of society.

CHAPTER OUTLINE

I.   INTRODUCTION
        Robert Chambers served fifteen years for manslaughter in a case that created a media frenzy. In 1988, Chambers was charged with murdering Jennifer Levin, although he claimed that the death was accidental and a result of "rough sex." Chambers' defense attorneys and prosecutors plea bargained a manslaughter conviction because the jury deadlocked. From the initial investigation of police to serving "hard time" in a high-security prison including five years in solitary confinement, Chambers experienced all of the stages of the criminal justice system.

II.   THE GOALS OF CRIMINAL JUSTICE

A.   Introduction
        1.   In 1967, the **President's Commission on Law Enforcement and Administration of Justice** described the criminal justice system as an apparatus society uses to "enforce the standards of conduct necessary to protect individuals and the community." Underneath this statement are three underlying goals:

B.   Doing Justice
        1.   Without a system founded on justice there would be little difference between criminal justice in the United States and that in authoritarian countries. Elements of the goal:
                a.   Offenders will be held fully accountable for their actions.
                b.   The rights of persons who have contact with the system will be protected.
                c.   Like offenses will be treated alike.
                d.   Officials will take into account relevant differences among offenders and offense

C.   Controlling Crime
        1.   The criminal justice system is designed to control crime by apprehending, prosecuting, convicting, and punishing those members of the community who do not live according to the law.
        2.   Constraint on the goal: Efforts to control crime must be carried out within the framework of law.

D.   Preventing Crime
        1.   The deterrent effect of the doing justice and crime control goals. Punishing those individuals who violate the law provides examples that are likely to deter others from committing wrongful acts.
        2.   The actions of citizens in taking simple precautions. Unfortunately many people leave homes and cars unlocked, and take other actions that facilitate crime.

E.   Technology Issues in Criminal Justice: **Backscatter X-Ray**
        1.   New technologies assist in preventing crime and gathering evidence but also cause problems in regard to invasions of privacy of individuals. For example, in 2003, reports surfaced that the federal government was experimenting with backscatter X-Ray devices to detect weapons or bombs being concealed by airline passengers. The idea of the government using X-Ray devices to view someone's unclothed body raised concerns about privacy rights.

III.   CRIMINAL JUSTICE IN A FEDERAL SYSTEM

A.   Introduction
        1.   Criminal justice is based upon the concept of **federalism** in which power is divided between a national government and state governments.
        2.   The **U.S. Constitution** gives the federal government specific powers over taxation, commerce, and national defense. Although it does not specifically discuss criminal justice institutions, there are federal law enforcement agencies and other aspects of national government involved in crime policy and the administration of justice.

B.   Two Justice Systems
        1.   Criminal laws are written and enforced primarily by agencies of the states (including counties and municipalities), yet the rights of defendants are protected by the constitutions of both state and national governments.
        2.   Although the large majority of criminal cases are heard in state courts, certain offenses (e.g., drug violations and transportation of a kidnap victim across state lines) are violations of *both* state and federal laws.
        3.   Example: when President Kennedy was assassinated in 1963, **Lee Harvey Oswald** was prosecuted for violating Texas law because Congress had not yet made it a federal offense to kill the President.

C.   <u>Expansion of Federal Involvement</u>
    1.   **Congress** has expanded the powers of the FBI and other federal agencies. Now the federal government pursues organized crime gangs dealing with drugs, pornography, and gambling on a national basis.
    2.   The FBI also has authority to help local police in certain situations, such as stolen property that may have been transported across state lines.
    3.   Disputes over jurisdiction may occur so federal and state officials need cooperation.
    4.   The existence of multiple criminal justice systems makes criminal justice in the United States highly decentralized.
    5.   In response to the terrorist attacks on September 11, 2001, Congress created the **Department of Homeland Security** to centralize the administration and coordination of many existing agencies.

IV.   CRIMINAL JUSTICE AS A SOCIAL SYSTEM

A.   <u>The System Perspective</u>
    1.   A **system** is a complex whole consisting of interdependent parts whose actions are directed toward goals and are influenced by the environment within which they function. The concept of system helps us to recognize that the agencies and processes of criminal justice are linked. One result is that the actions of the police, for example, have an impact on the other parts of the system prosecution, courts, and corrections.
    2.   One key concept is **exchange**, meaning the mutual transfer of resources among individual actors, each of whom has goals that he or she cannot accomplish alone.
        a.   **Plea bargaining** is an obvious example of exchange where a defendant's plea of guilty to a criminal charge with the expectation of receiving a reduced sentence.
        b.   The prosecutor and defense attorney reach agreement on the plea and sentence. Each actor, including the defendant and the judge, gains a benefit as a result.
        c.   The concept of exchange reminds us that decisions are the products of interactions among individuals in the system and that the subsystems of criminal justice are linked together by the actions of individual decision makers.

V.   <u>CHARACTERISTICS OF THE CRIMINAL JUSTICE SYSTEM</u>
A.   **<u>Discretion</u>**: At all levels of the justice process officials have significant ability to act according to their own judgment and conscience.
    1.   Police officers, prosecutors, judges, and correctional officials may consider a variety of circumstances and exercise many options as they dispose of a case.
    2.   The need for discretionary power has been justified primarily on two counts:
        a.   Resources: If every violation of the law were to be formally processed, the costs would be staggering.
        b.   Justice: Criminal justice practitioners believe that in many cases justice can be more fully achieved through informal procedures. For example, a judge may believe that justice is better served if a sex offender is sent to a mental hospital rather than to prison.
    IDEAS IN PRACTICE: Students play the role of a police chief who receives complaints from citizens about police officers failing to enforce traffic laws

B.   **<u>Resource Dependence</u>**: Criminal justice does not produce its own resources but is dependent on others for them. It must therefore develop special links with people responsible for the allocation of resources--that is, the political decision makers.
    1.   Criminal justice actors must be responsive to the legislators, mayors, and city council members who hold the power of the purse. Justice officials seek to maintain a positive image in news reports and seek to keep voters happy.

C.   **<u>Sequential Tasks:</u>** Every part of the criminal justice system has distinct tasks that are carried out sequentially.
    1.   Because a high degree of interdependence characterizes the system, the actions of one part of the system directly affect the work of the others.

2. The courts can deal only with the cases brought to them by the prosecutor, who can deal only with persons arrested by the police.

D. **Filtering**: The criminal justice process may be viewed as a filtering process through which cases are screened: some are advanced to the next level of decision making, and others are either rejected or the conditions under which they are processed are changed.
   1. Persons who have been arrested may be filtered out of the system at various points; very few of the suspects arrested are prosecuted, tried, and convicted.
   2. At each stage in the process decisions are made by officials as to which cases will proceed to the next level.
   3. The "funnel like" nature of the criminal justice system results in many cases entering at the top but only a few making it all the way to conviction and punishment.

VI. OPERATIONS OF CRIMINAL JUSTICE AGENCIES

A. Criminal Justice Subsystems
   1. The subsystems encompassing the police, prosecution and defense, courts, and corrections consist of over 60,000 public and private agencies that utilize an annual budget of over $146 billion, and a staff of more than 2 million people.

B. Police
   1. Complexity and fragmentation characterize the number and jurisdiction of the 18,769 public organizations in the United States engaged in law enforcement activities.
   2. Only fifty are federal law enforcement agencies; the rest are state and local.
   3. The responsibilities of police organizations fall into four categories:
      a. Keeping the peace: The protection of rights and persons in a wide variety of situations, ranging from street-corner brawls to domestic quarrels.
      b. Apprehending law violators and fighting crime: This responsibility actually accounts for only a small proportion of law enforcement agencies' time and resources.
      c. Engaging in crime prevention: Educating the public about the threat of crime and by reducing the number of situations in which crimes are most likely to be committed.
      d. Providing a variety of social services: Recover stolen property, direct traffic, provide emergency medical aid, get cats out of trees, help people who have locked themselves out of their apartments, etc.

C. Courts
   1. **Dual court system**: Separate judicial structure for each state in addition to a national structure.
   2. Interpretation of the law can vary from state to state. Judges have discretion to apply the law as they feel it should be applied until they are overruled by a higher court.
   3. Courts are responsible for **adjudication**--determining if defendants are guilty according to fair procedures.

D. Corrections
   1. On any given day about 6 million Americans are under the supervision of the corrections system.
   2. Only about a third of convicted offenders are actually incarcerated; the remainder are under supervision in the community through probation, parole, community-based halfway houses, work release programs, and supervised activities.
   3. The federal government, all the states, most counties, and all but the smallest cities are engaged in the corrections enterprise.
   4. Increasingly, nonprofit private organizations such as the YMCA have contracted with governments to perform correctional services.
   5. For-profit businesses have undertaken the construction and administration of institutions through contracts with governments.

WORK PERSPECTIVE: Lisa Zimmer, Drug Court Substance Abuse Counselor in Cincinnati, Ohio.

VII.   THE FLOW OF DECISION MAKING IN THE SYSTEM

A.   Discretionary Decisions
      1.   The disposition of cases in the criminal justice system involves a series of decisions.
      2.   made by police officers, prosecutors, judges, probation officers, wardens, and other officials who decide whether a case will move on to the next point or be dropped from the system.

B.   Steps in the Decision Making Process
      Remember that the formal procedures outlined may not always depict reality. The system looks like an assembly line as decisions are made about defendants. The process is shaped by the concepts of system, discretion, sequential tasks, filtering, and exchange.
      1.   **Investigation**: Police are normally dependent on a member of the community to report the offense.
      2.   **Arrest:** Taking a person into custody when police determine there is enough evidence indicating a particular person has committed a crime.
            a.   Under some conditions, arrests may be made on the basis of a warrant; an order issued by a judge who has received information pointing toward a particular person as the offender.
            b.   In some states, police officers may issue a summons or citation that orders a person to appear in court on a particular date, thus eliminating the need to hold the suspect physically until case disposition.
      3.   **Booking:** Procedure by which an administrative record is made of the arrest; a suspect may be fingerprinted, photographed, interrogated, and placed in a lineup for identification by the victim or witnesses. Bail may be set.
            a.   All suspects must be warned that they have the right to counsel, that they may remain silent, and that any statement they make may later be used against them.
      4.   **Charging:** Prosecuting attorneys determine whether there is reasonable cause to believe that an offense was committed and whether the suspect committed it.
      5.   Initial Appearance: Suspects must be brought before a judge to be given formal notice of the charge for which they are being held, to be advised of their rights, and to be given the opportunity to post bail. The judge determines if there is sufficient evidence to hold the suspect for further criminal processing.
            a.   The purpose of bail is to permit the accused to be released while awaiting trial. To ensure that the person will be in court at the appointed time, surety (or pledge), usually in the form of money or a bond, is required.
            b.   The amount of bail is usually based primarily on the judge's perception of the seriousness of the crime and the defendant's record.
            c.   For minor crimes, suspects may also be released on their own recognizance—a promise to appear in court at a later date.
            d.   Some suspects may be kept in custody if they are viewed as a threat to the community.
      6.   **Preliminary Hearing/Grand Jury**
            a.   The preliminary hearing, used in about half the states, allows a judge to determine whether probable cause exists to believe that the accused committed a known crime within the jurisdiction of the court. The case against the defendant may be dismissed or the accused is bound over for arraignment on an information.
            b.   In federal system and other states, the prosecutor appears before a grand jury composed of citizens who decide if there is enough evidence to allow the prosecutor to file an indictment.
            c.   The preliminary hearing and grand jury deliberations are designed to prevent hasty and malicious prosecutions, to protect persons from mistakenly being humiliated in public, and to discover if there are substantial grounds upon which a prosecution may be based.
      7.   **Indictment/Information**: The prosecutor prepares the formal charging document and enters it before the court.
      8.   **Arraignment:** The accused person is next taken before a judge to hear the indictment or information read and is asked to enter a plea. The judge must determine if a guilty plea is made voluntarily and whether the person has full knowledge of the possible consequences of the plea.

9. **Trial:** For the relatively small percentage of defendants who plead not guilty, the right to a trial by an impartial **jury** is guaranteed by the Sixth Amendment for defendants facing charges which carry six months or more of imprisonment.
    a. Most trials are summary or **bench trials** conducted by a judge without a jury.
    b. It is estimated that only about 10-15 percent of cases go to trial and only about 5 percent are heard by juries.
10. Sentencing: The judge's intent is to make the sentence suitable to the particular offender within the requirements of the law and in accordance with the retribution (punishment) and rehabilitation goals of the system.
11. **Appeal:** Defendants found guilty may appeal their convictions to a higher court based on claims that the rules of procedure were not properly followed or that the law forbidding the behavior is unconstitutional. Defendants lose about 80 percent of appeals. A successful appeal typically leads to a new trial rather than release.
12. Corrections: Probation, intermediate sanctions, incarceration are the sanctions most generally impose and supervised by the corrections subsystem.
    a. Probation allows convicted offenders to serve their sentences in the community under supervision. Violations of probation conditions can lead to imprisonment.
    b. Intermediate sanctions include intensive probation supervision, boot camp, home confinement, and community service.
    c. Incarceration: Offenders convicted of **misdemeanors** usually serve their time in city or county jails, while **felony** offenders serve their time in state prisons.
13. Release: Release may be accomplished through serving the full sentence imposed by the court or by returning to the community under supervision of a parole officer with restrictive conditions.

C. **The Criminal Justice Wedding Cake**
    1. The key concept for differentiating cases according to the way in which criminal justice officials and the public react to it.
    2. Layer 1: Very few **"celebrated"** cases that are exceptional, get great public attention, result in a jury trial, and often have extended appeals.
    3. Layer 2: Felonies that are deemed to be serious by officials, e.g., crimes of violence committed by persons with long criminal records against victims unknown to them.
    4. Layer 3: Felonies by offenders who are seen as of lesser concern than those in Layer 2; many cases are filtered out of the system, and plea bargaining is encouraged.
    5. Layer 4: Misdemeanors encompassing 90 percent of all cases handled in the criminal justice system; processes are speedy and informal, and fines, probation, or short jail sentences result. Assembly-line justice reigns.
    6. Close Up: The **Christopher Jones** Case. Illustrating the stages of the process in an actual criminal case.

D. Crime Control versus Due Process
    1. **Herbert Packer's** two competing models; ideal types designed to organize thinking about the criminal justice system. Packer recognizes that the administration of criminal justice operates within the contemporary American society and is therefore influenced by cultural forces that, in turn, determine the models' usefulness.
    2. **Crime Control Model:** Order as a Value
        a. Goal: Repression of Criminal Conduct
        b. Value: Efficiency
        c. Nature of Process: Administrative and filtering
        d. Decision Point: Police and Prosecutor (i.e., plea bargaining, discretionary dismissals)
        e. Basis for Decision Making: Discretion
        f. Analogy: Assembly Line

3. **Due Process Model:** Law as a Value
    a.   Goal: Preserve individuals' liberty
    b.   Value: Reliability (i.e., accurate decisions about guilt and innocence)
    c.   Nature of the Process: Adversarial
    d.   Decision Point: Courtroom (i.e., trial)
    e.   Basis for Decision Making: Law
    f.   Analogy: Obstacle course

VIII.   CRIME AND JUSTICE IN A MULTI-CULTURAL SOCIETY
A.   African-Americans, Hispanics, and other minorities are drawn into the criminal justice system at much higher rates than the white majority.
1.   African-Americans account for 1/3 of arrests and 1/2 of incarcerations
2.   Since 1980, the proportion of Hispanic-Americans among all inmates in U.S. prisons has risen from 7.7 percent to 16 percent.
3.   About 1/3 of all African-American males in their twenties are under criminal justice supervision.
4.   The crime victimization rate is 260 per 1,000 Hispanic households versus 144 per 1,000 non-Hispanic household
B.   Disparity is a difference between groups that can be explained by legitimate factors. But discrimination occurs when people are treated differently without regard to their behavior or qualifications.
C.   Three frequent explanations for racial disparities.
1.   Theory 1: African-Americans and Hispanics Commit More Crimes.
    a.   However, there is no evidence of an ethnic link to criminal behavior. Criminal behavior is evident among all groups.
    b.   There is a link between crime and economic disadvantages which disproportionately affect these minority groups. Unemployment rates are higher and average family income is lower among these minority groups.
    c.   Because most crime is intraracial rather than interracial, minority group members in poor neighborhoods also suffer from more significant victimization rates.
    d.   African-Americans and Hispanics are arrested more often and for more serious crimes on average than whites. Analysts question whether crime control efforts should shift to an emphasis on reducing social problems that may contribute to crime.
    e.   WHAT AMERICANS THINK: Most Non-Hispanics whites believe that blacks are treated fairly but most blacks do not think that blacks are treated fairly in the criminal justice system.
2.   Theory 2: The Criminal Justice System Is Racist
    a.   Research indicates that people of color are arrested more often for drug offenses even though they do not engage in drug use more often than whites. Also, unfounded arrests of African-Americans occur at four times the rate of unfounded arrests of whites.
    b.   The rate of incarceration for poor and minority citizens is greater than even their higher offense rates would justify.
    c.   Disparities need not be the result of overt racism. For example, if police patrols concentrate on poor neighborhoods, more arrests will be made there than elsewhere.
    d.   Poor people are less likely to make bail or hire their own attorneys, two factors that may contribute to a higher imprisonment rate.
3.   Theory 3: America Is A Racist Society.
    a.   There is some evidence of racism in the way that society asks the criminal justice system to operate. For example, federal sentencing guidelines punish users of crack cocaine about one hundred times more harshly than users of powder cocaine, even though the drugs are nearly identical. The only difference is that whites tend to use the powder form while people of color tend to use crack
    b.   Sentencing studies find a stronger link between unemployment and sentencing than between crime rates and sentencing. This suggests that prisons are being used to confine people who cannot find jobs.
    c.   Drug law enforcement is aimed primarily at low-level dealers in minority neighborhoods.

d.   Numerous examples of African-American and Hispanic professionals who have been falsely arrested when police saw a person of color whom they believed was "out of place."

4.   CLOSE-UP: Racial Profiling-Law enforcement officers relying upon stereotypes to profile criminals place an undue burden on innocent members of a wide variety of racial and ethnic groups.

5.   A QUESTION OF ETHICS: Should sentencing laws be changed because of a racial disparity?

REVIEW OF KEY TERMS

Fill in the appropriate term from the list for each statement below:

Department of Homeland Security
Backscatter X-Ray
system
booking
exchange
plea bargain
discretion
filtering process
dual court system
adjudication
arrest
warrant
information
indictment
felony
misdemeanor
Crime Control Model
preliminary hearing
Due Process Model
"wedding cake"
resource dependence
grand jury
arraignment
decentralization
bail
doing justice
controlling crime
preventing crime
U.S. Constitution
U. S. President's Commission on Law Enforcement and Administration of Justice
Congress
bench trial
jury trial
sequential tasks

1.   _____ is the authority to make decisions by using one's own judgment and conscience which provides the basis for individualization and informality in the administration of justice.

2.   _____ is a primary goal of criminal justice that provides the basis for distinguishing the American system from those of authoritarian countries.

3.   Most trials are _____ trials, meaning they are conducted without a jury.

4. _____ is a document charging an individual with a specific crime prepared by a prosecuting attorney and presented to a court at a preliminary hearing.

5. _____ is a characteristic of the criminal justice system that leads criminal justice officials to be responsive to elected officials and legislative bodies.

6. _____ consists of separate judicial structures for states and for the national government.

7. _____is intended to permit the release of defendants pending the processing of their cases if they do not pose a threat to the community.

8. _____ is the physical taking of a person into custody on the ground that there is probable cause to believe that he or she has committed a criminal offense.

9. The _____ emphasized the need for greater federal involvement in local crime-control and urged that federal grants be directed to the states to support criminal justice initiatives.

10. _____ is a complex whole consisting of interdependent parts whose actions are directed toward goals and are influenced by the environment within which they function.

11. _____ is a characteristic of the organization of law enforcement and other criminal justice agencies in the United States.

12. _____ is a characteristic of the criminal justice system that describes how one subsystem must complete its responsibilities before a case is passed to the authority of another subsystem.

13. In November 2002, Congress created _____ to address the threat of terrorism.

14. _____ is the system characteristic through which some cases are moved out of the criminal justice system and others are pushed ahead to later stages in the system.

15. _____ is a primary goal of criminal justice that involves apprehending, prosecuting, and punishing those who violate criminal laws.

16. _____ is the stage in the criminal justice process in which formal charges are read and the defendant enters a plea.

17. _____ is the institution that enacts national criminal laws for the U. S.

18. _____ is a stage in the criminal justice process in which defendants are normally photographed and fingerprinted.

19. The right to a trial by _____ is guaranteed by the Sixth Amendment.

20. _____ depicts the cases within the criminal justice system as having specific characteristics that lead various categories of cases to be processed in different ways.

21. _____ is a court order authorizing police officers to take certain actions, for example, to arrest suspects or to search premises.

22. _____ is a stage in the criminal justice process in which a judge determines whether or not there is sufficient evidence for a case to move forward for prosecution.

23. _____ depicts the criminal justice system as emphasizing reliable decisions that protect individuals' liberty through an adversarial process based on law.

24. _____ is a primary goal of criminal justice that relies on citizens to take precautions in their daily lives.

25. _____ does not include criminal justice among the federal government's specific powers.

26. _____ decides if there is enough evidence to file an indictment that will permit a prosecution to move forward.

27. _____ devices detect whether airline passengers are carrying weapons, bombs, or other contraband.

28. _____ are serious crimes carrying penalties of one year or more imprisonment.

29. _____ is the process of determining whether or not a defendant is guilty.

30. _____ is a mutual transfer of resources or information that flow from behavior based on decisions about the values and costs of alternatives.

31. _____ is a document returned by a grand jury as a "true bill" charging an individual with a specific crime.

32. A _____ is a defendant's admission of guilt to a criminal charge with the reasonable expectation of receiving a lighter penalty.

33. _____ are less serious offenses carrying penalties of no more than one year of incarceration.

34. _____ depicts the criminal justice system as one that emphasizes efficient repression of crime through the exercise of discretion in administrative processing of cases.

REVIEW OF KEY PEOPLE
Fill in the appropriate person from the list for each statement below:
Robert Chambers
Herbert Packer
Lee Harvey Oswald
Christopher Jones
Michael Kennedy

1. In 1997 reports surfaced indicating that the late _____, then a thirty nine year old lawyer and nephew of the late President John F. Kennedy, had carried on an affair with his children's 14 year old baby sitter.

2. Because Congress had not made killing the president a federal offense in 1963, the suspected assassin of John Kennedy, _____, would have been charged under Texas laws had he lived.

3. _____, a thirty-one-old man from Battle Creek, Michigan, was arrested, charged, and convicted of serious crimes arising from the police investigation of a series of robberies.

4. _____ described two competing models of the administration of criminal justice: the crime control model and the due process model.

5. _____ plead guilty to manslaughter and accepted a 15 year sentence for the death of Jennifer Levin in a highly publicized trial.

SELF-TEST SECTION

Multiple Choice Questions

1.1. Which of the following is NOT a goal of the American criminal justice system?
a) doing justice
b) preventing crime
c) consolidating power at the federal level
d) controlling crime
e) all of the above are goals of the criminal justice system

1.2. Which of the following is TRUE about the American criminal justice system?
a) citizens have authority to enforce the law
b) most people take steps to protect themselves against crime
c) there is little difference between the U. S criminal system and authoritarian countries
d) criminal justice officials are limited by the constitutional rights of individuals
e) criminal justice officials never fall short of doing justice

1.3.Which of the following is TRUE about discretion within the American system of criminal justice?
a) discretion not exist within the American system of criminal justice
b) discretion exists but for only a few participants
c) discretion exists for all participants but it does not limit the values of the American system
d) discretion exists and its use limits the values of the American system
e) discretion exists for only judges

1.4. Which of the following is TRUE about the American system of criminal justice?
a) very few suspects who are arrested are then prosecuted, tried, and convicted
b) all suspects who are arrested are then prosecuted, tried, and convicted
c) no suspects who are arrested are then prosecuted, tried, and convicted
d) a large percentage of suspects who are arrested are then prosecuted, tried, and convicted
e) none of the above are TRUE

1.5. Robert Chambers was sentenced to fifteen years in prison for manslaughter in the death of Jennifer Levin. What happened to Chambers?
a) Chambers was released after five years for good behavior
b) Chambers was murdered in prison by another inmate
c) Chambers was released after serving his entire fifteen year sentence
d) Chambers escaped from prison and remains at large.
e) Chambers remains in prison because he committed serious offenses in prison and had several years added to his sentence

1.6. What is the duty of the Federal Bureau of Investigation?
a) enact criminal laws
b) interpret criminal laws
c) evade criminal laws
d) enforce criminal laws
e) all of the above

1.7. How many state and local law enforcement agencies exist within the American system of criminal justice?
a) roughly 5,000
b) roughly 10,000
c) roughly 12,000
d) roughly 18,000
e) roughly 35,000

1.8. How many federal law enforcement agencies exist within the American system of criminal justice?
a) 3
b) 9
c) 17
d) 25
e) 50

1.9. What is the annual budget of the state and local law enforcement agencies within the American system of criminal justice?
a) more than $50 billion
b) more than $100 billion
c) more than $500 billion
d) more than $1 trillion
e) less than $100 million

1.10.Which of the following are major duties of police agencies?
a) keeping the peace
b) apprehending criminals
c) providing social services
d) preventing crime
e) all of the above

1.11. Which of the following duties is being performed if a police officer "directs traffic"?
a) solving crime
b) apprehending criminals
c) providing social services
d) preventing crime
e) all of the above

1.12. Which of the following duties is being performed if a police officer "provides emergency aid"?
a) solving crime
b) apprehending criminals
c) providing social services
d) preventing crime
e) all of the above

1.13. Which of the following accounts for the smallest amount of an officer's time?
a) keeping the peace
b) apprehending criminals
c) providing social services
d) preventing crime
e) all of the above account for a great deal of an officer's time

1.14. Which of the following engage in corrections?
a) federal government
b) state government
c) most counties
d) most cities
e) all of the above

1.15. What is the ratio of American adults who are under the supervision of state and federal corrections systems to the entire
adult population?
a) one in three
b) one in ten
c) one in fifteen
d) one in twenty
e) one in thirty

1.16. The right to a trial by an impartial jury is guaranteed by the...
a) First Amendment
b) Fifth Amendment
c) Sixth Amendment
d) Eighth Amendment
e) Tenth Amendment

1.17. How many percent of criminal cases go to trial?
a) two
b) ten to fifteen
c) twenty
d) thirty to forty
e) fifty

1.18. How many percent of criminal cases go before a jury?
a) five
b) fifteen to twenty
c) twenty
d) forty
e) fifty

1.19. What layer of the criminal justice wedding cake would include the O. J. Simpson trial ?
a) layer one (celebrated case)
b) layer two (serious felony case)
c) layer three (less important felony case)
d) layer four (misdemeanor case)
e) layer five (federal case)

1.20. What layer of the criminal justice wedding cake would prosecutors refer to as "heavy" cases with "tough" sentences?
a) layer one (celebrated cases)
b) layer two (serious felony cases)
c) layer three (less important felony cases)
d) layer four (misdemeanor cases)
e) layer five (federal cases)

1.21. What layer of the criminal justice wedding cake contains ninety percent of all cases?
a) layer one (celebrated cases)
b) layer two (serious felony cases)
c) layer three (less important felony cases)
d) layer four (misdemeanor cases)
e) layer five (federal cases)

1.22. Which of the following is NOT a layer of the criminal justice wedding cake?
a) layer one (celebrated case)
b) layer two (serious felony case)
c) layer three (less important felony case)
d) layer four (misdemeanor case)
e) layer five (federal case)

1.23. Which stage of the criminal justice process is crucial because it sets in motion the adjudication of a case?
a) arrest
b) charging
c) investigation
d) trial
e) sentencing

1.24. According to a study by Dozinger, what is the ratio of unfounded arrests that police make concerning African-Americans to whites?
a) police make unfounded arrests of African-Americans twice as often as whites
b) police make unfounded arrests of whites twice as often as African-Americans
c) police make unfounded arrests of African-Americans at the same rate as whites
d) police make unfounded arrests of African-Americans four times as often as whites
e) police make unfounded arrests of African-Americans ten times as often as whites

1.25. The link between crime and economic disadvantage is...
a) non-existent
b) slight
c) moderate
d) significant
e) a universal law of causal and effect

True and False
_____1.1. Robert Chambers was sentenced to death for the murder of Jennifer Levin.

_____1.2. The easiest goal of the American system of criminal justice is to do justice.

_____1.3. The U. S. Constitution does not provide for a national police force.

_____1.4. There are no federal law enforcement agencies in the U. S.

_____1.5. A suspect is fingerprinted at the booking stage of the criminal justice process.

_____1.6. Judges are responsible for imposing sentences.

_____1.7. Discretion is not an important concept within the American system of criminal justice.

_____1.8. The subsystems of the American system of criminal justice are interdependent.

_____1.9. Most cases go to trial in the American system of criminal justice.

_____1.10. African-Americans are treated fairly within the American system of criminal justice.

_____1.11. All fifty states in the U. S. have state law enforcement agencies.

_____1.12. Police are responsible for adjudication.

_____1.13. State courts are required by the U. S. Supreme Court to decide all cases in a similar fashion.

____1.14. Trial judges and other officials are ruled to have acted properly in eighty percent of appeals.

____1.15. Christopher Jones was arrested for loitering.

____1.16. Ninety percent of criminal cases involve serious felonies.

____1.17. The U. S. has a dual court system.

____1.18. There is a large disparity between the sentences imposed upon those convicted for crack cocaine and those convicted for powder cocaine.

____1.19. Michael Tonry argues that the "War on Drugs" was designed to disadvantage black youths.

____1.20. The link between crime and economic disadvantage is not significant.

WORKSHEET 1.1 SYSTEM ATTRIBUTES

Imagine that you are a county prosecutor. Briefly describe how the attributes of the criminal justice system (discretion, resource dependence, sequential tasks, and filtering) would affect your relationships, decisions, and actions with respect to each of the following.

Police_____

_____

_____

_____

Defense Attorneys_____

_____

_____

_____

Trial Judges_____

_____

_____

_____

News Media_____

_____

_____

_____

County Commissioners_____

_____

_____

_____

WORKSHEET 1.2 STEPS IN THE PROCESS
Briefly describe what happens at each of the following steps in the justice process.

Booking_____

_____

_____

Preliminary Hearing_____

_____

_____

_____

Grand Jury Proceeding_____

_____

_____

_____

Arraignment_____

_____

_____

_____

Trial_____

_____

_____

_____

Sentencing_____

_____

_____

_____

Appeal_____

_____

_____

CHAPTER 2

CRIME AND JUSTICE IN AMERICA

LEARNING OBJECTIVES

After covering the material in this chapter, students should understand:

1.   categorization of crime, including mala in se and mala prohibitia

2.   the extent of crime, crime trends, and related demographic influences;

3.   the sources for measuring crime and the weaknesses of those sources (especially UCR and NCVS);

4.   the existence of differences in criminal behavior patterns of men and women;

5.   the role of victims in precipitating crimes;

6.   classical and positivist theories about the causes of crime, including biological, psychological, and sociological approaches;

7.   the policy implications of the respective theories about the causes of crime.

CHAPTER SUMMARY

This chapter explores the problem of defining crime. While some acts are easily defined as criminal, such as murder, others are not so easily defined, such as euthanasia or abortion. Mala in se refers to acts that are wrong in themselves where the public can reach a consensus upon the criminality of the act. However, mala prohibita are acts that the government defines as criminal but the public might find conflictual. Examples are smoking marijuana or public drunkenness. Many scholars argue that the government use the law to impose values upon the public.

There are many different types of crime, such as occupational, organized, visible, political, crimes without victims, hate crimes, and cybercrime. Law enforcement authorities focus largely upon visible crime, which involves street crimes such as burglary or homicide, because people fear this type of crime more than any other. However, occupational crime, also known as white-collar crime, and political crimes can impose great costs upon society financially.

The crime problem today is a difficult issue for researchers because data on crime are not reliable. The Uniform Crime Reports provides data reported to police but does not track the dark figure of crime which is not reported to the police officials. The National Crime Victimization Survey involves interview of samples of the U. S. population by the government but people often inaccurately report their experiences to the government. Victimology surfaced in the 1950s as a field of criminology that studied the role of the victim in the criminal act. Young male residents of lower-income communities are the most likely to be victimized by crime. Because of the connection between race and social status in the United States, African Americans are more frequently victimized by crime than are whites. Most crime is intra-racial. A significant percentage of crimes are committed by acquaintances and relatives of victims, especially crimes committed against women.

Crime has a significant impact on all of society when one recognizes the financial and emotional costs it produces. Government agencies have begun to be more sensitive to the needs of crime victims. Thus, there are now programs in many places to provide services and compensation. Scholars have begun to study the role that victims may play in facilitating crimes. The classical school of criminology emphasized reform of the criminal law, procedures, and punishments. The rise of science led to the positivist school, which viewed behavior as stemming from social, biological, and psychological factors. Positivist criminology has dominated the study of criminal behavior in the twentieth century. The criminality of women has only recently been studied. It is argued that, as women become more equal with men in society, crimes committed by females will increase in number.

CHAPTER OUTLINE

I. INTRODUCTION

A.   The investigation into the murder of **Laci Peterson**, a happily married pregnant woman from middle-class suburbia, reinforces the idea that crime can happen anywhere to anyone. It also demonstrates how the news media and politicians keep the public focused on crime and cause people to be fearful when the actual risk from crime is quite small.

II. DEFINING CRIME

A.   **Mala in se** crimes, wrongs in themselves (murder, rape, assault), based on shared values: consensus.
B.   **Mala prohibitia** crimes are not wrongs in themselves but are punished because they are prohibited by government. There is often a lack of consensus about whether such actions should be illegal (e.g., use of marijuana; gambling, etc.).
C.   Legislators change the definitions of criminal activity as societal values change.

III. TYPES OF CRIME
    Crimes can be categorized as mala in se v. mala prohibitia; felonies v. misdemeanors. Other categories based on level of risk and profitability, degree of public disapproval, and cultural characteristics of offenders:

A.   **Visible Crime**
    Street crime or ordinary crime primarily by lower classes and run the gamut from shoplifting to homicide (i.e., violent crimes, property crimes public order crimes).
    1.   Visible crimes make up the FBI's Uniform Crime Reports
    2.   Theorists have argued that the predominantly lower class composition of correctional institutions reflects society's bias toward enforcing and punishing street crimes committed by the lower classes to a much greater extent than the crimes committed by people possessing greater status, wealth, and power.
B.   **Occupational Crime**
    Violation of law committed through opportunities created in the course of a legal business or profession. Often viewed a shrewd business practices rather than as illegal acts. They are crimes that are often not discovered, if done right.
C.   **Organized Crime**
    Social framework for the perpetration of criminal acts rather than specific acts themselves. Organized criminals provide goods and services to people, will engage in any illegal activity as long as it is low risk and high profit (e.g., pornography, **money laundering**, illegal disposal of toxic waste).
    1.   Organized crime has been associated with many different ethnic and immigrant groups as they struggled to gain access to legitimate economic opportunities when they became more accepted in American society.
    2.   Increasing problem of transnational criminal groups.
D.   **Crimes Without Victims**
    Offenses involving a willing and private exchange of goods or services, such as gambling, pornography, drug use, prostitution, etc. They are also called public order crimes.
    1.   Claimed justification for criminalizing such activities is the protection of society as a whole, including its moral fiber. Are these crimes really victimless if these people harm themselves?
    2.   Because these cases flood the courts, it is costly for society to enforce these laws.
    3.
WORK PERSPECTIVE: John H. Coleman, Police Officer in St. Petersburg, Florida

E. **Political Crime**
Includes activities such as treason, sedition (rebellion), and espionage which are carried out for an ideological purpose. American examples include acts of violence by those opposed to legal abortions.
   1. Crimes such as the Oklahoma City bombing may be politically motivated, but they are prosecuted as visible crimes rather than political crimes.

F. **Cybercrime**
The use of the computer or Internet to commit acts against persons, property, public order, or morality.
   1. The Internet is used to disseminate child pornography. Hackers create viruses that cause significant economic harm to businesses and government.
   2. Government has been slow to respond with new laws addressing newly developing harmful behaviors based on technology.

G. Technology Issues in Criminal Justice: Carnivore
Federal Bureau of Investigation has developed a software program called **Carnivore** that allows FBI agents to monitor email messages being transmitted on the internet. The use of Carnivore by the federal government presents problems in terms of Fourth Amendment violations because searches are conducted without probable cause or a search warrant

H. Close-Up: **Hate Crime**: A New Category of Personal Violence
Laws in most states target violent acts directed at victims because of their race, ethnicity, gender, religion, or sexual orientation. Controversies arise concerning whether such laws violate freedom of speech and association.

IV.   HOW MUCH CRIME IS THERE?

A. What Americans Think
Americans believe (erroneously) that there is more crime than in the prior year.
   1. Difficult to measure actual amount of crime because of the "**dark figure of crime**," namely large numbers of crimes that are not reported
   2. Homicide and auto theft regularly reported because, respectively, missing persons and located bodies must be accounted for, and crime reports are necessary for recovery on auto insurance.
   3. Rape, thefts, and other crimes reported less because of victims' and witnesses' fears, relationships with perpetrators, and unwillingness to get involved with police.

B. **Uniform Crime Reports (UCR)**
Flawed measure of crime because:
   a. Only counts crimes reported to police;
   b. Events labeled as crimes defined differently in different jurisdictions.
   c. However, changes are being instituted in the late 1990s using the **National Incident-Based Reporting System (NIBR)** which will provide detailed information on 46 offenses in 22 crime categories. The NIBRS will distinguish between attempted and completed crimes.

C. **National Crime Victimization Surveys (NCVS)** Surveys of households on crime victimization has enhanced knowledge about crime and probability of victimization. Valuable because has established stable patterns of victimization rates. However, flawed measure of crime because:
   a. People will not report their own participation in such crimes as prostitution, gambling, drug trafficking, and purchasing stolen property.
   b. Definition of criminal event depends on victim's perception of event.
   c. Memories of precise year in which event happened may fade over time.

D. Trends in Crime
Crime trends changed during 1980s
   1. UCR showed steady increase in crime rates until 1980, but NCVS showed stable victimization rates with declines during the 1980s.
      a. Since 1993, both the UCR and NCVS show declines in violent crimes, including homicides.
      b. Increased UCR crime rates attributable to increased willingness of cities to report crimes, the availability of "911" numbers, and neighborhood-level watch police patrol programs, so we cannot be certain about what increases show us about actual criminal behavior.

2. Age: Demographic Influences on Crime Trends: Crime trends affected by demographic trends, especially the number of people in the crime-prone age group, fourteen to twenty-four years.
   a. The number of legal abortions since 19 has decreased the number of people in the crime prone years in the late 1990s.
   b. Experts warned that of a projected increase in the number of teenage males at the start of the twenty-first century may lead to significant increases in crime. Such a rise in crime has not occurred.
3. Crack Cocaine
   Increases in violent crime and homicide in the 1980s are generally attributed to killings by young people under age 25. Killings were produced by spread of crack cocaine and availability of powerful handguns. The decline in crack use has apparently contributed to a reduction in violent crime.

V. CRIME VICTIMIZATION

A. Who Is Victimized?
Victimology subfield emerged in the 1950s and 1960s to focus attention on who is victimized, the impact of victimization, and role of victims in precipitating attacks.
   1. Lifestyle-exposure theory: i.e., urban poverty: Violent crime primarily is an urban phenomenon, in areas with high incidence of physical deterioration, economic insecurity, poor housing, family disintegration, and transiency.
   2. African-Americans more likely than whites to be victims; most violent crime is intra-racial (i.e., offender and victim are same race). Young more likely than old to be victims. Men and low-income city dwellers more likely to be victims.
   THE POLICY DEBATE: Have Tough Crime-Control Policies Caused A Decline in Crime?
B. Acquaintances and Strangers
   1. Two-thirds of violent crimes against women are committed by acquaintances and relatives.
   2. Less than half of the violent crimes against men are committed by acquaintances or relatives.
A QUESTION OF ETHICS: What should a person do when they suspect that a family members is involved in drug use and/or drug trafficking?
C. The Impact of Crime
   1. Estimates of total tangible losses from crime(medical bills, lost property, work time) are put at $105 billion. The intangible costs to victims (pain, trauma, lost quality of life)are put at $450 billion.
   2. The cost of operating the criminal justice system is over $146 billion per year for taxpayers.
   3. The foregoing costs estimates do not include consideration of the costs to consumers of organized and occupational crime.
   4. Fear as an Impact of Criminality
      a. Fear of crime rose sharply from the 1960s until 1973 and then stabilized.
      b. Fear of crime greatest in urban areas; stimulates movement of jobs and businesses outside of cities and limits activities of city residents, especially at night.
      c. Women, elderly, and upper-income suburbanites more frightened than the average citizen.
      d. Fear exceeds reality; fear may be fed by television, news media, personal communication in social networks, etc.
   5. Level of fear also affected by both likelihood of victimization seriousness of offense. Thus in some places people are more fearful of burglary than murder since burglary is more likely to occur.
   6. Reduction in crime rates has not reduced fear of crime. News and entertainment on television and movies emphasize crime and may contribute to fear.
   7. WHAT AMERICANS THINK: Is there any area where you would be afraid to walk alone at night? 30 percent of respondents answered "Yes" which represents a significant segment of the American public.

D. The Experience of Victims in the System
1. Victims traditionally overlooked and forgotten; often felt interrogated and poorly treated by criminal justice officials in addition to their emotional, economic, and physical injuries.
2. During past two decades, justice agencies have taken new interest in the treatment and welfare of crime victims.
3. Proposed "Victim's Rights" constitutional amendment and various other state and federal enactments have placed more emphasis on victims.
4. Programs of counseling, compensation, and assistance have been instituted.

E. The Role of Victims in Crime
1. Victims may voluntarily act in ways that invite crime or the opportunity for crime.
2. Conclusions of studies:
   a. Some citizens do not take proper precautions
   b. People can provoke or entice criminal act
   c. Victims in certain nonstranger crimes are unwilling to assist officials with investigation and prosecution.
   d. Andrew Karmen points out that some victims are partly to blame for motor vehicle theft because of **negligence**, **precipitation**, and provocation.

VI. CAUSES OF CRIME

A. Classical and Positivist Theories
1. **Classical Criminology**: Up through the 18th century, most Europeans saw criminal behavior in religious terms: wrongdoers were under the devil's influence.
2. **Cesare Beccaria's** *Essay on Crimes and Punishments* published in Italy in 1764. First, secular explanation for crime caught the attention of thinkers in Europe and North America. Beccaria argued that crime is rational behavior and that most people have the potential to engage in criminal behavior. It is fear of punishment that keeps people in check. Argued for a rational link between gravity of crime and severity of punishment: the punishment should fit the crime.
3. Classical notions remain of interest among scholars who argue that crime results from rational choices and lawbreakers weighing the risks and benefits of crime.
4. **Neoclassical Criminology**: In the 1980s, new interest in classical criminology emerged as some scholars argued that crimes may result from rational choices by people weighing the costs and benefits of illegal activities. These ideas have influenced sentencing reform, criticisms of rehabilitation, and greater use of incarceration.
5. **Positivist Criminology**: The dominant approach. New focus in nineteenth century assumed:
   a. Human behavior is controlled by physical, mental, and social factors, not by free will.
   b. Criminals are different from noncriminals.
   c. Science can be used to discover the causes of crime and to treat deviants.
6. The particular theory of crime causation accepted by society will affect the definition of laws and crime policies.

B. **Biological Explanations**
Cesare Lombroso claimed that certain people are **criminogenic**- born criminals and have traits that mark them as more primitive and savage than other people. Some genealogical studies have found many lawbreakers within individual family trees. Led to policies favoring sterilization of institutionalized persons.
1. Biological explanations rejected as racist following World War II, but gained renewed exposure in 1970s through sociobiology theories.
2. **James Q. Wilson** and **Richard Herrnstein's** book *Crime and Human Nature* (1985) reviewed the scholarly literature and claimed that certain "constitutional factors" such as sex, age, body type, intelligence, and personality, predispose some people to crime.
3. Research gives some support to notion that certain factors may be related to violent behavior in some people.
4. Policy implications: A policy based on biological explanations would attempt to identify people with specific traits and then treat them with drug therapy, supervision, or incapacitation.

5.   Proposals calling for the chemical castration of repeat sex offenders are erroneously based on biological explanations.

C.   **Psychological Explanations**

1.   **Sigmund Freud's** (1856-1939) proposed theories of early childhood experiences in the unconscious and also developed psychoanalysis, a technique for the treatment of personality disorders. Freud's personality theory said that the personality is comprised of three parts: id, ego, and superego.

2.   Psychiatrists have linked criminal behavior to such concepts as innate impulses, psychic conflict, and the repression of personality.

3.   **Psychopathology**: Related theories claimed that some people were "psychopaths," "sociopaths," or has anti-social personalities." Critics, however, have noted that it is difficult to identify and measure emotional factors in order to isolate people thought to be criminogenic.

4.   Policy Implications: Develop policies to and treat people with personality disorders.

D.   Sociological Explanations

1.   Sociological explanations of crime assume that the offender's personality and actions are molded by contact with the social environment and such factors as race, age, gender, and income.

2.   University of Chicago researchers in the 1920s looked closely at the ecological factors that gave rise to crime: poverty, inadequate housing, broken families, and the problems of new immigrants.

3.   **Social Structure Theory**: attribute criminal behavior to the stratified nature of Western societies, giving particular prominence to the fact that classes control very different amounts of wealth, status, and power. Thus deprivations and inequality lead the lower classes to crime.

     a.   **Robert Merton** extended the idea that the structure of society often permits the situation of **anomie** to develop: social conditions in which rules or norms to regulate behavior have weakened or disappeared. Deviant behavior may appear for individuals who are anomic or frustrated because they are unable to achieve their aspirations.

4.   Policy Implications: Society should take actions to address the social conditions that breed crime by, for example, expanding education, job training, urban development, and health care.

5.   **Social Process Theory**: Because criminal behavior is not limited to the poor, social process theorists believe that criminality results from the interactions of people with the institutions, organizations, and processes of society. Thus everyone has the possibility of being a criminal, regardless of social status or education. There are subgroups of social process theories:

     a.   **Learning theories**: Criminal activity is normal learned behavior with family and peers as primary influences. **Edwin Sutherland** developed **differential association theory**, which states that criminal behavior is learned through interactions with other persons, especially family members and other close associates.

     b.   **Control theories**: All members of society have the potential to commit crimes, but most people are restrained by their ties to such conventional institutions and individuals as family, church, school, and peer groups. Criminality results when these primary bonds are weakened and the person no longer follows the expected norms for behavior.

     c.   **Labeling theories**: By breaking rules, certain individuals come to be labeled as deviant by society. The stigmatized individuals then come to believe that the label is true and they assume a criminal identity and career. By arguing, in effect, that the criminal justice system creates criminals by labeling individuals as such, this approach advocates the decriminalization of certain offenses to avoid needlessly placing labels on people.

6.   Policy Implications: If crime is learned behavior, then people must be treated in ways that build conventional bonds, develop positive role models, and avoid labeling. Thus there should be policies to promote stable families and develop community agencies to assist those in need.

7.   **Social Conflict Theory**: Argues that criminal law and criminal justice are mainly the means of controlling society's poor and have-nots. The rich commit crimes but are much less likely to be punished.

     a.   Critical, radical, or Marxist criminologists argue that the class structure of society results in certain powerless groups in society being labeled as deviant. When the status quo is threatened, criminal laws are altered to label and punish threatening groups and deviant criminals.

8.   Policy Implications: Develop policies to reduce class-based conflict and injustice. Give equal enforcement attention and punishment to crimes committed by upper-class offenders.

IDEAS IN PRACTICE: Students can role play that they are an advisor to a governor who wants to address the root causes of crime.

E.   Women and Crime
    1.   Most theories about the causes of crime are based almost entirely on observations of males. Except with respect to prostitution and shoplifting, little crime research focused on women prior to the 1970s. It was assumed that women did not commit serious crimes because of their nurturing, dependent nature. Women offenders were viewed as moral offenders: "fallen women."
    2.   **Freda Adler's** work stressed the role of the women's movement in changing women's roles and making their criminal behavior more similar in the 1970s and thereafter.
    3.   **Rita Simon** emphasized greater freedom and opportunities in the job market as the source of changes in women's criminality
    4.   Research shows that the number of women being arrested seems to be growing faster than the growth of men in crime. However, the number of women arrested is still relatively small.
    5.   Some researchers believe that women will become more involved in economic and occupational crimes as more women pursue careers in business and industry.
    6.   In general, like male offenders, women arrested for crimes tend to come from poor families in which physical and substance abuse are present.
F.   Assessing Theories of Criminality
All of the theories focus on the visible crimes of the poor, but pay less attention to organized crime and white-collar crimes. Theorists have also paid primary attention to criminality by males. There is a need for a theory that can help integrate various explanations that seem to apply to certain kinds of crimes or offenders.

REVIEW OF KEY TERMS
Fill in the appropriate term from the list for each statement below:
money laundering
sociological explanations
differential association
victimology
classical criminology
positivist criminology
biological explanations
psychological explanations
social structure theories
anomie
social process theories
learning theories
control theories
labeling theories
social conflict theories
criminogenic factors
crimes without victims
mala in se
mala prohibita
Carnivore
occupational crimes
organized crime
visible crime
political crimes

cybercrime
hate crime
National Incident-Based Reporting System (NIBRS)
Uniform Crime Reports (UCR)
National Crime Victimization Survey (NCVS)
dark figure of crime
precipitation
negligence

1. _____ assert that crime is normal behavior which may be undertaken by anyone depending on the social forces and groups that influence their behavior.

2. _____ asserts that criminal behavior stems from free will, and therefore the system should demand accountability from offenders through deterrence-oriented punishments.

3. _____ emphasize that the causes of criminal behavior are not found in the individual but in the social process that defines certain acts as deviant or criminal..

4. _____ assert that criminal law and the criminal justice system are primarily means of controlling the poor.

5. _____ is a state of normlessness caused by a breakdown in the rules of social behavior.

6. _____ assert that crime is learned behavior.

7. _____ assert that criminal behavior is caused by physiological and neurological factors.

8. _____ assert that crime is the creation of a lower-class culture as poor people respond to poverty and deprivation.

9. _____ assert that criminal behavior results when the bonds that tie an individual to others in society are broken.

10. _____ includes the study of how victims may precipitate crimes.

11. _____ asserts that criminal behavior stems from social, biological, and psychological factors.

12. _____ are influences that are thought to bring about criminal behavior in an individual.

13. _____ assert that mental processes and associated behaviors are the cause of criminal behavior.

14. _____ assert that people become criminals when they identify with family members and individuals who regard criminal activity as normal and usual.

15. _____ assert that social conditions that bear on the individual are the causes of crime.

16. _____ is the metaphor for the amount of crime that goes unreported to the police.

17. _____ is generated from a compilation of reports from law enforcement agencies throughout the country.

18. _____ is also known as street crime or ordinary crime.

19. _____ involve the willing and private exchange of illegal goods and services that are in strong demand.

20. _____ are offenses that are wrong by their very nature.

21. _____ measures the amount of crime from the perspective of victims.

22. _____ is the means through which each police officer will record and report each offense in a crime incident instead of merely describing the most serious crime in the incident.

23. _____ are criminal offenses committed through opportunities created in a legal business or occupation.

24. _____ are acts usually done for ideological purposes, such as treason and sedition, that constitute threats against the state.

25. _____ are offenses that are prohibited by law but are not inherently wrong.

26. _____ is a framework for the perpetration of criminal acts providing illegal services that are in great demand.

27. _____ moving the proceeds of criminal activities through a maze of businesses, banks, and brokerage accounts so as to disguise their origin.

28. The e-mail surveillance system used by the FBI is called _____.

29. A victim who leaves the keys in the vehicle contributes to motor vehicle theft through _____.

30. A victim who leaves a car in a vulnerable spot contributes to motor vehicle theft through _____.

31. An offense committed through the use of computers is called a _____.

32. Violent acts aimed at individuals because of their race are called _____ crimes.

REVIEW OF KEY PEOPLE
Fill in the appropriate person from the list for each statement below:
Laci Peterson
Edwin Sutherland
Cesare Lombroso
Cesare Beccaria
Sigmund Freud
Robert Merton
James Q. Wilson & Richard Hernnstein

1. _____: associated with the theory that criminality is biologically determined.

2. _____: wrote book examining research on links between biological factors and criminal behavior.

3. _____: associated with social structure theories of criminality and the idea that anomie within society influences criminal behavior.

4. _____ : developed theory that behavior can be caused by mental activity that takes place outside of our conscious awareness.

5. _____ : developed differential association theory.

6. _____ : regarded as the originator of classical criminology.

7. _____ : a pregnant woman who disappeared on Christmas Eve, 2002. Her body was later recovered from the San Francisco Bay and her husband was charged with her murder.

SELF-TEST SECTION
Multiple Choice Questions
2.1. In April 2003, who was charged with the murder of Laci Peterson and her infant son?
a) David Myers
b) Scott Peterson
c) the Mafia
d) James Kopp
e) Eric Rudolph

2.2. Which of the following are involved in organized crime?
a) African-Americans
b) Russians
c) Asians
d) Hispanics
e) all of the above

2.3. Which of the following is an example of politicians being tough on crime"?
a) adding 100,000 police officers to the streets
b) building more prisons
c) requiring parolees to register with the police
d) all of the above
e) none of the above

2.4. Which of the following is TRUE about gambling, prostitution, and drug use?
a) Everyone agrees that they should be crimes
b) Everyone agrees that prostitution should be a crime, but not drug use or gambling
c) Everyone agrees that drug use should be a crime, but not prostitution or gambling
d) Everyone agrees that gambling should be a crime, but not drug use or prostitution
e) Everyone does NOT agree that they should be crimes

2.5. Which of the following is TRUE about theories of criminality?
a) they focus on both the rich and the poor
b) they focus on visible and less visible crimes
c) some theories can predict criminality
d) they overemphasize the role of women
e) all of the theories contain a bit of truth

2.6. How did the Roe v. Wade (1973) decision impact the criminal justice system?
a) Roe ended the criminalization of early-term abortions
b) Roe ended the criminalization of homosexuality
c) Roe ended the death penalty for juveniles
d) Roe ended the "three strikes and you're out" laws
e) Roe ended the criminalization of euthanasia

2.7. Which of the following refers to crime committed using one or more computers?
a) online crime
b) high-tech crime
c) visible crime
d) cybercrime
e) intelcrime

2.8. The "war on drugs" is associated with what type of crime?
a) occupational crime
b) crimes without victims
c) visible crime
d) organized crime
e) cybercrime

2.9. What type of crime is the murder of an abortion doctor ?
a) occupational crime
b) victimless crime
c) visible crime
d) organized crime
e) political crime

2.10. What type of crime is homicide?
a) occupational crime
b) victimless crime
c) visible crime
d) organized crime
e) political crime

2.11. What type of crime is committed most often by "respectable well-to-do people"?
a) occupational crime
b) victimless crime
c) visible crime
d) organized crime
e) political crime

2.12. What type of crime is burning a cross?
a) occupational crime
b) victimless crime
c) hate crime
d) organized crime
e) cybercrime

2.13. A Seattle study found that the most feared crime was…
a) homicide
b) residential burglary
c) arson
d) forcible rape
e) embezzlement

2.14. What is the most accurate measure of crime in America?
a) Uniform Crime Reports
b) dark figure of crime
c) National Incident-Based Reporting System
d) National CrimeVictimization Survey
e) there is no accurate measure

2.15. How did the Lawrence v. Texas (2003) decision impact the criminal justice system?
a) Lawrence ended the criminalization of early-term abortions
b) Lawrence ended the criminalization of homosexuality
c) Lawrence ended the death penalty for juveniles
d) Lawrence ended the "three strikes and you're out" laws
e) Lawrence ended the criminalization of euthanasia

2.16. What freedoms might be violated by the Carnivore system used by the FBI?
a) right to free speech
b) right against cruel and unusual punishment
c) right to a trial by jury
d) right against unreasonable search and seizure
e) right to free press

2.17. Which measure of crime relies upon more detailed reports of crime by police agencies?
a) FBI Statistics Data
b) dark figure of crime
c) National Incident-Based Reporting System
d) National CrimeVictimization Survey
e) there is no such measure

2.18.Which of the following is a consequence of crime?
a) higher taxes
b) higher prices
c) increased levels of fear in society
d) all of the above
e) none of the above

2.19.Which of the following is FALSE about victims?
a) most victims of crime are young males who are nonwhite
b) many victims behave in ways that invite crime
c) victims of crimes by their own relatives are more willing to help in the investigation
d) all of the above are TRUE
e) all of the above are FALSE

2.20. Which of the follow is an example of a person who is criminogenic?
a) person becomes a criminal because of a dysfunctional childhood
b) person becomes a criminal because of poverty
c) person becomes a criminal because of a personality disturbance
d) person becomes a criminal because of huge jaws
e) all of the above

2.21. Which twentieth century thinker proposed a psychoanalytic theory of criminal behavior?
a) Cesare Lombroso
b) Cesare Beccaria
c) Sigmund Freud
d) Henry Goddard
e) Ada Jukes

2.22. Which of the following is TRUE concerning social process theory?
a) the poor are the only people who commit crimes
b) criminal behavior is abnormal behavior
c) people commit crimes because of the circumstances in their lives
d) social process theory gained recognition in the nineteenth century
e) all of the above are TRUE

2.23. Which of the following is TRUE concerning social structure theory?
a) the poor are the only people who commit crimes
b) criminal behavior is inborn
c) people commit crimes because of their physical traits
d) social structure theory is associated with social class
e) all of the above are TRUE

2.24. Which of the following is TRUE concerning social conflict theory?
a) the poor are the only people who commit crimes
b) criminal behavior is abnormal behavior
c) people commit crimes because of personality disorders
d) one type of social conflict theory is Marxism
e) all of the above are TRUE

2.25. Which of the following is TRUE about women and crime?
a) the number of crimes committed by women has increased recently
b) women commit the same types of crime as men
c) there has been more research about women as opposed to men
d) women account for one-half of all arrests
e) all of the above are TRUE

True and False Questions

_____ 2.1. The actual risk from crime is quite large.

_____ 2.2. Mala prohibita are acts prohibited by government.

_____ 2.3. Mala in se are acts wrong by nature.

_____ 2.4. The U. S. has only one source of data on crime, the Uniform Crime Reports.

_____ 2.5. Law enforcement officials focus largely upon visible crime.

_____ 2.6. The 2001 attacks on the World Trade Center are an example of a political crime.

_____ 2.7. Persons usually provide accurate information when interviewed about their experiences with crime.

_____ 2.8. Organized crime is associated with many different ethnic and racial groups.

_____ 2.9. Cybercrimes rarely involve the theft of personal funds.

_____ 2.10. The rise in crime in the 1970s has been blamed on the post-World War II baby boom.

_____ 2.11. Classical criminologists argue that laws and punishments should be hidden from the public.

_____ 2.12. Learning theory is a biological explanation for criminal behavior.

_____ 2.13. Fear of crime does NOT limit freedom.

_____ 2.14. Theories about the causes of crime are most often based on the observations of men.

_____ 2.15. Positivist criminologists argue that criminals are different from noncriminals.

_____ 2.16. Women commit far more crimes than men.

_____ 2.17. Freda Adler connects the increase in female crimes to the women's movement.

_____ 2.18. Murder, or criminal homicide is a Part I (Index Offense).

_____ 2.19. The persons most likely to be victimized by crime are whites and people with high-incomes.

_____ 2.20. Demographic factors (age gender, and income) affect lifestyle which, in turn, affects people's exposure to dangerous places.

WORKSHEET 2.1: THEORIES ABOUT THE CAUSES OF CRIME

On his way home from school, a fourteen-year-old boy from a poor family stops at a convenience store. When he thinks the clerk is not looking, he puts a bottle of orange juice under his coat and heads for the door. The clerk catches him and calls the police. How might one explain the boy's criminal action according to each of the following theories about causes of crime?

Biological Explanations_____

_____

_____

_____

_____

Psychological Explanations_____

_____

_____

_____

_____

Social Structure Theory_____

_____

_____

_____

_____

Social Process Theory_____

_____

_____

_____

_____

WORKSHEET 2.2: MULTIDISCIPLINARY PERSPECTIVE

Discuss how the following persons have contributed to the study of criminal behavior:

Edwin Sutherland_____

_____

_____

_____

_____

Robert Merton_____

_____

_____

_____

_____

Cesare Lombroso_____

_____

_____

_____

_____

Cesare Beccaria_____

_____

_____

_____

_____

Freda Adler _____

_____

_____

_____

_____

Rita Simon _____

_____

_____

_____

_____

CHAPTER 3

CRIMINAL JUSTICE AND THE RULE OF LAW

LEARNING OBJECTIVES

After covering the material in this chapter, students should understand:

1.   the development of American criminal law from the English common law system;

2.   the sources of criminal law;

3.   the principles of substantive criminal law;

4.   the accepted defenses and their justifications in substantive criminal law;

5.   the importance of procedural due process;

6.   the expansion of the meaning of the Bill of Rights and its protections for criminal defendants.

CHAPTER SUMMARY

Criminal law focuses on prosecution and punishment by the state of people who violate specific laws enacted by legislatures, while civil law concerns disputes between private citizens or businesses. Criminal law is divided into two parts: substantive law that defines offenses and penalties, and procedural law that defines individuals' rights and the processes that criminal justice officials must follow in handling cases. The common law tradition, which was inherited from England, involves judges' shaping law through their decisions. Criminal law is found in written constitutions, statutes, judicial decisions, and administrative regulations.

Substantive criminal law involves seven important elements that must exist and be demonstrated by the prosecution in order to obtain a conviction: legality, *actus reus,* causation, harm, concurrence, *mens rea,* punishment. The *mens rea* element, concerning intent or state of mind, can vary with different offenses, such as various degrees of murder or sexual assault. The element may also be disregarded for strict liability offenses that punish actions without considering intent. Criminal law provides opportunities to present several defenses based on lack of criminal intent: entrapment, self-defense, necessity, duress (coercion), immaturity, mistake, intoxication, and insanity. Standards for the insanity defense vary by jurisdiction with various state and federal courts using several different tests: M'Naghten Rule, Irresistible Impulse Test, Durham Rule, Comprehensive Crime Control Act Rule, the Model Penal Code rule.

The provisions of the Bill of Rights were not made applicable to state and local officials by the U.S. Supreme Court until the mid-twentieth century, when the Court incorporated most of the Bill of Rights' specific provisions into the due process clause of the Fourteenth Amendment. The Fourth Amendment prohibition on unreasonable searches and seizures has produced many cases questioning the application of the exclusionary rule. Decisions by the Burger and Rehnquist Courts during the 1970s, 1980s, and 1990s have created several exceptions to the exclusionary rule and given greater flexibility to law enforcement officials. The Fifth Amendment provides protections against compelled self-incrimination and double jeopardy. As part of the right against compelled self-incrimination, the Supreme Court created *Miranda* warnings that must be given to suspects before they are questioned. The Sixth Amendment includes the right to counsel, the right to a speedy and public trial, and the right to an impartial jury. The Eighth Amendment includes protections against excessive bail, excessive fines, and cruel and unusual punishments.

CHAPTER OUTLINE

I.   INTRODUCTION

A.   The bombing of the Murrah Federal Building in Oklahoma City on April 19, 1995 killed 168 people. **Timothy McVeigh** received a death sentence and executed in June 2001 for his integral role in the attack. Terry Nichols, a co-conspirator in the bombing, was convicted and received a life sentence in December 1997. The federal trials of McVeigh and Nichols demonstrate the dual nature of the American criminal justice system. A possibility remains that Nichols might be tried at the state level and given a death sentence for his role in the bombing. A second prosecution of Nichols illustrates that both the federal and state governments have the power to define crimes covering events in the same location, but they do not necessarily prosecute the same sets of crime. A second prosecution of Nichols also raises questions about the constitutional rights of the defendant in a second trial. Would this violate the double jeopardy clause of the Fifth Amendment or the right to a speedy trial in the Sixth Amendment? Hence, the two primary functions of the American criminal justice system are to define criminal behavior and to describe the procedures to be followed in order to respect the rights of criminal defendants.

II.   FOUNDATIONS OF THE CRIMINAL LAW

A.   Law must proscribe an act before it can be regarded as a crime and have accompanying punishment. **Civil law** concerns contracts, property, and personal injuries. **Criminal law** concerns conduct punishable by government.

B.   Criminal law is divided into substantive and procedural law:
    1.   **Substantive law:** stipulates the types of conduct that are criminal and the punishments to be imposed.
    2.   **Procedural law:** sets forth the rules that govern the enforcement of the substantive law.

III.   SUBSTANTIVE CRIMINAL LAW

A.   Seven Principles of Criminal Law
    1.   Legality: existence of a law defining the crime; the U.S. Constitution prohibits **ex post facto** laws.
    2.   **Actus reus:** behavior of either commission or omission; bad intentions alone or status alone (i.e., such as being a drug addict) is insufficient; must have act or omission
    3.   **Causation**: causal relationship between the act and the harm suffered.
    4.   Harm: damage inflicted on legally protected value (e.g., person, property, reputation); also includes the potential for harm: **inchoate offenses** when conspire to commit offense even if harm does not actually occur.
    5.   Concurrence: the simultaneous occurrence of the intention and the act.
    6.   **Mens rea** (a guilty state of mind): guilty mind requires intention to commit the act.
    7.   Punishment: the stipulation in the law of sanctions to be applied against persons found guilty of the forbidden behavior.

B.   Elements of a Crime
    1.   Attendant circumstances
    2.   **Actus rea** (the act)
    3.   **Mens rea** (state of mind)
        a.   Burglary example: entering a building or occupied structure (**actus rea**), with the intent to commit a crime (**mens rea**), when the premises are not open to the public or the actor is not privileged to enter (attendant circumstances).

C.   Statutory Definitions of Crimes
    1.   Definitions of crimes vary from state to state.

2.   Murder and Nonnegligent Manslaughter: murder requires **"malice aforethought"** or some other requirement of a higher level of intent

D.   Responsibility for Criminal Acts
   1.   **Mens rea**: key element for establishing perpetrator's responsibility; not necessarily whether person acted with consciousness of guilt, but whether a reasonable man in the defendant's situation and with his physical characteristics would have had a consciousness of guilt ("objective *mens rea*").
   2.   Accidents are not crimes because of the absence of *mens rea*, although acts of extreme negligence or recklessness may be criminal. Different levels of intent in criminal law. Depending on the statute, criminal acts may be done either intentionally, knowingly, recklessly, or negligently.
   3.   **Entrapment** is a defense claiming the absence of intent when the defendant lacks predisposition and government induced a law-abiding citizen to commit a crime.
        a.   1992 Supreme Court found entrapment in case of federal agents sending solicitations to Nebraska farmer to offer to sell him child pornography. According to Justice White's opinion: the government may not "originate a criminal design, implant in an innocent person's mind the disposition to commit a criminal act, and then induce commission of the crime so that the government may prosecute."
   4.   **Self-Defense:** person who feels in immediate danger of being harmed by another's unlawful use of force may ward off the attack in self-defense; generally must use only the force level necessary to defend yourself.
        a.   Atlanta Falcons football player, T. J. Duckett, defended himself when he was attacked by three assailants. He knocked one attacker unconscious and severely injured another. Duckett was entitled to defend himself with reasonable force against an unprovoked attack.

IDEAS IN PRACTICE: Can a person be charged with manslaughter if he or she used excessive force in defending him or herself?

   5.   **Necessity:** for one's own preservation or to avoid a greater evil, inflict a harm on a person who was not responsible for the imminent danger (i.e., person speeding in order to take a sick child to the hospital): famous example of survivors in lifeboat killing and eating cabin boy in order to survive
   6.   **Duress** (Coercion): a person who has been forced or coerced to commit an act has acted under duress.
        a.   During a bank robbery, if an armed robber forces a bank customer to drive the getaway car, the customer could claim duress to avoid criminal prosecution.
   7.   **Immaturity**: traditionally Anglo-American law has excused criminal behavior by children under the age of seven on the ground that they are immature and not responsible for their actions; arguments could be made concerning the capacity of seven- to fourteen-year-olds to contest whether they had sufficient maturity to be responsible for their actions.
   8.   Mistake: under the Model Penal Code a reasonable mistake of law or fact may be a defense.
   9.   **Intoxication:** voluntary intoxication is normally not a defense unless the crime required specific rather than general intent; a person tricked into consuming an intoxicating substance can use intoxication as a defense.
        a.   1996 U.S. Supreme Court decision approved Montana statute barring introduction of evidence of intoxication to negate intent element of crime.
   10.   **Insanity:** controversial and relatively rare defense successful in only about one percent of cases. Usually accompanied by civil commitment statute permitting insane acquittee to be hospitalized until condition improves. Five variations on insanity rule used by various states:
        a.   **M'Naghten Rule:** did not know what he was doing or did not know it was wrong.
        b.   **Irresistible Impulse Test**: could not control his own conduct.
        c.   **Durham Rule:** the criminal act was caused by his mental illness.
        d.   Model Penal Code (Substantial capacity test): lacks substantial capacity to appreciate the wrongfulness of his conduct or to control it.

e. Federal rule: lacks capacity to appreciate the wrongfulness of his conduct or wrongfulness of act a result of severe mental disease or defect. Implemented through the Comprehensive Crime Control Act of 1984.

f. After **John Hinckley's** assassination attempt on the life of President Ronald Reagan, the insanity defense was reexamined and eight states adopted the defense of "guilty but mentally ill" that allows conviction but requires psychiatric care during imprisonment. Federal law shifted burden of proof to defendant to prove insanity.

11. Close-Up: The Insanity Defense and Its Aftermath: A former teacher who tortured a student to death might be released from a mental facility after being acquitted through the insanity defense. By contrast, a man who broke a window in Virginia still held in a mental hospital thirteen years later a much longer period of confinement than if convicted of the crime.

IV. PROCEDURAL CRIMINAL LAW

A. Introduction
Accused persons in criminal cases must be accorded certain rights and protections in keeping with the adversarial nature of the proceeding and they must be tried according to legally established procedures.

1. Procedures may seek to advance truth seeking (e.g., trial by jury) or to prevent improper governmental actions (e.g., unreasonable searches and seizures).

2. What Americans Think: College freshman increasingly believe that courts show too much concern for the rights of criminals.

B. **Bill of Rights**
Ten amendments added to the U.S. Constitution in 1789 including protections against self-incrimination and double jeopardy.

1. *Barron v. Baltimore* **(1833):** initially determined that Bill of Rights only provided protection for individuals against actions by the federal government, not actions by state governments. The constitutions of many states contained their own lists of protections for people within those states.

C. The **Fourteenth Amendment** and Due Process
1. Post-Civil War amendment stating that "no State shall" deprive people of:
   a. the privileges and immunities of citizenship
   b. life, liberty, or property without due process of law
   c. equal protection of the laws
   These vague terms are subject to interpretation by the U.S. Supreme Court.

2. During the twentieth century the Supreme Court gradually made most of the provisions of the Bill of Rights applicable against the states by saying that individual rights had been incorporated into the 14th Amendment right to due process which was good against actions by states. This process was called **incorporation**.
   a. Several early cases caused the Supreme Court to identify due process rights possessed by people against the states: Powell v. Alabama (1932) concerning quick death sentences given to African-American defendants in unfair proceedings.
   b. Concept of **"fundamental fairness"** to determine which specific rights were applicable against the states as a component of the 14th Amendment right to due process.

WORK PERSPECTIVE: Amy Cruice, Case Investigator, American Civil Liberties Union, Annapolis, Maryland

D. **The Due Process Revolution**
Supreme Court applied specific provisions of the Bill of Rights against the states by incorporating into due process right of the 14th Amendment; most of the criminal defendants' rights in the Bill of Rights were incorporated during the 1960s.

1. **Earl Warren,** Chief Justice from 1953 to 1969
2. Warren Burger, Chief Justice from 1969 to 1986

E. **Fourth Amendment:** Protection Against Unreasonable Searches and Seizure
1. What is unreasonable?

2. Problems of the **Exclusionary Rule**: applicable against federal government in 1914 (**Weeks v. United States**); **Mapp v. Ohio (1961)** applied the exclusionary rule against state and local law enforcement officials after Cleveland police made a warrantless search of a home; exceptions created during the Burger and **Rehnquist** Court eras (e.g., **United States v. Leon**-good faith exception).
   a. Conservatives argue that exclusion is not effective against police misconduct and that it exacts a high price from society.
   b. Liberals argue that it is better for a few guilty people to go free than to permit police to engage in misconduct.
3. Recent Supreme Court decisions give greater flexibility to police for conducting searches.

F. <u>**Fifth Amendment**</u>: Protection Against Self-Incrimination & Double Jeopardy
   1. **Self-Incrimination:** Warren Court era decisions shifted focus from courtroom to defendants' initial contacts with police; thus require access to counsel (**Escobedo v. Illinois, 1964**) and to be informed of rights, including right to remain silent (**Miranda v. Arizona, 1966).**
      a. Statements obtained in violation of **Miranda warnings** can be excluded from evidence unless they fall under one of the exceptions created by the Burger Court (e.g., public safety, inevitable discovery rule).
   2. Suspects continue to confess. Police have adapted their interrogation techniques.
   3. **Double Jeopardy:** a person charged with a criminal act may be subjected to only one prosecution or punishment for that offense in the same jurisdiction; if a case dismissed before trial, a subsequent prosecution is permissible.
      a. Does not preclude the possibility of successive prosecutions in different (i.e., state or federal) jurisdictions. (Rodney King case had subsequent federal prosecution of police officers after initial state court acquittal).
      b. TECHNOLOGY ISSUES IN CRIMINAL JUSTICE: Detecting Guilt. What if technology such as polygraph machines or brain wave monitors allow law enforcement officials to read whether a person is being truthful?

G. <u>**Sixth Amendment**</u>: The Right to Counsel and Fair Trial
   1. **Right to Counsel: Gideon v. Wainwright (1963)** required appointed counsel for indigent state court defendants facing six months or more of incarceration. Right to counsel extended to other points in the process (preliminary hearings, etc.). However, no right to counsel for discretionary appeals or in trial with only fine as sentence. The Court reinforced Miranda in **Dickerson v. United States (2000).**
   2. Speedy and Public Trial: public trial is to protect defendant from arbitrary conviction.
   3. Impartial Jury: jury is supposed to serve a representative function; jury trial must be available in states to defendants facing serious charges. Jury is supposed to be drawn from fair cross-section of the community. There is no guarantee that the jury will be representative. Impartiality best achieved through random selection of jury pool; avoids exclusion of identifiable groups.
   4. Most Americans (64%) think that it is a bad idea for the government to listen in on conversations between attorneys and their clients.

H. <u>**Eighth Amendment**</u>: Protection Against Excessive Fines, Excessive Bail, and Cruel and Unusual Punishment
   1. Release on Bail: release not required, bail simply cannot be "excessive"; federal statute permits holding defendants in jail after a finding that they may be dangerous to the community or that no conditions of release would prevent flight from the jurisdiction (**United States v. Salerno and Cafero).**
   2. Excessive Fines: **Austin v. United States (1993),** justices unanimously returned to the lower court for re-hearing a case involved forfeiture of an estimated $40 million in real estate and businesses. In 1998, the Court actually identified an excessive fine when a traveler at an airport forfeited $357,000 for failing to report that he was transporting more than $10,000.

3.   Cruel and Unusual Punishment: Supreme Court determined in 1958 (**Trop v. Dulles**) that the term "cruel and unusual punishments" must be defined according to contemporary standards.

A QUESTION OF ETHICS: Should a criminal defendant who will not behave during court proceedings be given electric shock with a stun belt?

V. CONSTITUTIONAL RIGHTS AND CRIMINAL JUSTICE PROFESSIONALS

A.   In response to Supreme Court decisions involving constitutional rights, police, prosecutors, and correctional officers have been forced to develop guidelines for criminal justice professionals. Many people question whether the Court has struck the proper balance between the protection of constitutional rights and the need to punish criminal offenders.

VI. MY AFFAIR WITH HEROIN: Inside the Criminal Justice System and Beyond: One Man's Journey, written by Chuck Terry

REVIEW OF KEY TERMS

Fill in the appropriate term from the list for each statement below
United States v. Leon
Weeks v. United States
Trop v. Dulles
The Queen v. Dudley & Stephens
Escobedo v. Illinois
United States v. Salerno and Cafaro
Barron v. Baltimore
Mapp v. Ohio
Gideon v. Wainwright
Austin v. United States
Furman v. Georgia
Dickerson v. United States
Wyoming v. Houghton
Miranda v. Arizona
civil law
self-defense
substantive criminal law
inchoate offenses
mens rea
ex post facto
actus reus
causation
necessity
procedural due process
duress
incorporation
immaturity
exclusionary rule
M'Naghten Rule
Durham Rule
Irresistible Impulse Test
insanity defense
malice aforethought
intoxication
Bill of Rights
fundamental fairness

Fourth Amendment
New York v. Quarles
self incrimination
Fifth Amendment
capital punishment
Sixth Amendment
double jeopardy
Eighth Amendment
right to counsel
Fourteenth Amendment
entrapment

1. _____ defines the acts that the government will punish and specifies the punishments for such offenses.

2. The Court ruled in _____ that evidence obtained from improper questioning could be used if a situation posed an immediate threat to public safety.

3. _____ may be used with reasonable force to protect against criminal attacks.

4. _____ is a legal doctrine supporting the idea that so long as a state's conduct maintains basic standards of fairness, the Constitution has not been violated.

5. _____ is the portion of the Constitution used by the Supreme Court to bar states from violating people's right to due process of law.

6. _____ is a crucial element of intent for murder charges.

7. _____ is the claim that someone lacked the appropriate mental capacity to be held responsible for a criminal act.

8. _____ is the body of rules that regulate the relationships between or among individuals, usually involving property, contracts or business disputes.

9. _____ is a constitutional right that attempts to assure that criminal defendants' rights are protected during the processing of cases.

10. _____ is the extension of the Due Process Clause of the Fourteenth Amendment to make binding on state governments the rights guaranteed in the Bill of Rights.

11. _____ is a defense with its historical roots in sailors' cannibalism while lost at sea.

12. _____ is a defense that is rarely available unless someone unwittingly ingested alcohol.

13. _____ prevents the use of torture and mutilation as punishment.

14. _____ means "guilty mind" or blameworthy state of mind, necessary for legal responsibility for a criminal offense.

15. _____ is a criminal law written to punish an act that has already occurred.

16. _____ is the required action component of criminal laws.

17. _____ provides a defense in some jurisdictions when a defendant could not control his own conduct.

18. _____ is a defense when someone physically forces someone else to commit a crime.

19. _____ provides the right against double jeopardy.

20. _____ is the necessary relationship in criminal law between an action and the harm suffered.

21. _____ is the act of exposing oneself to prosecution by being forced to respond to questions whose answers may reveal that one has committed a crime.

22. _____ is the constitutional provision that seeks to make people feel secure against unwarranted intrusions into their homes and property.

23. _____ provides assurances that accused persons in criminal cases will be accorded certain rights and will be tried according to legally established procedures.

24. _____ is the most severe punishment in the American criminal justice system which is governed by rules against cruel and unusual punishments.

25. _____ provides a defense that police induced a particular individual to commit a crime.

26. _____ provides a defense in some jurisdictions when a defendant did not know what he was doing or did not know that was he was doing was wrong.

27. _____ the principle that illegally obtained evidence must be excluded from trial.

28. _____ provides the right to trial by jury.

29. _____ contains a list of rights added to the Constitution and initially applicable only against the federal government.

30. _____ is a defense when someone is considered too young to form the necessary intent to be held responsible for a criminal act.

31. _____ provides the right against excessive fines.

32. _____ provides a defense in some jurisdictions when the criminal act was caused by mental illness.

33. _____ is a right against being tried twice in the same jurisdiction for the same offense.

34. _____ are crimes that include conduct that is criminal even though the harm that the law seeks to prevent has not been done but merely planned or attempted.

35. _____ is the case that required an attorney be provided to suspects when they are taken into custody.

36. _____ is the case that required states to provide attorneys for felony defendants who could not pay for an attorney themselves.

37. _____ is the case in which the Supreme Court applied the exclusionary rule against state and local officials in cases of improper searches and seizures.

38. _____ is a case that created an exception to the exclusionary rule.

39. _____ is the case that required police officers to inform suspects of their due process rights upon arrest or else confessions could not be admitted as evidence.

40. _____ is the case in which the Supreme Court determined that the Excessive Fines Clause of the Eighth Amendment applies to seizures of property by the government.

41. _____ is the case that examined the necessity defense for cannibalism on the high seas.

42. _____ is a U. S. Supreme Court ruling that the protections of the Bill of Rights apply only to actions of the federal government.

43. _____ is the case that reinforced the Miranda warnings by upholding the Miranda v. Arizona precedent.

44. _____ is the case in which the Supreme Court upheld the Bail Reform Act which permits federal judges to detain without bail suspects considered dangerous to the public.

45. _____ is the case from 1914 that decided evidence must be excluded when federal law enforcement officials conduct an improper search.

46. _____ is the case that decided police can search auto passengers' purses, suitcases, and other containers if the driver of the car is found in possession of drugs or other contraband.

47. _____ is the case that decided the meaning of the Eighth Amendment's cruel and unusual punishments clause shall be defined by evolving societal standards.

REVIEW OF KEY PEOPLE
Fill in the appropriate person from the list for each statement below
Earl Warren
Timothy McVeigh
John Hinckley
King John of England
William Rehnquist

1. The current Chief Justice on the U. S. Supreme Court who was appointed in 1986 is _____.

2. Chief Justice _____ led a liberal revolution that changed the meaning and scope of constitutional rights.

3. In 1215, _____ issued the Magna Carta, the first written guarantee of due process.

4. _____ was found guilty of planning and carrying out the Oklahoma City bombing and he was executed in June 2001.

5. _____ attempted to assassinate President Ronald Reagan in 1981.

SELF-TEST SECTION

Multiple Choice Questions

3.1. Who was executed in June 2001 for the Oklahoma City bombing?
a) Terry Nichols
b) Timothy McVeigh
c) John Hinckley
d) Michael Fortier
e) all of the above were executed for their part in the bombing

3.2. What type of law governs business deals, contracts, and real estate?
a) civil law
b) criminal law
c) authoritarian law
d) substantive law
e) common law

3.3. What is another name for substantive criminal law?
a) common law
b) civil law
c) procedural criminal law
d) moral code
e) penal code

3.4. Which of the following write substantive criminal law?
a) Congress
b) state legislatures
c) city councils
d) all of the above
e) none of the above

3.5. Who summarized in a single statement the major principles of Western criminal law?
a) William Rehnquist
b) Earl Warren
c) Jerome Hall
d) Warren Burger
e) King John

3.6. What is legal scholar, Jerome Hall, known for in the area of criminal law?
a) Hall created the Durham Rule for insanity defenses
b) Hall summarized the major principles of Western criminal law in a single statement
c) Hall is known for defining self-defense in criminal cases
d) Hall wrote the Comprehensive Crime Control Act while serving as a legal counsel in the U. S. Senate
e) Hall wrote an article that launched the incorporation of the Bill of Rights upon the states

3.7. What distinguishes murder from manslaughter?
a) exclusionary rule
b) common law
c) civil law
d) procedural criminal law
e) malice aforethought

3.8. Which of the following principles of criminal law is crucial in establishing responsibility for the criminal act?
a) legality
b) causation
c) punishment
d) mens rea
e) concurrence

3.9. Which of the following has been used as a test for insanity?
a) M'Naghten Rule
b) Irresistible Impulse Test
c) The Durham Rule
d) Substantial Capacity Test
e) all of the above

3.10. The U. S. Supreme Court struck down a California law that made it a crime to be addicted to drugs in the case of...
a) Cohen v. California (1971)
b) Rochin v California (1954)
c) Chimel v. California (1969)
d) O. J. Simpson v. California (1995)
e) Robinson v. California (1962)

3.11. What did the Supreme Court rule in *Montana v. Egelhoff*?
a) states may NOT enact laws that prevent the use of an intoxication defense
b) states may enact laws that prevent the use of an intoxication defense
c) states may NOT enact laws that prevent the use of an immaturity defense
d) states may enact laws that prevent the use of an immaturity defense
e) states must enact laws that prevent the use of an insanity defense

3.12. What did the Supreme Court decide in *U. S. v. Leon (1984)*?
a) the Court created a "good-faith" exception to the exclusionary rule
b) the Court created a "public safety" exception to the exclusionary rule
c) the Court created an "inevitable discovery" exception to the exclusionary rule
d) the Court ruled that no exceptions existed to the exclusionary rule
e) the Court created the exclusionary rule

3.13. What did the Supreme Court decide in *New York v. Quarles (1984)*?
a) the Court created a "good-faith" exception to the exclusionary rule
b) the Court created a "public safety" exception to the exclusionary rule
c) the Court created an "inevitable discovery" exception to the exclusionary rule
d) the Court ruled that no exceptions existed to the exclusionary rule
e) the Court created the exclusionary rule

3.14. What did the Supreme Court decide in *Kyollo v. U. S. (2001)*?
a) police may use lie detectors during questioning of suspects
b) police may NOT use lie detectors during questioning of suspects
c) police may be use force against a suspect if it is reasonable
d) police may use thermal imaging devices to detect the presence of heat
e) police may NOT use thermal imaging devices to detect the presence of heat in a home

3.15. The level of force used in self-defense cannot exceed the...
a) police's reasonable perception of the threat
b) person's (using self-defense) reasonable perception of the threat
c) judge's reasonable perception of the threat
d) average person's reasonable perception of the threat
e) threat as perceived by the person who is the attacker (not the person exercising self-defense)

3.16. Which of the following is TRUE about the Bill of Rights and state power?
a) only one amendment of the Bill of Rights applies to state power
b) a few of the amendments in the Bill of Rights apply to state power
c) most of the amendments in the Bill of Rights apply to state power
d) all of the amendments in the Bill of Rights apply to state power
e) none of the amendments in the Bill of Rights apply to state power

3.17. Under the Fifth Amendment, how many times can a person be prosecuted or punished for an offense in the same jurisdiction?
a) once
b) twice
c) three times
d) four times
e) unlimited number of times

3.18.Who issued the Magna Carta?
a) King Edward
b) King George
c) King John
d) Queen Victoria
e) Prince Alfred

3.19. Prior to the 1960s, the Supreme Court was unwilling to allow confessions that were beaten out of suspects under the doctrine of…
a) fundamental fairness
b) prior restraint
c) clear and present danger
d) self-incrimination
e) Miranda warnings

3.20. What three amendments were added to the U. S. Constitution immediately after the Civil War?
a) First, Second, and Third
b) Fourth, Fifth, and Sixth
c) Tenth, Eleventh, and Twelfth
d) Thirteenth, Fourteenth, and Fifteenth
e) Twentieth, Twenty-First, and Twenty-Second

3.21. Which chief justice led a liberal revolution that expanded the scope of constitutional rights?
a) William Rehnquist
b) Oliver Wendell Holmes
c) Hugo Black
d) Earl Warren
e) John Jay

3.22. Which U. S. Supreme Court decision applied the exclusionary rule to the states?
a) Marbury v. Madison (1803)
b) Barron v. Baltimore (1833)
c) Durham v United States (1954)
d) Mapp v. Ohio (1961)
e) Gibbons v. Ogden (1824)

3.23. Which of the following best explains Chief Justice Rehnquist's philosophy is cases dealing with criminal justice?
a) Rehnquist has expanded the rights of criminal suspects
b) Rehnquist has eliminated the rights of criminal suspects
c) Rehnquist has endorsed the actions of police officers and prosecutors
d) Rehnquist has supported all state and local judges, regardless of ideology
e) Rehnquist has refused to hear cases dealing with criminal justice

3.24. What is the standard established in the Fourth Amendment for a warrant to be issued?
a) reasonable doubt
b) probable cause
c) reasonable suspicion
d) preponderance of the evidence
e) each judge decides his or her own standard

3.25. During what era did the Supreme Court apply most criminal justice rights in the U. S. Constitution against the states?
a) 1935 to 1948
b) 1962 to 1972
c) 1983 to 1990
d) 1994 to 2002
e) the Supreme Court has only applied a few of the rights in the U. S. Constitution to the states

True and False Questions

_____ 3.1. A civil trial involves relationships between individuals.

_____ 3.2. The U. S. criminal justice system operates according to civil law.

_____ 3.3. Substantive criminal law answers the question "What is illegal"?

_____ 3.4. The judiciary defines certain acts as crimes.

_____ 3.5. Americans are fond of saying "we have a government of men, not of laws."

_____ 3.6. States may enact laws that prevent the use of an intoxication defense.

_____ 3.7. The current rule for establishing an insanity defense is the Durham Rule.

_____ 3.8. A person cannot be arrested for simply being under the influence of drugs.

_____ 3.9. Men and women today show little difference in their support for criminal defendants' rights.

_____ 3.10. The Bill of Rights was nationalized through the Fifteenth Amendment.

_____ 3.11. Chief Justice Earl Warren limited the interpretation of criminal defendants' rights.

_____ 3.12. Self-defense is based on the defending person's perception of the threat.

_____ 3.13. The criminal defendants' rights are found in the Fourth, Fifth, Sixth, and Seventh Amendments.

_____ 3.14. Timothy McVeigh was the only person involved in the Oklahoma City bombing.

_____ 3.15. The Bill of Rights was ratified by the states at the same time as the U. S. Constitution.

_____ 3.16. The cruel and unusual punishment clause is found in the Eighth Amendment.

_____ 3.17. The double jeopardy clause is found in the Fifth Amendment.

_____ 3.18. The process of incorporation occurred during the Burger Court era.

_____ 3.19. The Bill of Rights contains the first ten amendments to the U. S. Constitution.

_____ 3.20. Chief Justice William Rehnquist supports criminal defendants and their rights more often than he supports the actions of police officers.

WORKSHEET 3.1: PRINCIPLES OF CRIMINAL LAW

Acting in response to complaints about smokers gathering in the lobby of the library, the Board of Trustees of the Jonesville Public Library approves the following new rule on the evening of February 6th. The new rule states:

"It shall be unlawful for anyone to smoke at the public library. This rule shall take effect as soon as the Jonesville City Council meets to approve it."

The Jonesville City Council is scheduled to consider the new rule at its 7 p.m. meeting on February 15th. The Library's new smoking rule is the third item scheduled for discussion on the Council's agenda.
At 7:05 p.m. on February 15th, Sam Johnson leaves the public library. At the front door to the library he encounters his brother John. John is struggling while using both hands to carry ten overdue books. He has a lighted cigarette dangling from his mouth. "Hey, John," says Sam, "I don't think that you're supposed to smoke in the library anymore." "Really, I hadn't heard that," said John. "Say, while you're holding the door for me, Sam, can you take this cigarette and put it in that ashtray in the lobby? Thanks a million." As Sam took the cigarette from his brother's lips and walked toward the ashtray, a police officer coming out of the lobby arrested him for violating the library's anti-smoking rule.

You are asked to serve as Sam's attorney. Use four of the seven principles of criminal law to formulate arguments on Sam's behalf about why he should not be found guilty of violating the rule.

1._____

_____

_____

_____

2._____

_____

_____

_____

3._____

_____

_____

_____

4._____

_____

_____

WORKSHEET 3.2: INSANITY DEFENSE

Over the course of seven years, a mother has five babies and they all die during the first months of their lives. Doctors conclude that each child died from Sudden Infant Death Syndrome (SIDS) -- commonly known as "crib death" -- the unexplainable cause of death for 7,000 to 8,000 American babies each year. The woman's family doctor publishes an article about her family to show how SIDS tragically seems to run in families, perhaps for unknown genetic reasons. Years later a prosecutor notices the article and charges the woman with murdering all of her children. The woman initially confesses during police questioning but later claims that the police pressured her to confess. You are hired as her defense attorney. A psychiatrist friend of yours tells you that your client might suffer from a psychiatric condition known as "Munchausen's syndrome by proxy." You hope to use this information to consider presenting an insanity defense.

1. Go to the library and locate a book on medicine or psychiatry that can define for you "Munchausen's syndrome by proxy." What is the definition?

_____

_____

_____

2. Briefly explain whether or not your client's condition can fulfill the requirements of the various tests for the insanity defense.

M'Naghten:_____

_____

_____

Irresistible Impulse:_____

_____

_____

Durham:_____

_____

_____

Substantial Capacity:_____

_____

_____

Federal Comprehensive Crime Control Act:_____

_____

_____

WORKSHEET 3.3: FOURTH AMENDMENT AND EXCLUSIONARY RULE

A woman called the police to her home after her daughter was severely beaten earlier in the day by the daughter's boyfriend. The daughter agreed to use her key to let the officers into the apartment where the man was sleeping. The officers did not seek to obtain either an arrest warrant or a search warrant. After the daughter unlocked the apartment door, the officers entered and found a white substance, which later proved to be cocaine, sitting on a table. They arrested the sleeping man and charged him with narcotics offenses. The defendant sought to have the drugs excluded from evidence because the officers' warrantless search was based on permission from the girlfriend who had moved out of the apartment several weeks earlier and therefore had no authority to give the officers permission to enter and search.

As the prosecutor, think about possible exceptions to the exclusionary rule, such as those discussed for the Fourth and Fifth Amendments, to make arguments about why the evidence should not be excluded.

1._____

_____

_____

2._____

_____

_____

Now, imagine that you are the judge. Decide whether the evidence obtained in the warrantless search should be excluded. Provide reasons for your decision. Consider the words of the Fourth Amendment, the purposes of the Amendment, and the potential effects on society from the rule you formulate for this case.

_____

_____

_____

_____

_____

_____

_____

_____

_____

[Compare with *Illinois v. Rodriguez*, 110 S.Ct. 2793 (1990)].

WORKSHEET 3.4: FIFTH AND SIXTH AMENDMENTS

After arresting a suspect for burglary, police officers learned that the suspect's nickname was "Butch." A confidential informant had previously told them that someone named "Butch" was guilty of an unsolved murder in another city. The police in the other city were informed about this coincidence and they sent officers to question the suspect about the murder. Meanwhile, the suspect's sister secured the services of a lawyer to represent her brother on the burglary charge. Neither she nor the lawyer knew about the suspicions concerning the unsolved murder case. The lawyer telephoned the police station and said she would come to the station to be present if the police wished to question her client. The lawyer was told that the police would not question him until the following morning and she could come to the station at that time. Meanwhile, the police from the other city arrived and initiated the first of a series of evening questioning sessions with the suspect. The suspect was not informed that his sister had obtained the services of a lawyer to represent him. The suspect was not told that the lawyer had called the police and asked to be present during any questioning. During questioning, the suspect was informed of his *Miranda* rights, waived his right to be represented by counsel during questioning, and subsequently confessed to the murder.

1. If you were the defense attorney, what arguments would you make to have the confession excluded from evidence?

_____

_____

_____

_____

_____

2. If you were the judge, would you permit the confession to be used in evidence? Provide reasons for your decision.

_____

_____

_____

_____

_____

_____

[Compare your decision with *Moran v. Burbine*, 475 U.S. 412 (1985)]

CHAPTER 4

POLICE

LEARNING OBJECTIVES

After covering the material in this chapter, students should understand:

1.   the English origins from which American police eventually developed;

2.   the history of American police, including the Political Era, the Professional Model era, and the Community Model era;

3.   organization of the police in the American federal system, including federal, state, county, municipal, and Native American Tribal agencies

4.   styles of policing, including watchman, legalistic, and service;

5.   police functions and the extent of those functions, including order maintenance, law enforcement, and service;

6.   the nature of police work, including citizen-police encounters and the role of discretion;

7.   the underlying issues and development of practices to address domestic violence.

8.   Police dealing with special populations, multi-cultural populations and the movement toward community crime prevention.

CHAPTER SUMMARY

The police in the United States have their roots in the early nineteenth-century developments of policing in England. Similar to England, the American police have limited authority, are under local control, and are organizationally fragmented. Three eras of American policing are: the political era (1840-1920), the professional era (1920-1970), and the community policing era (1970-present). In the U.S. federal system of government, police agencies are found at the national, state, county, and municipal levels. Improvements have been made during the past quarter-century in recruiting more officers who are women, racial and ethnic minorities, and well-educated applicants. The functions of the police are order maintenance, law enforcement, and service. Police executives develop policies on how they will allocate their resources according to one of three styles: the watchman, legalistic, or service styles. Discretion is a major factor in police actions and decisions. Patrol officers exercise the greatest amount of discretion. The problem of domestic violence demonstrates the connection between police encounters with citizens, their exercise of discretion, and police actions. Police face challenges in dealing with special populations, such as the mentally ill and homeless, who need social services, yet often attract the attention of police because they disturb or offend other citizens as they walk the streets. Policing in a multicultural society requires an appreciation of the attitudes, customs, and languages of minority-group members. For police to be effective they must maintain their connection with the community.

CHAPTER OUTLINE

I.   INTRODUCTION.

The terrorist attacks on September 11, 2001 demonstrated that we are not completely secure in our society. Before the destruction of the World Trade Center, most Americans had little reason to recognize the number of agencies with law enforcement responsibilities and their particular areas of emphasis. As a result of September 11th, we are more aware and appreciative of the law enforcement agencies at all of levels of the American criminal justice system.

II.   THE DEVELOPMENT OF THE POLICE IN THE UNITED STATES

A.   The English Roots of the American Police
1.   Three major traditions passed from England to the United States:
a.   limited authority
b.   local control
c.   organizational fragmentation
2.   In early England, **frankpledge** system required that groups of ten families, called tithings, agree to uphold the law, maintain order, and commit to court those who had violated the law. Every male above the age of twelve was required to be part of the system. The tithing was fined if members did not perform their duties.
3.   Parish constable system established in England in 1285 under the **Statute of Winchester**. All citizens required to pursue criminals under direction of constables. Traditional system of community law enforcement maintained well into the eighteenth century.
4.   **Bow Street Runners**, amateur volunteer force in London impressed authorities with their effectiveness, but concept unable to spread around the country after death of founder, **Henry Fielding**, in 1754.
5.   In 1829, under Home Secretary **Sir Robert Peel**, Parliament established the Metropolitan Constabulary for London, which was structured along the lines of a military unit. The Home Secretary was responsible for supervising the **"bobbies"** (named after Robert Peel).
6.   Early English police mandate was to maintain order while keeping a low profile; attempted to use nonviolent methods and minimize conflict between police and public. Leaders feared that if the police were too powerful or too visible, they might threaten civil liberties. Four-part mandate:
a.   Prevent crime without repressive use of force and avoid military intervention in community disturbances;
b.   Manage public order nonviolently, using force to obtain compliance only as last resort;
c.   Minimize and reduce conflict between the police and the public;
d.   Demonstrate efficiency by means of the absence of crime and disorder rather than by physical evidence of police actions in dealing with problems.

B.   Policing in the United States
1.   Before the Revolution, Americans shared English belief that community members had a basic responsibility to help maintain order. Over time, ethnic diversity, local political control, regional differences, the opening up of the West, and the violent traditions of American society were factors that brought about a different development of police in the United States compared with that in England.
2.   **The Political Era**: 1840-1920
a.   Growth of cities led to pressure for modernization of police forces. Cities faced ethnic conflicts as a consequence of massive immigration, hostility toward non-slave African-Americans, mob actions against banks and other institutions during economic declines: raised fears about the survival of democratic institutions.
b.   Large cities, such as Boston and Philadelphia, took first steps toward adding daytime police force to supplement night watchmen.
c.   In urban North, close ties developed between police and local political leaders; political party machine recruited and maintained the police and the police acted on behalf of local politicians. Police performed crime prevention, order maintenance, and service functions in decentralized manner by responding to problems individually as they encountered them.

d. In the South, first organized police patrols in cities with large slave populations because whites feared revolts. "Slave patrols" had full powers to search, arrest, and administer corporal punishment against African-Americans.

e. The frontier West often governed by vigilante justice. Local sheriffs depended on the assistance of men in the community. Federal marshals were primarily responsible for courtroom security and custody of prisoners.

3. **The Professional Model Era**: 1920-1970

a. Progressive reform movement pushed by upper-middle-class, educated Americans sought to rid government of party politics and patronage. Reformers influenced by the Progressive movement sought to professionalize police and remove the connections between police and local politicians. Two primary goals of Progressives were to create efficient government and us e government services to improve services for the poor.

b. Six elements emphasized in model of professional policing:
   i. Police force should stay out of politics.
   ii. Members should be well-trained, highly disciplined, and tightly organized.
   iii. Laws should be equally enforced.
   iv. Police should take advantage of technological developments;
   v. Merit rather than political patronage should be the basis of personnel decisions;
   vi. Crime fighting should be prominent.

c. Switch to crime fighting emphasis from order maintenance emphasis did more to change the nature of American policing than did any of the other aspects of the professionalism model.

d. Reformers such as **August Vollmer** and **O.W. Wilson** introduced motorized patrols, radio communication, rapid response plans, and rotating beat assignments. Diminished connections between individual police officers and specific neighborhoods and citizens. The emphasis on professionalism encouraged the creation of national organizations such as the International Association of Police Chiefs.

e. By the 1930s and thereafter, police emphasized their concern with serious crimes as the police increased their reliance on technology, centralized decision making, and equal enforcement of the laws.

f. During the 1960s, the civil rights and anti-war movements as well as urban riots raised questions about the professional model. Police were isolated from the communities that they were supposed to serve and their attempts to maintain order appeared to focus on maintaining the status quo at the expense of political minorities, such as inner-city residents.

4. **The Community Model Era**: 1970-Present

a. Research questioned the professional model's effectiveness. Important research findings clashed with major tenets of the professional crime-fighter model. These findings included:
   i. Increasing number of police officers in neighborhood was found to have little effect on crime rate.
   ii. Rapid response to calls for service does not greatly increase the arrest of criminals.
   iii. It is difficult if not impossible to improve rates of solving crimes.

b. Critics argued that professional model, especially use of motorized patrol, isolated police from the community.

c. **James Q. Wilson** and **George Kelling** argued in their **"broken windows theory"** that a reorientation to little problems, such as maintenance of order, provision of services, and strategies to reduce the fear of crime, would be most beneficial for reducing community fear and improving quality of life by preventing neighborhood disorder and deterioration. Also would improve public attitudes toward the police by moving to a problem-oriented approach.

d.   Remains to be seen whether this new orientation, which has its critics, will increase police effectiveness. Much depends on exactly what the public and government leaders expect police to accomplish.

III. LAW ENFORCEMENT AGENCIES

A.   **Federal Agencies**
Have taken dominant role in eyes of media and public although fewer in number than state and local agencies.

1.   **Federal Bureau of Investigation**: broadest range of control; investigates all crimes not under control of other federal agencies.

   a.   **J. Edgar Hoover** became Director in 1924; made major changes to increase professionalism and reduce reputation for corruption and violation of civil liberties. After Hoover, the FBI has been criticized for its responsiveness to the policies of particular presidential administrations.

2.   Specialization in Federal Law Enforcement:

   a.   Drug Enforcement Administration (DEA)

   b.   Bureau of Alcohol, Tobacco, and Firearms (BATF)

   c.   **Secret Service**; Div. of Treasury Dept. (responsible for counterfeiting, forgery, protection of the president).

   d.   Internal Revenue Service

   e.   Bureau of Postal Inspection

   f.   Border Patrol; Div. of Immigration and Naturalization Service

   g.   U.S. Coast Guard

   h.   National Parks Service

3.   Federal Agencies after September 11: In the aftermath of 9-11, there has been an expansion and reorganization, especially among federal law enforcement agencies. A key development has been the creation of the **Department of Homeland Security** which is responsible for protecting the U. S. from terrorist attacks.

   a.   The President requested $36.2 billion to the Homeland Security Office to develop and coordinate the implementation of a comprehensive strategy to secure the U. S. from terrorist attacks.

   b.   The Department of Homeland Security is divided into four directorates:

      i.   Border and Transportation Security

      ii.   Emergency Preparedness and Response

      iii.   Science and Technology

      iv.   Information Analysis and Infrastructure Protection

   c.   With the events of 9-11, the role of federal law enforcement agencies is being reoriented to focus more on international and domestic terrorism and less on local street crimes.

WORK PERSPECTIVE: Maureen Pawlak, Special Agent for the U. S. Department of Education

B.   State Agencies
Every state except Hawaii has **state police**; in many states they fill the void for enforcement in rural areas; also may have state crime lab available for all local law enforcement agencies.

C.   County Agencies
Sheriffs are found in almost all of the 3,100 counties in the U.S.; traditionally have had responsibility for rural policing; sheriff often also has responsibility for local jail; may be selected by election or by political appointment depending on state.

D.   Native American Tribal Police:
Native American tribes have significant autonomy. Tribal law enforcement agencies may enforce laws on Native American reservations.

E.   Municipal Agencies:
The police departments of cities and towns have general law enforcement authority. City police forces range in size from 40,000 full-time sworn offices to only one in small towns.

IV.   POLICE FUNCTIONS

A.   Introduction
Complete list includes facilitating movement of people and vehicles, resolving conflicts, identifying problems, creating and maintaining feeling of security in community, and assisting those who cannot care for themselves.

B.   **Order Maintenance**
Order Maintenance: prevent disturbances and threats to public peace. It requires the exercise of significant discretion when officers decide how to handle situations as they arise.

IDEAS IN PRACTICE: Can a police officer make a situation worse by intervening in a dispute?

C.   **Law Enforcement**
Situations in which the law has been violated and only the identity of the guilty needs to be determined. Victims frequently delay calling the police, thereby reducing the likelihood of apprehending the offender.

D.   **Service**
First aid, rescuing animals, and extending social welfare services, especially to lower class citizens. Most calls to police are unrelated to crime and many are merely seeking information. Many of these functions may assist crime control, such as checking the doors of buildings, dealing with runaways and drunks, etc.

E.   Implementing the Mandate
1.   Police administrators have learned that they can gain greater support for their budgets by emphasizing the crime-fighting function.
2.   David Bayley argues that police do not prevent crime.
    a.   There is no connection between number of officers and the crime rate.
    b.   Primary strategies adopted by the police have not been shown to affect crime. These core strategies are patrolling the street by uniformed officers, rapid response to emergency calls, and expert investigation by detectives.

V.   POLICE POLICY
Police use their discretion in determining how to deploy resources and which criminal behaviors to address or overlook.

CLOSE-UP: HIGH SPEED PURSUIT- High speed pursuits are dangerous and controversial. Most states have written policies to govern high speed chases. Guidelines exist but officers still must analyze the situation, use discretion in a highly emotional environment.

A QUESTION OF ETHICS: Should a police officer handle a situation differently because the youths involved are from a wealthy community?

A.   Styles of Policing
Community influence on policing: **James Q. Wilson** found that political culture, reflecting socioeconomic characteristics of city and the
organization of city government exerted major influence over police operational style:
1.   **Watchman style**: emphasize order maintenance in declining industrial town, partisan mayor-council form of government; ignore minor violations, especially traffic and juvenile.
2.   **Legalistic style**: emphasize law enforcement in good government council-manager form of government; police acted as if there was a single standard of community conduct; police professionalism; large number of traffic tickets and misdemeanor arrests.

3. **Service style**: emphasize balance between maintaining order and law enforcement; less likely than the legalistic to make arrests in suburban communities; burglaries and assaults taken seriously, but seek to avoid arrests for minor offenses.

VI. POLICE ACTIONS

A. Technology Issues in Criminal Justice : Computers in Patrol Cars
   1. Computers in patrol cars have improved police efficiency. Police officers are able to gather information quickly but computers also impose financial costs and unintended consequences such as the need to train officers and safety concerns over computers becoming projectiles in high speed chases or collisions.

B. Encounters Between Police and Citizens
   1. The accessibility of the police to the citizen, the complainant's demeanor and characteristics, and the type of violation all structure official reaction and the probability of arrest. However, many people fail to call the police to report crimes because they believe that it is not worth the effort and the cost to the citizens' time. Thus citizens exercise control over police work by the decisions about whether or not to call the police.
   2. What Americans Think: Americans appear to have confidence in police.

C. Police Discretion
   Discretion is a characteristic of organizations: officials are given the authority to base decisions on their own judgment rather than on a formal set of rules.
   1. Discretion increases as one moves down the organizational hierarchy: patrol officers have the greatest amount of discretion in maintaining order and enforcing highly ambiguous laws (e.g. disorderly conduct, public drunkenness, breach of the peace, etc.)
   2. Officers exercise discretion in a number of ways: noninvolvement, arrest, informal handling of incident, etc.
   3. Four factors especially important in affecting officers' exercise of discretion:
      a. Nature of the crime.
      b. Relationship between the alleged criminal and the victim.
      c. Relationship between the police and the criminal or victim.
      d. Race/Ethnicity, age, gender, class.
      e. Departmental policies.
   4. Formal rules cannot cover all situations; officers must have a shared outlook that provides a common definition of situations they are likely to encounter.

D. **Domestic Violence**
   1. Domestic violence perpetrated by men against women is consistent across racial and ethnic boundaries. African-American women, women aged 16-24 , from urban areas, and from lower income families are the most likely to be victims of violence by an intimate. Thirty percent of all female murder victims were killed by an intimate.
   2. Until mid-1970s, often not treated as serious criminal matter despite the fact that many women are victimized repeatedly. Concerns were expressed that police would make the situation worse for the victim by intervening into a "private family matter."
   3. Intervention in domestic disputes was also dangerous to police officers: volatile, emotional situations; police officer in field feels challenged to choose appropriate response to the situation.
   4. In the past, officers tried to calm the couple and make a referral to social service agencies. Police departments began to reconsider their practices after research in Minneapolis and other cities found that abusive husbands who were arrested and briefly jailed were less likely to commit acts of domestic violence again.
   6. Research in Milwaukee indicated that factors such as the victim's injuries and the defendant's arrest record influenced the prosecutor's decision to charge.
   7. Policy changes were also enacted as a result of lawsuits against departments by injured women who claimed that police ignored evidence of criminal assaults. Police agencies have developed training programs for their officers concerning domestic violence.

VII.   POLICE AND THE COMMUNITY

A.   **Special Populations**.
1. Urban police have the complex task of working with social service agencies in dealing with special populations such as the homeless, runaways, mentally ill, drugs addicts, and alcoholics.

B.   Policing a Multicultural Society
1.   Circumstances for effective police functions difficult, especially in urban areas where there is distrust of police and a lack of cooperation among some citizens.
2.   The United States is growing more ethnically diverse, partly through immigration. Police relations with citizens may be hampered by stereotypes, cultural differences, and language barriers.
3.   Two reasons that some urban residents resent the police are permissive law enforcement in poor neighborhoods which provides residents with unequal police protection, and allegations of police brutality.
4.   Studies show that many police have biased attitudes toward the poor and members of racial minority groups.
5.   The military organization of police and the "war on crime" mentality many encourage violence by police toward inner city residents.
6.   Frequent experience of African Americans being hassled and framed by the police
7.   Difficulties in police relationship to minority communities. Police may not strictly enforce some laws, yet be more aggressive in treating poor people or minority group members as potential suspects for other kinds of crimes.
8.   What Americans Think: African-Americans and Hispanics are significantly more afraid than whites that police will stop and arrest when you are completely innocent.

C.   **Community Crime Prevention**
1.   There is now recognition that control of crime and disorder cannot rest on police; requires community cooperation and involvement: thus citizens' crime watch groups have proliferated.
2.   Neighborhood watch; crime stopper programs on television and radio, other mechanisms for community involvement. Baltimore example of residents in a neighborhood working to improve area and reduce crime.

REVIEW OF KEY TERMS

Fill in appropriate term from the list for each statement below
frankpledge
order maintenance function
service function
law enforcement function
watchman style
legalistic style
Bow Street Runners
Political Policing Era
Statute of Winchester
Federal Bureau of Investigation
Secret Service
federal agencies
state police
"posse comitatus"
Professional Policing Era
Community Policing Era
"broken windows theory"
discretion
service style

domestic violence
sheriff
special
community crime prevention
bobbies

1. _____ are responsible for many crimes that cross state boundaries.

2. _____ emphasizes strict enforcement of all laws.

3. _____ constitutes the contemporary era in American policing history that seeks to reconnect law enforcement officers with the citizens.

4. _____ emphasizes order maintenance and arrests only for major infractions but historically associated with discriminatory practices.

5. _____ exists everywhere except Hawaii and serves useful functions for law enforcement on highways and in rural areas.

6. _____ was the name commonly applied to the London law enforcement group established by Henry Fielding in the eighteenth century.

7. _____ can be enhanced if government agencies and neighborhood organizations cooperate.

8. When police deal with the mentally ill, the homeless or drug addicts, they are dealing with _____ populations.

9. _____ emphasizes that fear of crime grows from disorder in society.

10. _____ is the primary federal law enforcement agency in the U. S. that deals with such crimes as bank robbery and kidnapping.

11. _____ is the historical era in which modern technologies were developed and applied to policing.

12. _____ is employed by police in dealing with tense confrontations and disputes on the streets.

13. _____ is the function of controlling crime by intervening in situations in which the law has been clearly violated and the police need to identify and apprehend the guilty person.

14. _____ was formed upon the call of local law enforcement officials in frontier areas who needed the citizens' help in fighting crime.

15. _____ is a style which creates avoidance of arrests for minor offenses and use of nonarrest sanctions because the police emphasize other goals and activities.

16. _____ a system in old English law in which a group of ten families pledged to be responsible for keeping order and bringing violators of the law to court.

17. _____ emphasizes the prevention of behavior that either disturbs or threatens to disturb the public peace.

18. _____ constituted the earliest era in the American policing history.

19. _____ is the primary federal agency that deals with counterfeiting.

20. _____ is often an elected official.

21. _____ is assaultive behavior involving adults who are married or who have a prior or ongoing intimate relationship.

22. _____ provides assistance to the public, usually in matters unrelated to crime.

23. The English police officers named after Sir Robert Peel were called _____.

24. _____ established the parish constable system in England.

REVIEW OF KEY PEOPLE

<u>Fill in appropriate person(s) from the list for each statement below</u>
Henry Fielding
Sir Robert Peel
J. Edgar Hoover
O.W. Wilson
August Vollmer
James Q. Wilson & George Kelling

1. _____ was responsible for professionalizing the FBI.

2. _____ developed the "broken windows thesis."

3. _____ established the first unofficial police force in London.

4. _____ was chief of police in Berkley, California from 1909 to 1932 and advocated professional policing.

5. _____ oversaw the development of the official police force in England.

6. _____ was an ardent proponent of motorized patrols and rapid response as the means to facilitate effective crime fighting.

SELF-TEST SECTION
Multiple Choice Questions
4.1. How many families were in a tithing?
a) one
b) two
c) five
d) seven
e) ten

4.2. Which federal agencies were involved in responding to the terrorist attacks on September, 11, 2001?
a) Federal Bureau of Investigation
b) Drug Enforcement Administration
c) Department of Defense
d) Bureau of Alcohol, Tobacco, and Firearms
e) all of the above

4.3. Federal law enforcement agencies are part of what branch of government?
a) judiciary
b) executive
c) legislative
d) local
e) state

4.4. When was the Bureau of Investigation (later renamed the FBI) established?
a) 1908
b) 1924
c) 1972
d) 1980
e) 1994

4.5. Which of the following is involved with federal law enforcement?
a) Department of Homeland Security
b) Secret Service
c) Drug Enforcement Agency
d) Customs Service
e) all of the above

4.6. Although crime has historically been a state and local issue in the U. S., the "federalization"
of crime has been a mainstay of American criminal justice policy since...
a) 1920s
b) 1940s
c) 1960s
d) 1980s
e) 1990s

4.7. What image of police is firmly rooted in the minds of the public and is the main reason given by recruits for joining the force?
a) crime fighter
b) social service provider
c) maintaining order
d) social service investigator
e) all of the above

4.8. What is stressed in the watchman style of policing?
a) exercising discretion
b) professionalism
c) fairness and justice
d) minor infractions dealt with informally
e) all of the above

4.9. What community often experiences the service style of policing?
a) reform-minded city
b) middle class suburban
c) mixed socio-economic
d) blue collar
e) all of the above

4.10. What is stressed in the legalistic style of policing?
a) exercising discretion
b) professionalism
c) deal with misdeeds of locales in a personal, nonpublic way
d) minor infractions dealt with informally
e) all of the above

4.11. What style of policing would you most likely find minor laws, such as traffic laws, enforced in a harsh way toward some groups?
a) watchman style
b) service style
c) legalistic style
d) all of the above
e) none of the above

4.12. Racial discrimination is most likely produced from the...
a) watchman style
b) service style
c) legalistic style
d) all of the above
e) none of the above

4.13. Who developed the three styles of policing-watchman, legalistic, and service?
a) Robert Peel
b) James Q. Wilson
c) J. Edgar Hoover
d) Henry Fielding
e) August Vollmer

4.14. Who was chief of police in Berkeley, California (1909-1932) and a leading advocate of professional policing?
a) Robert Peel
b) James Q. Wilson
c) J. Edgar Hoover
d) Henry Fielding
e) August Vollmer

4.15. Which of the following is TRUE about Native American Tribal Police?
a) they maintain a limited degree of legal autonomy from the American system
b) they cannot enforce tribal criminal laws against non-Native Americans, even on their land
c) most tribes are recognized by the federal government
d) The gambling operations on reservations has resulted in an increase in criminal jurisdiction disputes
e) all of the above are true

4.16. What are the three historical periods of policing?
a) political, professional, and community model
b) pre-colonial, colonial, and post-colonial
c) crime fighter, crime preventer, and service provider
d) watchman, legalistic, and service
e) crime control, crime and order, and order

4.17. As chief of police of Wichita, Kansas, who promoted the use of motorized patrols and rapid response?
a) Robert Peel
b) James Q. Wilson
c) J. Edgar Hoover
d) O. W. Wilson
e) August Vollmer

4.18. Who wrote the article, "Broken Windows: The Police and Neighborhood Safety" about how police should work more on little problems?
a) Robert Peel and Bat Masterson
b) O. W Wilson and August Vollmer
c) J. Edgar Hoover and Henry Fielding
d) George Kelling and James Q. Wilson
e) Wyatt Earp and Mark Moore

4.19. What U. S. organization was formed in 1915 to emphasize police professionalism by promoting training standards and a code of ethics?
a) Central Intelligence Agency
b) Federal Bureau of Investigation
c) Fraternal Order of Police
d) Department of Homeland Security
e) U. S. Border Patrol

4.20. What International organization was formed in 1902 to promote police professionalism by promoting training standards and a code of ethics?
a) Interpol
b) International Association of Chiefs of Police
c) International Homeland Security
d) United Nations
e) The Hague

4.21. Where did the term "posse" originate?
a) Latin term for " police"
b) French term for "public"
c) Old English term for "possessing the convict"
d) Latin term for "power of the country"
e) German term for "capture of prisoners"

4.22. What policing era was influenced by the Progressives?
a) political
b) professional
c) community
d) all of the above
e) none of the above

4.23. During what policing era does close personal contact between officers and citizens occur?
a) political
b) professional
c) community
d) all of the above
e) none of the above

4.24. During what policing era does the use of motorcycle units occur?
a) political
b) professional
c) community
d) all of the above
e) none of the above

4.25. During what policing era do party machines dominate?
a) political
b) professional
c) community
d) all of the above
e) none of the above

True and False Questions

_____ 4.1. The roots of American policing derive largely from England.

_____ 4.2. The terrorist attacks on September 11th did NOT change federal law enforcement tactics.

_____ 4.3. British police officers were called "peelers" after Sir Robert Peel.

_____ 4.4. The professional era of policing involved staying out of politics.

_____ 4.5. The urban riots of the 1960s did not affect the assumptions of the professional model.

_____ 4.6. Community policing involved more foot patrols.

_____ 4.7. The phrase "Just the facts, ma'am" is most commonly associated with the professional model era of policing.

_____ 4.8. Providing first aid is an example of a service function.

_____ 4.9. The service style of policing is most likely found in a declining industrial city.

_____ 4.10. American policing did not develop differently in the South as opposed to the Northeast.

_____ 4.11. Race is the only factor that affects attitudes toward police.

_____ 4.12. In the United States, police power resides with the federal government.

_____ 4.13. A majority of people have a great deal of confidence in the police.

_____ 4.14. Community policing began in the 1920s.

_____ 4.15. A tithing is a group of two families.

_____ 4.16. The political era of policing involved police corruption.

_____ 4.17. The Federal Bureau of Investigation places great emphasis upon white-collar crime.

_____ 4.18. The service style of policing places a balance between law enforcement and order maintenance.

_____ 4.19. The watchman style of policing emphasizes law enforcement.

_____ 4.20. Public confidence is important for police if they are to do their job well.

WORKSHEET 4.1: ORGANIZATION OF THE POLICE

Imagine that you are a member of Congress. One of your staff assistants brings you a proposal to nationalize law enforcement throughout the United States. The proposal calls for abolishing state police agencies, county sheriffs, and local police departments. Instead, Congress would create a new U.S. Department of Law Enforcement. A Secretary of Law Enforcement would oversee a national police agency which would have units established in each state, county, city, and town. Your assistant argues that the new organization would save resources by coordinating the work of every law enforcement officer in the nation and creating a standard set of law enforcement policies and priorities. In addition, the plan would standardize training, salary, and benefits for police officers everywhere and thus raise the level of professionalism of police, especially in small towns and rural areas.

Before you decide whether or not to present this proposal to Congress, respond to the following questions.

1. Are there any undesirable consequences that could develop from putting this plan into action?

_____

_____

_____

_____

_____

_____

2. As a politician, you are concerned about how others will react to the plan. How do you think each group would react and why?

a. Voters_____

_____

_____

b. State and local politicians_____

_____

_____

c. Police officers_____

_____

_____

3. Will you support the proposal? Why or why not?

_____

_____

WORKSHEET 4.2: POLICE POLICY

You are a retired police chief. A state government has hired you to provide advice on the appropriate police policy to implement in several jurisdictions. You advise them on whether to choose the watchman, legalistic, or service style. Explain why.

A. A city of 100,000 that contains a diverse mixture of Whites, African-Americans, Asian-Americans, and Hispanics. The unemployment rate is high. Few wealthy people live in the city. Most people are middle-class, but 25 percent of the citizens qualify for government assistance. The police department reflects the racial/ethnic mix of the city's population.

B. A small town of 2,000 residents. Most residents work in one lumber mill or in businesses that serve loggers and farmers who live in the area. The town's population is almost entirely white, except when large numbers of people from various minority groups arrive in the summer and fall to work on local farms.

C. A suburb with 15,000 residents. Twenty percent of the residents are members of minority groups. Nearly all of the town's residents are white-collar or professional workers with high incomes. Most people commute to a big city to work.

A._____

_____

_____

_____

_____

_____

B._____

_____

_____

_____

_____

_____

C._____

_____

_____

_____

_____

CHAPTER 5

POLICE OFFICERS AND LAW ENFORCEMENT OPERATIONS

LEARNING OBJECTIVES

After covering the material in this chapter, students should understand:

1.   the recruitment, training, and socialization of police officers;

2.   the recruitment and integration of women and minority officers;

3.   the police subculture, including the working personality and the elements of danger and authority;

4.   the organization of police departments and their allocation of resources;

5.   police action and decision making, including organizational response and productivity issues;

6.   the role of detectives and the investigation function, including the apprehension process and forensic techniques;

7.   the role of specialized operations in traffic, vice, and drug enforcement and technology issues such as DNA databases.

CHAPTER SUMMARY

The police must recruit and train individuals who will uphold the law and receive citizen support. Improvements have been made during the past quarter- century in recruiting more officers who are women, racial and ethnic minorities, and well-educated applicants. The police work in an environment greatly influenced by their subculture. The concept of the working personality helps us understand the influence of the police subculture on how individual officers see their world. The isolation of the police strengthens bonds among officers but may also add to job stress. Police operations are shaped by their formal organizational structures and also influenced by social and political processes both within and outside the department. The police are organized along military lines so that authority and responsibility can be located at appropriate levels. Police services are delivered through the work of the patrol, investigation, and specialized operations units. The patrol function has three components: answering calls for assistance, maintaining a police presence, and probing suspicious circumstances. The investigation function is the responsibility of detectives in close coordination with patrol officers. The felony apprehension process is a sequence of actions that includes crime detection, preliminary investigation, follow-up investigation, clearance, and arrest. Specialized units dealing with traffic, drug, and vice are found in large departments.

CHAPTER OUTLINE

I.   INTRODUCTION

Officer Jeff Postell captured one of the FBI's most wanted fugitives, **Eric Rudolph.** Rudolph was wanted for the 1996 Olympic Park bombing and attacks on abortion clinics in Alabama and Georgia. Postell was a rookie police officer on routine patrol when he noticed Rudolph crouching near a dumpster behind a grocery store. Postell' success underscores the importance of regular police officers and performing their daily activities that serve the functions of law enforcement, order maintenance and service. Police officers must be organized, deployed and supervised in an effective manner in order to be successful.

II.   WHO ARE THE POLICE?

A.   Recruitment
    1.   People have various motivations in seeking a career in law enforcement: public service, secure government work, adventure, etc.
    2.   Minimum standards and low pay will attract only those unable to enter more attractive occupations. Need to have desirable pay and benefits.
    3.   Increasingly departments are able to attract college educated recruits.
        a.   Recruits must pass physical exam, background check, physical fitness test, and psychological tests.
    4.   Federally funded Police Corps program provides reimbursement of college expenses for college grads who agree to serve for four years on a police force.

B.   The Changing Profile of the Police
    1.   Changes away from all white, all male police forces spurred by:
        a.   Police-community relations problems.
        b.   Urban riots of the 1960s that were caused by conflict between white police and minority communities.
        c.   **Equal Employment Opportunity Act of 1972** bars state and local governments from discriminating in their hiring practices.
    2.   Minority Police Officers
        a.   Studies show increased representativeness in many of the country's largest departments.
        b.   Election of African-American or Hispanic mayor does not necessarily mean that the police department will become more open and representative.
    3.   Women on the Force
        a.   First woman officer in 1905 in Portland, Oregon. Only 1.5 percent of officers women in 1970; up to only 10 percent twenty years later. Women may make up 16 percent of force in large cities of 250,000 or more, but about half of U.S. police agencies employ no women.
        b.   Most women have easily met performance requirements, but it is at the social level that they have met their greatest resistance. Male officers often doubt that women can physically back them up in a crime situation or disturbance.
        c.   Resistance may also be based on cultural expectations by male officers and public about women's role and behavior. Women may be subjected to sexual harassment.

C.   Training
    1.   Police academy run by large departments or by the state for rural and town recruits.
    2.   Recruits told that real learning will take place on the job.
    3.   **Process of socialization** includes learning informal practices as well as formal rules.
    4.   Officers work in an organizational framework in which rank carries privileges and responsibilities.
        a.   Performance measured by their contribution to the group's success.

III.   THE POLICE SUBCULTURE

A.   Introduction
    1.   **Subculture** is made up of the symbols, beliefs, values, and attitudes shared by members of a subgroup within the larger society. The subculture of the police helps define the "cop's world" and each officer's role in it. Police develop shared values that affect their view of human behavior and their role in society.

B.   **The Working Personality**
    1.   One's occupational environment shapes the way one interprets events. Two important elements in police working personality: danger and authority.
    2.   Danger
        a.   Police are especially attentive to signs of potential violence because they work in dangerous situations.

b. Socialization process teaches recruits to be cautious and suspicious. Orientation toward watching and questioning can contribute to tension and conflict in contacts with the public.

c. Police officers constantly on edge watching for unexpected dangers, on duty and off duty.

3. Authority

a. Police officers, a symbol of authority with low occupation status, must often be assertive in establishing authority with citizenry. This can lead to conflict, hostility, and perhaps overreaction and police brutality.

b. Officer expected to remain detached, neutral, and unemotional even when challenged and in situations of conflict.

C. Public Morality

1. In his field observations of L. A. patrol officers, **Steve Herbert** found a high sense of morality in the law enforcement culture. Morality helps police overcome dilemmas.

2. Dilemma of contradiction between the goal of preventing crime and police inability to do so.

      i. Dilemma of using discretion to handle situations that do always strictly follow established procedure.

      ii. Dilemma of police must invariably act against at least one person's interest, including the possibility of injuring or killing someone.

3. Morality is helpful in encouraging police to serve the public under difficult conditions, but may also lead to negative impact if police use morality to engage in stereotyping in categorizing people.

D. Police Isolation

1. Public generally supportive of police, but police perceive public to be hostile; officers tend to socialize primarily with other officers.

2. Officers' contacts with the public are frequently during moments of conflict, crisis, and emotion.

3. Because police officers are so identified with their jobs, members of the public frequently treat them as police, even when off-duty. Increases the need for bonding and socializing between officers, officers' families, and families of other officers. Develop group identity.

4. Officers may be unable to step back from jobs and separate their professional and personal lives. What Americans Think: Racial differences in Americans' assessments of police honesty and ethics.

E. Job Stress

1. Working environment and subculture affect physical and mental health in form of marital problems, health problems, and drinking problems. Suicide can be a problem.

a. **External stress:** real threats and dangers on the job.

b. **Organizational stress:** produced by paramilitary character of police forces -- odd hours, changing schedules, detailed rules and procedures.

c. **Personal stress:** may be affected by racial or gender status, or by not adjusting to group-held values.

d. **Operational stress:** total effect of the need to confront daily the tragedies of urban life.

2. Police departments had been slow to address issue of stress, but many have developed counseling, liberal disability rules and other mechanisms.

IV. ORGANIZATION OF THE POLICE

A. Bureaucratic Elements

1. Division of Labor: Police are organized with a structure of ranks and allocation of officers according to management, support services, investigation, and field operations. (Ex: Phoenix department) This allows for allocation of resources and supervision of personnel.

2. Chain and Unity of Command: Military character of police departments is illustrated by the chain of command according to ranks-officer, commander, sergeant, lieutenant, captain, major, and chief.

B.	Operational Units
	1.	Separate functional units may be established for: **patrol**, investigation, traffic, vice, and juvenile.
	2.	Usually only middle-sized to large cities maintain specialized vice and juvenile units.

C.	The Police Bureaucracy and the Criminal Justice System
	1.	The role of the police bureaucracy in the broader criminal justice system:
		a.	Police are the gateway to the justice system through which information and individuals enter. Officers' use of discretion in arresting individuals and investigating cases defines the nature and quality of cases entered.
		b.	Police officers' administrative decisions are influenced by the fact that others determine the ultimate outcome of the case. Officers may feel that they are ignored or looked down upon by prosecutors, lawyers, or judges.
		c.	Police officers are expected to observe rules and obey superiors while simultaneously exercising independent, discretionary judgments.

V.	POLICE RESPONSE AND ACTION
	1.	Police in democracy organized mainly to be **reactive** (citizen-invoked calls for service) rather than **proactive** (police-invoked).
	2.	Police arrive after the fact, thus reports by victims and observers define the boundaries of policing.
	3.	The public has come to expect that police will respond to every call. This results in **incident-driven policing.**
	4.	Police employ proactive strategies such as surveillance in some contexts. As more police personnel are allocated to proactive operations, the number of resulting arrests are likely to rise.

A.	Organizational Response
	1.	Administrative environment and organization of department affect the way in which calls are processed as well as the nature of police response.
	2.	Centralization of communications (i.e, 911 numbers and two-way radios) has altered past practices of individual officers observing and addressing crime problems in neighborhoods. Now police react to instructions from
communications center and can report back for further instructions and assistance.
	3.	Police departments use **differential response strategies** for calls. Dispatchers make decisions about whether or not a patrol car needs to rush to the scene of each call. A delayed response may be just as effective depending on the nature of the call.
	4.	Advocates of community policing believe that advances in communication technology further isolate the officers from the community and prevent them from building rapport.
	5.	Close-Up: Holding the 911 Line. An examination of a day in the life of a 911operator demonstrates the stress associated with a very important occupation.
	IDEAS IN PRACTICE: How should a police chief measure productivity?

B.	**Productivity**
	1.	Following the lead of New York City's Compstat program, several cities now emphasize accountability at the precinct level. Local commanders must explain the results of their efforts to combat crime.
	2.	Police have difficulty in measuring the quantity and quality of their work.
	3.	Crime rates and **clearance rates** are problematic measures of police productivity.
	4.	The clearance rate is the percentage of crimes that police believe they have solved through an arrest. It varies by the nature of the offense.
	5.	Police often use "activity" as a measure (i.e., tickets issued, arrests made, suspects stopped for questioning), although this does not necessarily reflect, for example, the complete range of order maintenance functions. It may actually be more beneficial for society when police spend their time calming conflicts, becoming acquainted with citizens, and providing services and information for people.

What Americans Think: Favorable attitudes toward the ability of the police to combat crime.

VI.   DELIVERY OF POLICE SERVICES
    1.   **Line functions**: directly involved in operational activities, accounts for approximately 84 percent of personnel. Patrol bureau generally the largest, accounting for two-thirds of all **sworn officers**. **Staff functions** supplement or support the line functions.

A.   Patrol Functions
    1.   Patrol officers make up two-thirds of all sworn officers. In small communities, the patrol force constitutes the entire department.
    2.   Patrol function has three components.
        a.   Answering calls for assistance
        b.   Maintaining a police presence.
        c.   Probing suspicious circumstances.
    3.   When not responding to calls, officers engage in **preventive patrol**--making the police presence known to deter crime and to be available to respond to calls.
    4.   Patrol officers' presence in a community can be major factor in reducing fear of crime. Patrol may also improve community relations and increase citizen cooperation with police.
    5.   Patrol work is low status, entry level, often viewed as boring, thankless and taken for granted, yet patrol officers carry the major burden of the criminal justice system in confronting difficult conflict situations and making discretionary decisions.

B.   **Investigation**
    1.   Detective Responsibilities All units usually involved with investigation, but patrol unit's preliminary investigation is crucial because success in some cases is linked to the speed of identifying and arresting the offender. When offender not immediately apprehended, then investigation often transferred to detectives: higher status and pay, less supervision, and devoted to crime fighting rather than other functions
    2.   Detectives often organized by type of crime that they investigate (homicide, robbery, etc.). One criticism of detectives is that they may duplicate work of patrol or break continuity of investigation by transferring case to separate unit. Detectives in small departments must be generalists.
    3.   Detectives involved when:
        a.   Serious crime occurs and offender immediately identified and apprehended. Detective prepares case for prosecutor.
        b.   Offender is identified but not apprehended, so detective tries to locate individual.
        c.   When offender is not identified but there are several suspects, the detective conducts investigation aimed at either confirming or disproving suspicions.
        d.   When there is no suspect, the detective must start from scratch.
    4.   Detectives rely on technical expertise in their department and from cooperating police forces.
WORK PERSPECTIVE: Mary Peterson, Detective in Glenview, Illinois

    5.   **Apprehension**:
    Stages in Process: 1) Crime detected, 2) Preliminary investigation, usually by patrol officer, 3) follow-up investigation, 4) clearance and arrest:

    6.   **Forensic Techniques**
        a.   Use of science to aid in gathering evidence: fingerprints, blood sample analysis, DNA analysis. Forensic component of investigation hampered if there is a lack of facilities that can do the complete range of tests. Localities often rely on state crime lab or on FBI crime lab.
        b.   Full implementation of **DNA fingerprinting** must wait until enough labs fully equipped for such analysis. Hold great potential for investigating various crimes.

7. Research on Investigation
    a. Research suggests that the police have overrated the importance of investigation as a means of solving crimes and shows that most crimes are cleared because of arrests made by the patrol force at or near the scene. Response time -- time from commission of crime to arrival of police -- is very important element in apprehension as is the identification of the suspect by the victim.
    b. Detectives important because high status gives patrol officers a goal to seek and fulfills public's expectation that police will conduct investigations.

TECHNOLOGY ISSUES IN CRIMINAL JUSTICE: National DNA Database. Many states and the federal government are building a national database of DNA records that is maintained by the FBI. The project is known as **CODIS**, which stands for Combined DNA Index System. CODIS began in 1990 as a pilot project to serving a few states and localities and it has grown to include 47 states and the District of Columbia

C. Special Operations
    1. **Traffic**: authorities disagree about whether or not to create separate units for traffic responsibilities. Traffic work is highly discretionary and essentially proactive, and the level of enforcement can be considered a direct result departmental policies and norms. Traffic enforcement is one area in which departments enforce norms of productivity.
    2. **Vice**: enforcement against prostitution, gambling, narcotics, etc. depends on proactive police work. Because of the nature of the crimes, political influence is sometimes brought to bear to dampen enforcement. Increasingly police are using electronic surveillance and undercover work. Frequent reliance on informants creates problems. Critics fear that such operations move away from opening policing and thereby threaten civil liberties.
    3. Drug Law Enforcement: many large cities have separate drug bureaus within police departments. Different strategies employed, including flooding "drug market" areas with police officers aggressively making arrests. Police activities may only move drug dealers to different location. Law enforcement efforts have not stopped sales and use of illegal drugs.

REVIEW OF KEY TERMS

Fill in the appropriate term from the list for each statement below
CODIS
line functions
patrol
sworn officers
incident-driven policing
differential response
reactive patrol
proactive patrol
vice
traffic
productivity
DNA "fingerprinting"
staff functions
external stress
operational stress
organizational stress
personal stress
preventive patrol
S.W.A.T.
Equal Employment Opportunity Act of 1972
free patrol
CSI

subculture
clearance rate
forensic techniques
socialization
working personality

1.   The word _____ is thought to be derived from a French word which means "to tramp about in the mud."

2.   _____ are those that directly involve field operations, such as patrol and traffic.

3.   _____ is something difficult to measure because of the varied responsibilities of police officers, although arrests, traffic tickets, and other indicators have been used for this purpose.

4.   _____ is the typical American patrol strategy that involves officers response to notification that a crime has been committed.

5.   The _____ bars state and local governments from discriminating in their hiring practices.

6.   _____ is a reactive approach to policing emphasizing a quick response to calls for service.

7.   _____ is the name used for officers parking and walking.

8.   _____ is made up of the symbols, beliefs, values, and attitudes shared by members of a subgroup in society.

9.   _____ are police employees who have taken an oath and been given powers by the state to make arrests and use force in accordance with their duties.

10.   _____ is the police subdivision involving strategic weapons and tactics.

11.   _____ involves the scientific analysis of fingerprints, semen, blood, hair, soil, and textiles.

12.   _____ is the general patrol strategy in which officers search for offenders without waiting for a crime to be reported; used heavily for traffic and vice enforcement.

13.   _____ is a measure of police productivity based on the percentage of crimes solved through an arrests.

14.   _____ is a strategy involving dispatchers prioritizing calls for service and using various response options.

15.   A _____ unit often involves the use of undercover agents and informers.

16.   _____ unit involves accident investigation, parking problems and fire emergency.

17.   The public has become aware of scientific testing techniques used for law enforcement purposes through the television drama _____.

18.   _____ are performed by supplemental police staff not involved in direct operations.

19.   _____ is a proactive patrol strategy which involves making the police presence known, deterring crime, and make officers respond quickly to calls.

20.   A set of emotional and behavioral characteristics developed by members of an occupational group is called

21.   The process by which the rules, symbols, and values of a group are learned by its members is called
_____.

22.   _____ is produced by real threats and dangers.

23.   _____ reflects the total effect of dealing with thieves.

24.   _____ is the national database of DNA records.

25.   _____ can be caused by an officer's racial or gender status among peers.

26.   _____ is produced by the nature of the work in a paramilitary structure.

27   _____ involves identifying people through their distinctive gene patterns.

REVIEW OF KEY PEOPLE
Fill in the appropriate person from the list for each statement below
Lola Baldwin
Eric Rudolph
Jeff Postell
Steve Herbert

1.   In his field observations of L. A. patrol officers, _____ found a high sense of morality in the law enforcement subculture.

2.   _____ was the rookie police officer who arrested Eric Rudolph in May, 2003.

3.   _____ was arrested in May, 2003 for the bombing of abortion clinics in Alabama and Georgia and the 1996 Olympic Park bombing in Atlanta.

4.   The first female police officer was _____ in 1905 in Portland, Oregon.

SELF-TEST SECTION

Multiple Choice Questions
5.1. What bars state and local governments from discriminating in their hiring practices?
a) Equal Employment Opportunity Act of 1972
b) Civil Rights Act of 1866
c) Jim Crow laws
d) Equal Access Employment Act of 1987
e) Article V of the U. S. Constitution

5.2. Which of the following is a line function?
a) patrol
b) investigation
c) traffic control
d) vice
e) all of the above

5.3. What is the clearance rate for prostitution arrests?
a) 10 %
b) 25%
c) 50%
d) 75%
e) 100%

5.4. Why was a rookie police officer, Jeff Postell, able to capture Eric Rudolph?
a) Postell was trained by the CIA in special investigative techniques
b) Postell was simply a small town police officer on a routine patrol doing his job
c) Postell spent several years researching the behavioral patterns of Rudolph
d) Postell was working as a security officer and captured Rudolph minutes after the bombing of Olympic Park in Atlanta
e) Postell had been friends with Rudolph in high school and knew his hiding spots in the woods of North Carolina

5.5. What type of stress is produced by real threats and dangers?
a) external stress
b) organizational stress
c) personal stress
d) operational stress
e) none of the above

5.6. What type of stress is produced by the nature of police work being paramilitary?
a) external stress
b) organizational stress
c) personal stress
d) operational stress
e) none of the above

5.7. What type of stress is produced by gender status among peers?
a) external stress
b) organizational stress
c) personal stress
d) operational stress
e) none of the above

5.8. What type of stress is produced by being lied to on the job by a thief?
a) external stress
b) organizational stress
c) personal stress
d) operational stress
e) none of the above

5.9. What is TRUE about the profile of the American police officer in the 21st century?
a) women and minorities represent a smaller percentage of police departments than in the past
b) women represent a smaller percentage but minorities represent a larger percentage of police departments than in the past
c) women and minorities represent a larger percentage of police departments than in the past
d) minorities represent a smaller percentage but women represent a larger percentage of police departments than in the past
e) women and minorities represent the same percentage of police departments as in the past

5.10. What is the acronym for the national database of DNA?
a) SWAT
b) CSI
c) CODIS
d) DNA
e) there is no acronym

5.11. What is the origin of the word "patrol"?
a) from a Scottish word meaning "rolling police"
b) from a German word meaning "police action"
c) from a French word meaning "to tramp around in the mud"
d) from a Spanish word meaning "to dance in the streets"
e) from a Latin word meaning "walking with authority"

5.12. Who was the 21-year old rookie police officer who arrested Eric Rudolph, an alleged bombing suspect?
a) Lola Baldwin
b) Jeff Postell
c) Steve Herbert
d) David Bayley
e) an entire SWAT team

5.13. Which of the following can be analyzed scientifically?
a) blood
b) fingerprints
c) hair
d) semen
e) all of the above

5.14. Which of the following is TRUE concerning arrests for drug sales and possession in the U. S.?
a) arrests for drug sales and possession have declined dramatically
b) arrests for drug sales and possession have increased slightly
c) arrests for drug sales and possession have stayed the same
d) arrests for drug sales and possession have increased dramatically
e) arrests for drug sales and possession have declined slightly

5.15. Which of the following is NOT a function of a well-organized police department?
a) clear lines of authority
b) division of labor
c) each working separately to achieve goals
d) a chain of command
e) rules to guide the activities of staff

5.16. All but the smallest police departments assign officers to operational...
a) units
b) wards
c) precincts
d) classes
e) categories

5.17. Which of the following is an example of a proactive strategy?
a) responding to a citizens' call
b) undercover work
c) citizen approaching police on the street with information
d) all of the above
e) none of the above

5.18. Which of the following is an example of a reactive strategy?
a) surveillance
b) undercover work
c) waiting for a citizen to approach police on the street with information
d) all of the above
e) none of the above

5.19. How can a police officer best handle stress?
a) work harder
b) keep to yourself
c) seek counseling
d) all of the above
e) none of the above

5.20. Which of the following is a change in policing in the past thirty years?
a) more women are police officers
b) more nonwhites are police officers
c) minimum height and weight requirements have changed
d) all of the above are examples of changes in the past thirty years
e) none of the above are examples of changes in the past thirty years

5.21. Which of the following is TRUE about police work and stress?
a) policing is one of the ten most stress-producing jobs
b) stress is not a problem today for police, but it was in the past
c) In relation to the general population, a lower proportion of officers have marital and drug problems
d) all of the above are TRUE
e) all of the above are FALSE

5.22. If a police officer feels uncomfortable because of his/her race, this is an example of...
a) external stress
b) organizational stress
c) personal stress
d) operational stress
e) occupational stress

5.23. If a police officer experiences stress because of constant schedule changes, this is an example of...
a) external stress
b) organizational stress
c) personal stress
d) operational stress
e) occupational stress

5.24. If a police officer experiences stress because of a high speed chase, this is an example of ...
a) external stress
b) organizational stress
c) personal stress
d) operational stress
e) occupational stress

5.25. If a police officer experiences stress because he/she is afraid of a lawsuit being filed, this is an example of...
a) external stress
b) organizational stress
c) personal stress
d) operational stress
e) occupational stress

True and False Questions

_____ 5.1. Women are prohibited from being police office in major cities with high crime rates.

_____ 5.2. The investigation function involves detectives working independent of patrol officers.

_____ 5.3. Before the 1970s, many police departments did not hire nonwhites.

_____ 5.4. Police officers are generally well-paid.

_____ 5.5. Police have only one strategy to deal with drug dealing.

_____ 5.6. Lola Baldwin was the first female police officer.

_____ 5.7. Police can identify an offender's DNA with only a single droplet of blood.

_____ 5.8. Patrol officers account for less than ten percent of all sworn officers.

_____ 5.9. Line functions are those that directly involve field operations.

_____ 5.10. In police work, it is important for police officers to focus on the success of the group.

_____ 5.11. Police agencies are organized in a military manner.

_____ 5.12. Police do not use proactive strategies.

_____ 5.13. Police assign priorities to calls for service.

_____ 5.14. Most police action is initiated by an officer in the field.

_____ 5.15. All police departments have vice squads.

_____ 5.16. In the U. S., almost all police labs are equipped to perform DNA analysis.

_____ 5.17. The clearance rate is the percentage of crimes solved through an arrest.

_____ 5.18. Arrests for drug selling has a 100 percent clearance rate.

_____ 5.19. The Supreme Court ruled that it is unconstitutional for the federal government and the states to build a national database of DNA because it infringes on the right to privacy.

_____ 5.20. Enforcement of vice laws depends on reactive police work.

WORKSHEET 5.1: RECRUITMENT AND TRAINING OF POLICE OFFICERS

1. What qualifications would you require for someone to be hired as a police officer? Why?

_____

_____

_____

_____

_____

_____

2. What salary and benefits would you offer in order to attract the police officer-candidates that you described?

_____

_____

_____

_____

_____

3. What are the three most important subjects that should be taught to new police recruits? Why?

_____

_____

_____

_____

_____

_____

_____

4. Could you use training to combat any negative aspects of the police subculture and working personality? If so, how?

_____

_____

_____

WORKSHEET 5.2: DETECTIVES

A study has raised questions about whether or not your police department should keep a separate investigation division containing detectives. There are questions about whether or not detectives solve many crimes because most arrests result from the work of patrol officers or the assistance of citizens. Pretend that you have to draft a report making recommendations about the future of the detective bureau. How would you address the following questions?

1. What is the job of the detectives? (write a job description)

_____

_____

_____

_____

_____

_____

2. How are investigations conducted and what is the role of the detectives in investigations?

_____

_____

_____

_____

3. What is the relationship between detectives and patrol officers?

_____

_____

_____

_____

_____

4. How would the police department be different if there were no detectives?

_____

_____

_____

CHAPTER 6

POLICE AND CONSTITUTIONAL LAW

LEARNING OBJECTIVES

After covering the material in this chapter, students should understand:

1.   police officers' responsibility to control crime under the rule of law;

2.   search and seizure issues

3.   arrest and interrogation issues

4.   circumstances justifying warrantless searches

5.   Miranda warnings and their consequences

6.   the exclusionary rule, its application to the states, and exceptions to the rule.

CHAPTER SUMMARY

The Supreme Court has defined rules for the circumstances and justifications for stops, searches, and arrests in light of the Fourth Amendment's prohibition on "unreasonable searches and seizures." Most stops must be supported by reasonable suspicion and arrests, like search warrants, must be supported by enough information to constitute probable cause. The plain view doctrine permits officers to visually examine and seize any contraband or criminal evidence that is in open sight when they are in a place that they are legally permitted to be. Searches are considered "reasonable" and may be conducted without warrants in a number of specific circumstances such as borders, airports, and other situations required by special needs beyond the normal purposes of law enforcement. Limited searches may be conducted without warrants when officers have reasonable suspicions to justify a stop-and-frisk for weapons on the streets; when officer make a lawful arrest; when exigent circumstances exist; when people voluntarily consent to searches of their persons or property; and in certain situations involving automobiles. The Fifth Amendment privilege against compelled self-incrimination helps to protect citizens against violence and coercion by police as well as to maintain the legitimacy and integrity of the legal system. The Supreme Court's decision in *Miranda v. Arizona (1966)* required officers to inform suspects of specific rights before custodial questioning, although officers have adapted their practices to accommodate this rule and several exceptions have been created. The exclusionary rule is a remedy designed to deter police from violating citizens' rights during criminal investigations by barring the use of illegally obtained evidence in court. The Supreme Court has created several exceptions to the exclusionary rule, including the inevitable discovery rule and the "good faith" exception in defective warrant situations.

CHAPTER OUTLINE

I.   INTRODUCTION
     In September 2001, letters containing a deadly biological agent, anthrax, were delivered to media personalities such as Tom Brokaw and politicians such as Senator Thomas Daschle. The anthrax letters killed five people and demonstrated the vulnerability of American society to bioterrorism. Because the letters potentially could have affected thousands of persons randomly through cross-contamination, the U. S. government made the anthrax letters a high priority in terms of apprehending the person(s) responsible for the bioterror attack. A critical dilemma in times of emergencies such as the anthrax letters involves the amount of power given to government officials to protect large numbers of American citizens balanced with a need to protect the liberties of those same citizens. A scientist by the name of **Steven Hatfill** was investigated for mailing the anthrax letters in June 2002 but was not charged after government officials searched his home.

II.   LEGAL LIMITS OF POLICE INVESTIGATIONS

A.   In a democratic society, police are expected to control crime while complying with the rule of law as it protects the rights of citizens, including criminal suspects. Evidence used against suspects must be admissible evidence.

B.   **Search and Seizure Concepts**
        1.   The **Fourth Amendment** prohibits unreasonable searches and seizures. The Supreme Court defines searches as actions by law enforcement officials that intrude upon people's reasonable expectations of privacy. If people are not free to leave when officers' assert their authority to halt someone's movement, then a seizure has occurred and the Fourth Amendment requires that the seizure be reasonable. Government officials interference with an individual's freedom for a duration of minutes is called a stop. Stops must be justified by a **reasonable suspicion**, or a police officer's belief based on facts that would be recognized by others in a similar situation as indicating that criminal activity is afoot and requires further investigation that will intrude on a reasonable expectation of privacy.

C.   The Concept of **Arrest**
        1.   Seizure of an individual by government official who takes suspect into custody. Courts prefer arrest warrants for felonies, but have not required them. The Fourth Amendment also speaks of seizures (e.g., arrests) being based on probable cause.
        WORK PERSPECTIVE: Keri Middleditch, Assistant County Prosecutor of Oakland County, Michigan

D.   **Warrants and Probable Cause**
        1.   Officer must show reliable information establishing **probable cause** to believe that a crime has been or is being committed. The particular premises and pieces of property to be seized must be identified and the officer must swear under oath that they are correct.
        2.   To justify the existence of probable cause, officers are required to present evidence to a judicial officer supported by an oath or affirmation, or swearing that all information presented is true. Police officers may present an affidavit which is a written statement confirmed by oath or affirmation.
        3.   **Totality of circumstances** is a flexible test established by the Supreme Court in Illinois v. Gates (1983) to identify whether probable cause exists to justify a judge's issuance of a warrant.

III.   **PLAIN VIEW DOCTRINE**: during a search, incident to arrest or with a warrant, officers can seize and examine items in plain view even if not listed on warrant, if those items may be evidence of illegal activity.

A.   Open Fields Doctrine: property owners have no reasonable expectation of privacy in open fields on and around their property.

B.   Plain Feel and Other Senses: Police officers can justify a warrantless search based upon smell or odor and also based upon feel (Minnesota v. Dickerson 1993)

C.   TECHNOLOGY ISSUES IN CRIMINAL JUSTICE: Monitoring Computer Keystrokes
        1.   Should the U. S. government use technology to combat terrorism by monitoring electronic communications or should the Fourth Amendment apply to computers and electronic communications?

IV.   WARRANTLESS SEARCHES
A.   Special Needs Beyond the Normal Purpose of Law Enforcement: Officers do not need any suspicion to justify a search in specific contexts, such as airline passengers or border searches.
        1.   U.S. Customs Service Policies for Personal Searches
        2.   Close Up State Supreme Courts and Constitutional Rights: state courts can make authoritative decisions about many of their own affairs. State courts control the interpretation of their own state constitutions.

WHAT AMERICANS THINK. 47 % of Americans support the FBI using wiretaps and searching homes and computers of Americans who are suspected of having links to foreign terrorists and 30% oppose these methods of investigation.

B.   **Stop and Frisk** on the Streets: brief questioning and pat down searches (stop and frisk) permitted based on reasonable judgment of police officers (**Terry v. Ohio, 1968**) that a crime as occurred or is about to occur, and that the stopped person may have a weapon.
IDEAS IN PRACTICE: When does a patrol officer have the right to conduct a "stop and frisk" search?

C.   **Search Incident to Lawful Arrest:** police can search person and areas in immediate vicinity for weapons when a lawful arrest is made (**Chimel v. California, 1969**).

D.   **Exigent Circumstances**: officers might find themselves in the middle of an urgent situation where they must act swiftly and do not have time to go to court to seek a warrant.

E.   **Consent** : citizen may waive Fourth Amendment and other rights and thereby allow police to conduct a search. Police may search an apartment based on the consent of someone whom police reasonably believe possesses the authority to consent even if the person does not actually possess such authority (*Illinois v. Rodriguez*, 1990).

F.   **Automobile Searches**: automobiles distinguished from homes in terms of people's expectations of privacy and the risk that evidence may be contained in a mobile vehicle (*Carroll v. United States*, 1925;*United States v. Ross*, 1982). Officers may search automobiles and containers in such vehicles if they have probable cause to do so.

V.   QUESTIONING SUSPECTS
A.   Miranda Rules
   1.   Upon arrest, suspects must be informed of their rights, based on Supreme Court decisions in Escobedo v. Illinois (1964) and **Miranda v. Arizona (1966). Miranda warnings** consist of police informing arrestee:
       a.   Of the right to remain silent (the **privilege against self-incrimination** found in the Fifth Amendment)
       b.   If they make a statement, it can and will be used against them in court
       c.   Of **right to have attorney** present during interrogation, or have an opportunity to consult with an attorney.
       d.   If they cannot afford an attorney, the state will provide one.
   2.   CLOSE-UP: *Miranda v. Arizona*, 384 U. S. 436 (1966) excerpts from the Court's opinion by Chief Justice Earl Warren.
   3.   Police officers can forego Miranda warnings if a there exists a threat to public safety. This is called the **"public safety exception" (New York v. Quarles, 1984)**.
   4.   Although some legal commentators and police officers criticize the Miranda warnings, the Supreme Court strongly endorsed the Miranda requirement in Dickerson v. United States (2000).

B.   The Consequences of Miranda
   1.   Police officers have adapted their techniques in various ways to question suspects and get information despite Miranda limitations. *Miranda* rights must be provided *before questions are asked* during custodial interrogations. Miranda does not apply if a police officer simply comes up to a person and starts to ask questions. The Supreme has ruled that people know that they can walk away from a police officer.
   2.   Departments train officers to read the *Miranda* warnings to suspects as soon as an arrest is made. This is done in order to make sure the warnings are not omitted as the suspect in processed in the system. The warnings may be read off a standard "Miranda card" to make sure that the rights are provided consistently and correctly. However, the courts do not require that police inform suspects of their rights immediately after arrest.
   3.   Officers are also trained in interrogation techniques that are intended to encourage suspects to talk despite *Miranda* warnings suspects of their rights immediately after arrest.

4. WHAT AMERICANS THINK? 45% of Americans agree that it will necessary to give up some of our liberties in order to curb terrorism; 47% agree that the government should be able to detain a non-citizen indefinitely if that person is suspected of belonging to a terrorist group; 23% agree that the government should be able to search property without a warrant on suspicion that a crime or terrorist attack is being planned.

5. A QUESTION OF ETHICS: Can police officers question a suspect who has been "informed" of his/her rights but doesn't really understand that an attorney should be present during the interrogation?

VI. **EXCLUSIONARY RULE**: illegally seized evidence must be excluded from court. The Supreme Court created the exclusionary rule in Weeks v. United States (1914) as a judicial remedy to guard against police corruption.

A. Application of the Exclusionary Rule to the States: The Supreme Court incorporated the Fourth Amendment upon the states in **Wolf v. Colorado (1949)** and later applied the exclusionary rule to the states in **Mapp v. Ohio (1961)** through the due process clause of the Fourteenth Amendment. Without the exclusionary rule, the Fourth Amendment has no meaning

B. Exceptions to the Exclusionary Rule: Since the Burger Court of the 1970s and 1980s, a number of conservative decisions have limited or created exceptions to the exclusionary rule. Among the modifications created:
1. **Good faith exception (United States v. Leon, 1984).**
2. **Inevitable discovery rule (Nix v.Williams, 1984).**

REVIEW OF KEY TERMS
Fill in the appropriate term from the list for each statement below
Chimel v. California (1969)
Fourth Amendment
search
search by consent
United States v. Leon (1984)
New York v. Class (1986)
search incident to a lawful arrest
reasonable suspicion
Mapp v. Ohio (1961)
totality of circumstances
search warrant
exigent circumstances
arrest
stop and frisk exception
plain view
right to counsel
public safety exception
good faith exception
inevitable discovery rule
exclusionary rule
Miranda warnings
probable cause
Terry v. Ohio (1968)
Miranda v. Arizona (1966)
stop
Nix v. Williams (1984)
automobile search
Wolf v. Colorado (1949)

1.	A(n)_____ is a government officials interference with an individual's freedom of movement for a duration that can be measured in minutes

2.	_____ established the "stop and frisk" doctrine permitting pat-down searches during field interrogations.

3.	_____ established the good faith exception to the exclusionary rule.

4.	_____ established that a gun protruding from under seat is within the scope of the plain view doctrine.

5.	_____ established the permissibility of searches incident to lawful arrests to ensure no weapons are on the arrestee or within reach of the arrestee.

6.	_____ established that police must inform arrestees of their rights.

7.	_____ applied the Fourth Amendment exclusionary rule to the states.

8.	_____ nationalized the Fourth Amendment upon the states, but not the exclusionary rule.

9.	_____ established the inevitable discovery exception to the exclusionary rule.

10.	The Supreme Court first addressed _____ in *Carroll v. United States (1925)*.

11.	_____ prevents police and prosecutors from using evidence that has been obtained through improper procedures.

12.	_____ is one avenue to conduct a search without a warrant because a citizen agrees to be searched.

13.	_____ is based on the idea that evidence should not be excluded when police officers acted on a warrant improperly issued by a magistrate..

14.	_____ was announced by the Supreme Court for situations in which exclusion of evidence is not required because officers took necessary actions to protect citizens.

15.	_____ is an exception to the warrant requirement because officers need to be sure there is no weapon on the person or within the person's reach.

16.	_____ permits the use of improperly obtained evidence that would have been found by the police eventually through proper means.

17.	_____ is a document issued by a judicial officer upon the sworn statement of a police officer.

18.	_____ is a Sixth Amendment protection included as part of the Miranda warnings.

19.	_____ is an exception to the warrant requirement because officers need not ignore illegal objects that are clearly visible.

20.	The _____ contains the search and seizure clause and the warrant clause.

21.	Government officials' examination of an hunt for evidence in or on a person or place that intrudes on reasonable expectations of privacy is called a(n) _____.

22.	An amount of reliable information indicating that it is more likely than not that evidence will be found in a specific location is called _____.

23.   A police officer's belief based on articulable facts that would be recognized by others in a similar situation as indicating that criminal activity is afoot is called _____.

24.   A flexible test established by the Supreme Court for identifying whether probable cause exists to justify a judge's issuance of a warrant is called _____.

25.   A(n) _____ is a significant deprivation of liberty because a person is taken into custody.
26.   _____ permits police officers to pat down the clothing of people if there is a reasonable suspicion of dangerous criminal activity.

27.   The right to remain silent is part of the _____ provided to suspects by police officers.

28.   _____ exist(s) when there is a threat to public safety or a risk that evidence will be destroyed.

REVIEW OF KEY PERSONS
Fill in the appropriate person from the list for each statement below
Tom Clark
Steven Hatfill
Warren Burger
Earl Warren
Nicodemo Sarfo Jr.
O. J. Simpson

1.   A warrantless search of football star _____'s house after his ex-wife was found murdered produced a bloody glove.

2.   _____ was a suspect in the mailed letters of anthrax during September 2001.

3.   The FBI installed a keystroke logging device on the computer of a suspected organized crime figure named _____.

4.   Justice _____ authored the Court's opinion in *Mapp v. Ohio (1961)*.

5.   Chief Justice _____ authored the Court's opinion in *Miranda v. Arizona (1966)*.

6.   After, _____ became Chief Justice, the Supreme Court began creating exceptions to the exclusionary rule.

SELF-TEST SECTION

Multiple Choice Questions

6.1.How does the U. S. Supreme Court define a "search"?
a) an action by a law enforcement official that creates tension between the official and a citizen
b) an action by a law enforcement official that intrudes upon people's "reasonable expectations of privacy"
c) when a law enforcement official speaks to a person
d) when a law enforcement official informs a person that a search is taking place
e) when a law enforcement official looks at a person

6.2. What did the Supreme Court rule in *New York v. Belton (1981)*?
a) the Supreme Court ruled that police cannot aggressively feel and manipulate people's property unless the luggage examination is part of a standard search in boarding a commercial airliner
b) the Supreme Court ruled that a search of the entire passenger compartment of the automobile for evidence or weapons is justified if the driver has been placed under arrest for violating the law
c) the Supreme Court approved warrantless bloodtests
d) the Supreme Court ruled that when officers are in hot pursuit of a fleeing suspected felon they need not stop to seek a warrant and thereby risk permitting the suspect to get away
e) the Supreme Court ruled that an unverified anonymous tip is not adequate as basis for a stop and frisk search

6.3. All arrests must be supported by ...
a) reasonable suspicion
b) reasonable doubt
c) preponderance of the evidence
d) probable cause
e) real evidence

6.4. Who was a key suspect identified by the government in the anthrax letters case of September 2001?
a) Tom Daschle
b) Tom Brokaw
c) Steven Hatfill
d) O. J. Simpson
e) Nicodemo Srafo Jr.

6.5. What is a written statement confirmed by oath or affirmation?
a) warrant
b) perjury
c) interrogatory
d) booking
e) affidavit

6.6. If a judicial officer makes a generalized determination about whether the evidence is both sufficient and reliable enough to justify a warrant, this is called the standard of..
a) reasonable suspicion
b) reasonable doubt
c) preponderance of the evidence
d) the totality of the circumstances
e) real evidence

6.7. Which of the following search does not require a warrant?
a) search incident to a lawful arrest
b) border searches
c) exigent circumstances
d) consent search
e) all of the above

6.8. Which of the following is contained within the Fourth Amendment?
a) the right to counsel
b) right against unreasonable search and seizure
c) warrant clause
d) b and c
e) all of the above

6.9. What did the Supreme Court rule in *Bond v. United States (2000)*?
a) the Supreme Court ruled that police cannot aggressively feel and manipulate people's property unless the luggage examination is part of a standard search in boarding a commercial airliner
b) the Supreme Court approved a warrantless search of an automobile
c) the Supreme Court approved warrantless bloodtests
d) the Supreme Court ruled that when officers are in hot pursuit of a fleeing suspected felon they need not stop to seek a warrant and thereby risk permitting the suspect to get away
e) the Supreme Court ruled that an unverified anonymous tip is not adequate as basis for a stop and frisk search

6.10. What did the Supreme Court rule in *Delaware v. Prouse (1979)*?
a) the Supreme Court ruled that police cannot aggressively feel and manipulate people's property unless the luggage examination is part of a standard search in boarding a commercial airliner
b) the Supreme Court approved a warrantless search of an automobile
c) the Supreme Court approved warrantless bloodtests
d) the Supreme Court prohibited random stops of vehicles by officers on patrol
e) the Supreme Court ruled that an unverified anonymous tip is not adequate as basis for a stop and frisk search

6.11. What did the Supreme Court decide in *New York v. Quarles (1984)* ?
a) the Court ruled that if the officer feels something that it immediately recognizable, as a weapon, the item may be seized
b) the Court approved a warrantless search of an automobile
c) the Court approved warrantless bloodtests
d) the Court ruled that a situation of urgency outweighs the need to respect individuals' rights
e) the Court ruled that an unverified anonymous tip is not adequate as basis for a stop and frisk search

6.12. What did the Supreme Court rule in *Flippo v. West Virginia (1999)*?
a) the Supreme Court ruled that police cannot aggressively feel and manipulate people's property unless the luggage examination is part of a standard search in boarding a commercial airliner
b) the Supreme Court ruled that police officers must obtain a warrant to open luggage, packages and file cabinets at a murder scene
c) the Supreme Court approved warrantless bloodtests
d) the Supreme Court ruled that when officers are in hot pursuit of a fleeing suspected felon they need not stop to seek a warrant and thereby risk permitting the suspect to get away
e) the Supreme Court ruled that an unverified anonymous tip is not adequate as basis for a stop and frisk search

6.13. What did the Supreme Court decide in *Carroll v. United States (1925)*?
a) the Supreme Court approved warrantless bloodtests
b) the Supreme Court approved a warrantless search of an automobile
c) the Supreme Court ruled that when officers are in hot pursuit of a fleeing suspected felon they need not stop to seek a warrant and thereby risk permitting the suspect to get away
d) the Supreme Court ruled that it would not permit thorough warrantless searches at crime scenes, even when a murder victim is discovered
e) the Supreme Court ruled that an unverified anonymous tip is not adequate as basis for a stop and frisk search

6.14. What did the Supreme Court decide in *Michigan v. Long (1983)*?
a) the Supreme Court expanded officers' authority to search automobiles even when no formal arrest has yet occurred
b) the Supreme Court approved warrantless bloodtests
c) the Supreme Court ruled that when officers are in hot pursuit of a fleeing suspected felon they need not stop to seek a warrant and thereby risk permitting the suspect to get away
d) the Supreme Court ruled that it would not permit thorough warrantless searches at crime scenes, even when a murder victim is discovered
e) the Supreme Court ruled that an unverified anonymous tip is not adequate as basis for a stop and frisk search

6.15. Which of the following is contained within the Fifth Amendment?
a) the privilege against self-incrimination
b) right to counsel
c) right to a jury trial
d) right to a public trial
e) all of the above

6.16. Which of the following movies is based on a true story in England in which police officers gain a confession from a bombing suspect whom they know to be innocent by placing a gun in the suspect's mouth and threatening to pull the trigger?
a) Minority Report
b) Clear and Present Danger
c) In the Name of the Father
d)The Sum of All Fears
e) Patriot Games

6.17. When can a police officer conduct a "stop and frisk"?
a) when probable cause exists
b) police officers can stop and frisk whenever they want to
c) whenever two police officers are present
d) whenever the person being searched is accompanied by a reliable witness
e) whenever reasonable suspicion exists

6.18. What did the U. S. Supreme Court decide in *Dickerson v. United States (2000)*?
a) the Supreme Court repeated its endorsement of the stop and frisk exception
b) the Supreme Court repeated its endorsement of the Miranda warnings
c) the Supreme Court repeated its endorsement of warrantless automobile searches
d) the Supreme Court repeated its endorsement of the probable cause standards
e) the Supreme Court repeated its endorsement of the plain feel doctrine

6.19. Which of the following is FALSE regarding the Miranda warnings?
a) a case must be dismissed if a police officer does not read a defendant the Miranda warnings
b) the warnings do not have to be provided until the police begin to ask questions
c) the warnings involve the Fifth and Sixth Amendments to the Constitution
d) the warnings are designed to deter police misconduct
e) all of the above are TRUE

6.20. Who wrote the opinion in *Mapp v. Ohio (1961)* where the U. S. Supreme Court nationalized the exclusionary rule?
a) Chief Justice Earl Warren
b) Justice Hugo Black
c) Justice William Day
d) Justice Tom Clark
e) Justice Felix Frankfurter

6.21. Which of the following exceptions to the exclusionary rule means that the officers acted with the honest belief that they were following the proper rules?
a) inevitability of discovery exception
b) public safety exception
c) good faith exception
d) "Honest Abe" exception
e) mistaken identity exception

6.22 . Which of the following is TRUE about automobile searches?
a) police always need a warrant to search an automobile
b) automobiles are treated no differently than homes
c) few automobile searches arise as a result of traffic stops
d) officers can search anywhere in the car for which they have probable cause to search
e) all of the above are true

6.23. After the September 11 terrorist attacks, which of the following was required by the U. S. government in order to place someone in jail?
a) a citizen had to be charged with a crime
b) a citizen had to be given access to court proceedings
c) a citizen had to be given the opportunity to meet with an attorney
d) the U. S. government had to meet all of the above requirements
e) the U. S. government was NOT required to meet any of the above requirements if a person was suspected of being an "enemy combatant"

6.24. During what era did the Supreme Court incorporate most of the criminal justice-related rights upon state governments?
a) Warren Court era
b) Taft Court era
c) Burger Court era
d) Rehnquist Court era
e) Hughes Court era

6.25. Which of the following is TRUE about the exclusionary rule?
a) it is specifically mentioned in the Fourth Amendment
b) it currently applies only to the federal courts
c) the Burger Court expanded criminal defendants' rights by supporting the exclusionary rule
d) it was created by the judiciary to deter police and prosecutors from misconduct
e) all of the above are TRUE

True and False Questions

_____ 6.1. Police must read suspects their Miranda rights immediately after arrest or else the arrest is invalid.

_____ 6.2. An arrest is only a limited intrusion upon one's liberty.

_____ 6.3. A warrant must be signed by a judicial officer.

_____ 6.4. Border searches without a warrant are an automatic violation of the Fourth Amendment.

_____ 6.5. The exclusionary rule applies to federal and state courts.

_____ 6.6. Consent searches without a warrant are a violation of the Fourth Amendment.

_____ 6.7. Following the terrorist attacks on September 11th, the U. S. government jailed many U. S. citizens without charging them with any crimes.

_____6.8. Chief Justice Earl Warren was a supporter of the exclusionary rule.

_____ 6.9. The Burger Court has created a number of exceptions to the exclusionary rule.

_____ 6.10. The Fourth Amendment does NOT contain the word "warrant."

_____ 6.11. The Fifth Amendment contains the right against unreasonable search and seizure.

_____ 6.12. The Sixth Amendment contains the right to counsel.

_____ 6.13. The right to remain silent is found in the Fourth Amendment.

_____ 6.14. The Supreme has concluded that it is sometimes necessary to risk setting a guilty criminal free in order to make sure that constitutional rights are protected.

_____ 6.15. Warrantless searches are justified if exigent circumstances exist.

_____ 6.16. If a police officer walks up to someone on the street and begins asking questions, the officer must inform the person of their rights.

_____ 6.17. Sobriety checkpoints violate the Fourth Amendment rights of citizens.

_____ 6.18. A large percentage of defendants file a motion to suppress, asking a judge to exclude evidence that has allegedly been obtained in violation of the defendant's rights.

_____ 6.19. Chief Justice William Rehnquist wrote the majority opinion in _Miranda v. Arizona (1966)._

_____ 6.20. Police officers can view the interior of an automobile without a search warrant.

WORKSHEET 6.1. THE JUSTIFICATION FOR WARRANTLESS SEARCHES

Warrantless searches are important for police officers in regard to gathering evidence that might otherwise be lost or endanger the safety of others in society. In the following exercise, students should list the basis for justifying the warrantless searches listed below. What purpose(s) are served by allowing law enforcement officers to conduct a search without a warrant? Are these searches justified in violating a person's rights based upon the purposes that you listed?

Stop and Frisk on the Streets _____

_____

_____

_____

Warrantless Search of Hispanics five miles from the Mexican border _____

_____

_____

_____

Search Incident to a Lawful Arrest _____

_____

_____

_____

Automobile Searches _____

_____

_____

Searching through someone's luggage at the airport _____

_____

_____

Consent searches_____

_____

CHAPTER 7

POLICING: ISSUES AND TRENDS

LEARNING OBJECTIVES

After covering the material in this chapter, students should understand:

1. police patrol activities, including issues of preventive patrol, response time, foot versus motorized patrol, aggressive patrol, and community-oriented policing;

2. police use of new technology and weapons in the fight against crime

3. police abuse, including police brutality and corruption;

4. civic accountability, including internal affairs divisions, civilian review boards, standards and accreditation, and civil liability;

5. the issues and problems posed by the increase in private policing.

CHAPTER SUMMARY

Police administrators must make decisions about possible patrol strategies, including directed patrol, foot patrol, and aggressive patrol. Community policing seeks to involve the citizens in identifying problems and working with police officers to prevent disorder and crime. The development of new technologies has assisted police investigations through the use of computers, databases, surveillance devices, and methods to detect deception. Police departments are seeking to identify non-lethal weapons that can incapacitate suspects and control unruly crowds without causing serious injuries and deaths. The problems of police misuse of force and corruption cause erosions of community support. Internal affairs units, civilian review boards, standards and accreditation, and civil liability suits are four approaches designed to increase police accountability to citizens. The expansion of security management and private policing reflects greater recognition of the need to protect private assets and plan for emergencies but it also produces new issues and problems concerning the recruitment, training, and activities of lower-level private security personnel.

CHAPTER OUTLINE

I. INTRODUCTION
   A. The Louima Case
      On August 9, 1997, New York City police brutalized a Haitian immigrant named **Abner Louima** which led to the imprisonment of at least one officer, **Justin Volpe**. The brutal attack of Louima illustrates the problem of police abusing their authority and violating the public trust.

II. ISSUES IN PATROLLING

   A. Assignment of Patrol Personnel: Distribution of police often focused on "problem" neighborhoods. Allocation decisions usually determined by: crime statistics, degree of urbanization, pressures from business and community groups, ethnic composition of area, socioeconomic conditions.
      1. **Preventive Patrol**: **Kansas City Preventive Patrol Experiment** on proactive crime-prevention patrol indicates that such patrols make little difference on crime or fear of crime. Officers spent much of their time on administrative tasks and other matters unrelated to patrolling. Findings contributed to shift in emphasis toward order maintenance and service in some departments.

2.   **Hot Spots:** Research indicates crime is not evenly distributed. Certain kinds of predatory crimes may be reduced if police focus on places with motivated offenders, suitable targets, and an absence of capable guardians. Knowledge of hot spots can permit officers to be assigned to **directed patrol,** a proactive form of patrolling that focuses on hot spots and hot times (i.e., times during the day when activity most likely to occur at a location).

3.   Rapid Response Time: Studies indicate police response time is not crucial factor in making arrests; instead it is citizen response time in reporting crime right away (**Spelman and Brown**).

    a.   Citizen delay is a major problem; citizens distracted by coping, lending assistance, interpreting ambiguous situation. Many departments now classify calls to determine which ones actually need immediate response.

    b.   Three major reasons for delay are not easily overcome by citizen education or other innovations:

       1) Some people find situations to be ambiguous and they are not sure whether to call the police.

       2) Other people are involved in coping activities (e.g., taking care of victim, directing traffic, otherwise helping out).

       3) Other people experience conflict in making decision about whether to call. They may avoid making immediate decision or seek the advice of others.

    c.   Elimination of citizen delay would only have partial impact on problem because many crimes, such as burglary, are not reported until after they are "discovered" -- long after perpetrator has left. In some other cases (robbery, rape, assault), the victim may know the perpetrator and therefore could call the police sooner.

4.   **Foot Patrol** versus **Motorized Patrol**: Many contemporary arguments for putting police back on foot patrol beat: better relationship with community, gain knowledge of neighborhoods, better able to detect criminal activity. Leads to higher citizen satisfaction and some evidence of lower crime rates. Motorized patrol changed police from watching to prevent crime to waiting to respond to crime.

IDEAS IN PRACTICE: Should a police chief risk endangering the lives of patrol officers to save money in the budget?

5.   One- versus Two-Person Patrol Units: One-person patrol is more economical, permits more cars to be out on streets at one time, can increase response time throughout city. One-person cars becoming more common. Despite being uneconomical, officers and union leaders believe it provides additional safety for the officers and the public. Policies often developed through negotiations between police chiefs, unions, and local government. By contrast, administrators believe that solo officers are less distracted with no partner for idle conversation.

6.   **Aggressive Patrol:** proactive strategy to maximize interventions and observations in the community. The city also uses proactive, plain clothes crime units that make a disproportionate number of arrests. Kansas City used aggressive traffic enforcement to find handguns that people were carrying. Sting" operations and repeat offender programs are expensive because officers are taken from usual duties. Most cost-effective strategy seems to be to create incentives for officers to increase number of traffic stops and field interrogations. Aggressive patrol in minority neighborhoods can produce tension with the police if people believe they are being singled out because of their race.

7.   THE POLICY DEBATE: Should the Police Aggressively Enforce **Public Order** Laws? Do "little" crimes lead to more serious crimes?

8.   **Community Policing**: Most commonly associated with attempts by police to involve community in making their neighborhoods safe.

    a.   Approach has emerged due to perceived deficiencies in crime-fighter orientation. Four elements:

       1) Community-based crime prevention,

       2) Reorientation of patrol activities to focus on nonemergency services,

                        3) Increased accountability of the police to the public,

                        4) Decentralization of police decision making so as to include citizens.

            b.   **Problem-oriented policing** (related approach):Attempts to ascertain what is causing citizens' calls for help. With knowledge of underlying problems, police can enlist help from community agencies and citizens to address the underlying problems. These problems may concern quality of life rather than crime.

B.   <u>The Future of Patrol</u>: Police patrol by itself does little to control many kinds of crime. New strategies need to maintain community cooperation, develop sensitivity to demographic characteristics of communities and neighborhoods, and emphasize attention to service, order maintenance, and fear of crime.

III.   POLICING AND NEW TECHNOLOGY.

          Questions exist about the accuracy of new technology as well as the dilemma posed by infringing upon the constitutional rights of citizens.

A. <u>Investigative Tools</u>
1.   One of the most rapidly advancing tools used by law enforcement is the computer, specifically portable computers in patrol cars. Computers are especially helpful in investigating cybercrime. Law enforcement are also employing a variety of surveillance and detection systems in public areas to apprehend criminals
2.   Scientists are looking to employ new technologies in questioning suspects because polygraph tests have been unreliable.

B. <u>Weapons Technology</u>
1.   Police are trying to develop alternative nonlethal weapons because officers and departments have been sued for using force against suspects resulting in injuring or killing persons.
2.   Alternative **nonlethal weapons** such as pepper spray or nets can be used to incapacitate a person temporarily with minimum harm.

TECHNOLOGY ISSUES IN CRIMINAL JUSTICE: Nonlethal Weapons

IV.   POLICE ABUSE OF POWER

A. <u>Use of Force</u>
1.   Issues and accusations of brutality more common in heightened racial conflict situations of major cities.
2.   Citizens use the term **police brutality** to describe a wide range of practices, from the use of profane or abusive language to physical force and violence.
3.   WHAT AMERICANS THINK? Most people approve of a police officer striking a citizen under certain circumstances.
4.   It is important to distinguish between police use of force and police use of excessive force.
5.   Police have authority to use force if necessary. However, police use of deadly force often causes great emotional upheaval within a community. Typical victim is from communities with economic inequality and large minority populations.
6.   Shooting of unarmed immigrant, **Amadou Diallo**, in New York City led to prosecution of police officers.
7.   In 1985, Supreme Court ruled for first time that police use of deadly force to apprehend an unarmed, nonviolent, fleeing felony suspect violated the Fourth Amendment guarantee against unreasonable seizure (case of unarmed 15-year-old shot and killed by Memphis Police в **Tennessee v. Garner**). Previously, police in many states followed common law principle that allowed the use of any force necessary to arrest a fleeing felon.
8.   In **Graham v. Connor (1989)** the Supreme Court established the "objective reasonableness" standard and said that the officer's use of force should be evaluated in terms of the "reasonableness of the moment."

9.   The risk of significant lawsuits by victims of improper police shootings looms over contemporary police departments and creates incentives for administrators to set and enforce standards for the use of force.

WHAT AMERICANS THINK: A large majority of Americans believe that police officers are justified in striking a citizen if they are threatened physically or verbally.

  B. Corruption
     1.   **Police corruption** is a long-standing problem in American history.
     2.   Corruption is not easily defined. Some see it in things as simple as accepting a free cup of coffee.
     3.   A Question of Ethics: a free meal given to a police officer at a restaurant.
     4.   **"Grass Eaters"** and **"Meat Eaters"**: "Grass eaters" are officers who accept payoffs that circumstances of police work bring their way. Most common form of corruption. "Meat eaters" aggressively misuse their power for personal gain. Recent examples of officers getting actively involved in crimes related to illegal drug trafficking, either working with drug dealers or else robbing drug dealers.
     5.   Corruption has been so rampant in some departments that it can=t be attributed to "a few bad apples." Most police work is out of public view, so norms of police work and department policies may shield corrupt officers from detection.
     6.   "Vice" and victimless crimes are so profitable and so unlikely to produce complaints that corruption is tempting and often easy.
     7.   Officers may suffer from role ambivalence. Officers responsible for protecting community but not given the necessary powers to do so. As a result, conscientious officers must often violate the law in order to perform their duties. Infractions by officers are overlooked. Eventually department's informal norms make types of illegal activity routinized. **Ellwyn Stoddard** uses the term "blue coat crime" to describe this identifiable informal code.
     8.   There are multiple effects from corruption:
        a.   Criminals are left free to pursue their illegal activities.
        b.   Departmental morale and supervision drop.
        c.   The image of the police suffers.
     9.   Some citizens do not equate police corruption with criminal activity.

V.   **CIVIC ACCOUNTABILITY**
     1.   Challenge of making police accountable to civilian control in order to give public confidence that officers are behaving according to governing laws and rules.

A.   **Internal Affairs**
     1.   Often lack formal mechanisms for public to register complaints effectively.
     2.   Risk that internal affairs investigators will view complaints by public as attacks on entire department.
     3.   Investigations by Internal Affairs units do not often fit Hollywood model: frequently investigating allegations of sexual harassment, substance abuse problems, or misuse of physical force rather than grand corruption
     4.   Internal affairs officers normally assigned only for set period (e.g., 8 years); work is stressful and makes it difficult to maintain relationships with other officers. Unit needs sufficient resources from department in order to be effective.
     5.   Often difficult to get officers to testify about other officers.

B.   **Civilian Review Boards**
     1.   Political battles over creation of such boards because police oppose civilians evaluating of their actions. Such boards exist in 36 of the 50 largest cities and in 13 of the next 50 largest cities.
     2.   Although officers believe such boards cannot understand and judge them fairly, the boards have not been harsh on police.
     3.   Because of the low visibility of actions that result in complaints, most complaints cannot be substantiated.

C.   Standards and Accreditation
      1.   Communities can gain greater accountability if they require that operations be conducted by
            nationally recognized standards. Commission on Accreditation of Law Enforcement Agencies
            (CALEA), for example, includes the creation of standards for the use of discretion.
      2.   **Accreditation** is voluntary. Certification may instill public confidence, provide management tool,
            and provide basis for educating officers about being accountable for their actions.

D.   **Civil Liability Suits**
      1.   Civil lawsuits against departments for misconduct are another avenue for civic accountability.
            Lawsuits for brutality, false arrest, and negligence are increasingly common.
      2.   **Monell v. Dept. of Social Services for the City of New York** in 1978 permitted suits against
            individual officials and agencies when person's civil rights violated by the "customs and usages"
            of the department.
      3.   Successful lawsuits and even the threat of lawsuits provides an incentive to improve the training
            and supervision of officers.
      4.   Insurance companies provide civil liability coverage for police departments and many officers
            have their own insurance policies.

VI.   SECURITY MANAGEMENT AND PRIVATE POLICING

A.   Introduction
      1.   **Private policing** has existed for a long time, including bounty hunters and strikebreakers in
            American history.
      2.   Private policing larger in terms of personnel and resources than federal, state, and local law
            enforcement combined.
      3.   The rise of private agencies occurred for a number of reasons:
            a.   An increase of crime in the workplace.
            b.   An increase in the fear of crime.
            c.   The fiscal crises of the states which have limited public protection.
            d.   Increased public and business awareness and use of more cost-effective private security
                  services.
WORK PERSPECTIVE: Rosa Weaver, Investigator, General Motors Global Security

B.   Functions of Security Management and Private Police
      1.   Top-level security managers have a range of responsibilities that call upon them to fulfill multiple
            roles that would be handled by a variety of separate individuals in the public sector.
      2.   Private sector corporations own and control security for vital facilities in the United States,
            including nuclear power plants, oil refineries, military manufacturing facilities, and other
            important sites. Fires, tornadoes, or earthquakes at such sites could release toxic materials into the
            air and water.
      3.   At lower levels, specific occupations in private security are more directly comparable to those of
            police officers. Many security personnel are the equivalent of private sector detectives.
      4.   Other activities are more directly comparable to those of police patrol officers, especially for
            lower level security officers who must guard specific buildings, apartments, or stores.

C.   Private Employment of Public Police
      1.   Private employers are eager to hire police. Twenty percent of police departments forbid police
            officers to **moonlight** for private security firms. Off-duty police retain their full authority and
            powers to arrest, stop and frisk, etc.
      2.   Conflict of Interest: police officers banned from being process servers, bill collectors,
            repossessors, investigators for criminal defense attorneys and bail bondsmen, or employees at
            gambling establishments.
      3.   Management Prerogatives: departments require officers to gain permission to accept outside
            work, and department may deny permission if work degrading to department, physically
            exhausting, dangerous, etc.

D. The Public-Private Interface
   1. Private employers' interests may not always coincide with the goals and policies of the local police department. Lack of communication between public and private agencies can lead to botched investigations, loss of evidence, and overzealousness by private officers.
   2. Some cooperative efforts and investigations have occurred between security and police.
   3. Private firms often bypass the criminal justice system.

E. Recruitment and Training
   1. Serious concerns of law enforcement officials and civil libertarians about the recruitment and training of private officers. Relatively little training provided in most places. Fewer than half of the states have licensing requirements.
   2. Because pay is low and many private officers work only temporarily, work often done by the young or the retired, with few formal qualifications.
   3. Regulations that exist tend to be aimed at contractual private police (agencies that work for fees) rather than proprietary (officers hired by a company to provide security for that company).

F. STEPPING INTO A NEW WORLD: ARRESTED, BOOKED, CHARGED, JAILED AND INVESTIGATED: In his journey through the criminal justice system, Terry Clark was arrested and booked for selling heroin.

REVIEW OF KEY TERMS

Fill in the appropriate term from the list for each statement below
preventive patrol
public order crimes
hot spots
Kansas City Preventive Patrol Experiment
directed patrol
foot
broken windows theory
legitimate force
motorized
aggressive patrol
excessive force
problem-oriented policing
nonlethal weapons
community policing
Graham v. Connor (1989)
police brutality
Tennessee v. Garner (1985)
police corruption
"grass eaters"
"meat eaters"
civic accountability
internal affairs units
civilian review boards
accreditation
civil liability suits
private policing
moonlighting
Monell v. Dept. of Social Services (1978)

1.   In the 1930s, _____ patrol came to be viewed as more effective than putting officers on the beat.

2.   _____ is a patrol strategy designed to maximize the number of police interventions and observations in the community.

3.   _____ argues that a patrol officer's moving through an area will keep criminals from carrying out illegal acts.

4.   _____ was a 15 beat area that concluded that changes in patrol strategies had no major effect on the amount of crime reported.

5.   _____ is the growing phenomenon of hiring personnel to be paid by corporate and other entities for crime control and order maintenance activities.

6.   _____ is an approach to policing in which officers routinely seek to identify, analyze, and respond to circumstances underlying the incidents that prompt citizens to call the police.

7.   In _____, the Supreme Court ruled that a person can sue a police department if he or she can show that wrongful acts were a product of the "customs, practices, and policies" of the department.

8.   Police may use _____ force to do their job.

9.   _____ is the general term for reviewing police behavior to ensure that law enforcement personnel perform within the boundaries of the law.

10.   If a police officer is employed part-time for a private employer, this is called _____.

11.   The zero-tolerance policing of the 1990s in New York City is an example of aggressive patrol linked to the _____.

12.   _____ are the divisions within police department responsible for investigating officers' misconduct.

13.   _____ is the Supreme Court case that found a Fourth Amendment violation in the shooting of an unarmed, nonviolent fleeing felony suspect.

14.   _____ consists of attempts by police to involve residents in making their neighborhoods safer.

15.   _____ is the use of the courts for recovering money damages for harms caused by improper police behavior.

16.   _____ are the supervisory entities opposed by police officers as an improper means to evaluate misconduct and discipline officers.

17.   _____ are "little crimes" that can lead to more serious offenses

18.   _____ are designed to incapacitate a suspect without inflicting serious injuries.

19.   _____ are places that produce the most crime.

20.   _____ is a voluntary program for certifying that police departments meet national standards.

21. _____ are officers who actively misuse their position and power in seeking illegal personal profit and other favors.

22. _____ is a general problem that is generated by officers' discretionary and low visibility opportunities to seek personal gain or mistreat the public through the use of their official positions.

23. In _____, the Supreme Court ruled that an officer's use of force should be judged in terms of the "reasonableness of the moment."

24. Studies have shown that _____ patrols are more costly and do not reduce crime, but they do make citizens less fearful.

25. _____ is a proactive form of patrolling that directs resources to known high-crime areas.

26. _____ are officers who accept personal gifts and profits that are presented to them in the course of performing their duties.

27. _____ is a term to describe a wide range of police misconduct from abusive language to physical force and violence

28. It is _____, in violation of departmental policies and state laws, that constitutes abuse of police power.

REVIEW OF KEY PEOPLE
Amadou Diallo
Ellywn Stoddard
Justin Volpe
Abner Louima
William Spelman
Dale Brown

1. In their study of rapid response time of police, _____ and _____ found that police succeeded in only 29 of 1,000 cases.

2. _____, a 32 year old Haitian immigrant, was arrested for disorderly conduct and brutally assaulted by New York City police officers.

3. _____ was sentenced to thirty years in federal prison for police brutality.

4. _____ studied blue-coat crime has said that it can become part of an "identifiable informal code"

5. _____, an unarmed West African immigrant, died in a fuselage of 41 bullets fired by four members of New York City's Street Crime Unit.

SELF-TEST QUESTIONS

Multiple Choice Questions

7.1. Who was convicted of police brutality and sentenced to thirty years in a federal prison?
a) Abner Louima
b) Justin Volpe
c) Amadou Diallo
d) Rodney King
e) Dale Brown

7.2. What "remains the most influential test of the general deterrent effects of patrol on crime"?
a) Uniform Crime Report
b) National Crime Victimization Survey
c) The Mollen Commission Study
d) Kansas City Preventive Patrol Experiment
e) Robert Peel's "Bobbies on Patrol Analysis"

7.3. In a study of "hot spots" in Minneapolis researchers found that...
a) 30 percent of streets and intersections produced 10 percent of calls to police
b) 3 percent of streets and intersections produced 50 percent of calls to police
c) 50 percent of streets and intersections produced 3 percent of calls to police
d) 20 percent of streets and intersections produced 20 percent of calls to police
e) 5 percent of streets and intersections produced 100 percent of calls to police

7.4. Which of the following is considered a proactive strategy?
a) tracking of high-risk parolees
b) firearms confiscation
c) sting operations
d) raid on a crack house
e) all of the above

7.5. In a study by William G. Spelman and Dale K. Brown, how often are police successful in using the rapid response approach?
a) 29 of 1,000 cases
b) 98 of 1,000 cases
c) 512 of 1,000 cases
d) 786 of 1,000 cases
e) 987 of 1,000 cases

7.6. . In the past, patrols were organized by "beats" because it was assumed that...
a) crime could happen anywhere
b) police could "beat" criminals at their game
c) police could use timing techniques to solve crimes
d) criminals were all "deadbeats"
e) all of the above

7.7. Which of the following is TRUE of aggressive patrol strategies?
a) aggressive patrol strategies may lead to citizen hostility
b) aggressive patrol strategies do NOT intrude on the rights of individuals
c) aggressive patrol strategies have been shown to increase crime
d) all of the above are true
e) all of the above are false

7.8. Why are police officials paying greater attention to public order crimes?
a) because nearly all police departments have surpluses in their budgets
b) because few civil liberties are violated in dealing with public order crimes
c) because research has shown that high levels of disorder are linked to high levels of crime
d) because most officers are uneducated
e) because there has been a reduction in more serious crimes and officers have more time

7.9. Which of the following is a component of community policing?
a) centralizing decision making
b) making police more accountable to the public
c) excluding residents from decision making
d) changing the focus of patrol activities to emergency services
e) all of the above are components

7.10. Who was the unarmed West African immigrant who died in a fusillade of 41 bullets fired by four members of the NYC Street Crime Unit?
a) Abner Louima
b) Justin Volpe
c) Amadou Diallo
d) Rodney King
e) Dale Brown

7.11. Which of the following is TRUE concerning "lie-detectors"?
a) lie detectors are admissible in court
b) it is illegal for police to use lie detectors
c) lie detectors are used often by police to exclude suspects but only can be used on willing suspects
d) lie detectors are 100% accurate
e) all of the above are false

7.12. What new technology did police officers use at the Super Bowl in 2001?
a) retinal scanning devices
b) facial recognition
c) thermal imaging cameras
d) all of the above
e) none of the above

7.13. What usually happens if an officer reports that another officer has done something unethical or illegal?
a) the reporting officer is given a promotion
b) the reporting officer is considered a snitch and ostracized
c) the reporting officer serves as a counselor for the offending officer
d) the reporting officer is given a job with internal affairs
e) the reporting officer is fired

7.14. According to research conducted in six urban jurisdictions, what percentage of arrests showed that no weapon was used by the police?
a) almost 1 percent
b) almost 10 percent
c) almost 50 percent
d) almost 75 percent
e) almost 98 percent

7.15. Which of the following is (are) considered a nonlethal weapon(s) by police departments?
a) gun
b) air-fired beanbags
c) pepper spray
d) b and c
e) all of the above

7.16. Higher-level security managers are increasingly drawn from …
a) college graduates with degrees in criminal justice
b) high school graduates with a strong interest in policing
c) high school dropouts who have a GED
d) college graduates with degrees in psychology
e) Ph. D. students who specialize in national security policy

7.17. Which of the following is TRUE concerning the private employment of public police?
a) private employment of public police is illegal
b) private employment never conflicts with an officers' public duties
c) private employment of public police can tire police officers and impair their ability to protect the public
d) private employment of public police is legal but private firms are not eager to hire public police
e) all of the above are false

7.18. What percentage of police departments forbid their officers to work for private employers?
a) 1 percent
b) 5 percent
c) 20 percent
d) 50 percent
e) 100 percent

7.19. How long has the public been aware of police abuse of power ?
a) since roughly 1875
b) since roughly 1900
c) since roughly 1930
d) since roughly 1980
e) since roughly 2002

7.20. What is the size of an Internal Affairs Department?
a) ten officers
b) twenty officers
c) thirty officers
d) fifty officers
e) it may vary between one officer and an entire section of officers

7.21. What is the term used if a police officer works part-time for a private employer?
a) internal affair time
b) stinging
c) moonlighting
d) hot spotting
e) aggressive patrolling

7.22. Which of the following is an example of a technological tool being used by law enforcement?
a) cameras
b) scanners
c) facial-recognition
d) computers
e) all of the above

7.23. In terms of costs and benefits, where are foot patrols most effective?
a) low density rural areas
b) high business or population density
c) suburban areas
d) low density urban neighborhoods
e) foot patrols are not effective anywhere

7.24. In Kansas City, Missouri, aggressive traffic enforcement was used as a way to seize firearms. How many guns were seized per traffic stop?
a) one gun per one traffic stop
b) one gun per five traffic stops
c) one gun per ten traffic stops
d) one gun per twenty-eight traffic stops
e) one gun per seventy-five traffic stops

7.25. What is the technical name for a "lie detector"?
a) polygraph
b) seismograph
c) retinal scanners
d) lie-recognition technology
e) thermal imaging camera

True and False Questions

_____7.1. Pepper spray can be used to incapacitate a person temporarily with minimum harm.

_____7.2. Police accreditation is voluntary.

_____7.3. Aggressive patrolling is a reactive strategy.

_____7.4. Stings, or antifencing efforts, are a widely used law enforcement technique.

_____7.5. Foot patrols are inexpensive.

_____7.6. Disorder, such as a broken window, creates fear in a community and increases crime problems.

_____7.7. Community policing changes the focus of patrol activities to nonemergency services.

_____7.8. Rapid response results in a 75 percent success rate for police.

_____7.9. Fingerprint evidence was used to convict offenders in the early twentieth century.

_____7.10. Polygraphs traditionally are considered reliable.

_____7.11. Police corruption is a relatively recent phenomenon with a short history in the U. S.

_____7.12. Abuse of police power is a major issue on the public's agenda.

_____7.13. Police may use "legitimate" force to do their job.

_____7.14. Police scandals rarely have occurred in the last quarter-century.

_____7.15. The use of new technology does not raise issues related to constitutional rights.

_____7.16. Officer Justin Volpe was acquitted of police brutality charges that he assaulted Abner Louima.

_____7.17. The Kansas City Preventive Control Experiment found that the changes in patrol strategies had major effects on the amount of crime reported.

_____7.18. Public order crimes are "serious crimes" that can lead to additional serious crimes.

_____7.19. Grass eaters, police officers who accept payoffs, are numerous.

_____7.20. Internal Affairs officers usually have good relationships with officers outside of their department.

WORKSHEET 7.1: PATROL STRATEGIES

You are the police chief in medium-sized city. In one residential neighborhood, citizens are alarmed (and complaining to city hall) because there has been a rash of burglaries. In the downtown area, an increase in muggings has the merchants concerned about losing business. At a city council meeting, representatives from both groups ask you how you can adjust patrol strategies to address the problems in each area. Pretend that you are responding to their questions in explaining below how each patrol strategy might impact (or not impact) the two problems areas in the city.

1. Preventive
Patrol_____

_____

_____

_____

_____

_____

_____

2. Foot Patrol_____

_____

_____

_____

_____

_____

3. Aggressive
Patrol_____

_____

_____

_____

_____

Whether or not you would adopt any of the foregoing patrol strategies, describe how you would address the crime problems in each area in order to reduce the problem and/or make the citizens feel less concerned.

_____

_____

CHAPTER 8

COURTS AND ADJUDICATION

LEARNING OBJECTIVES

After covering the material in this chapter, students should understand:

1.   the dual court system, the hierarchy of courts (general jurisdiction, appellate etc.) and the fragmented nature of the organization of courts in the United States;

2.   the judge's functions and roles in the criminal court;

3.   the methods used for selecting judges and the results of those selection methods;

4.   the decentralized organization of prosecution in the United States;

5.   the significant discretionary power of prosecutors to make unsupervised, low visibility decisions that shape criminal justice outcomes;

6.   the exchange relations between prosecutors and other actors that affect prosecutors' decisions (e.g., police, victims, court, community, etc.);

7.   the prosecutor's dilemma of seeking to win cases for the state while also ensuring that justice is served;

8.   the role conceptions of prosecutors: trial counsel for police; house counsel for police; representative of the court; and elected official;

9.   the nature of the accusatory process

10.   the Supreme Court's requirement for the appointment of defense counsel for indigent defendants facing incarceration;

11.   the difference between the television of image of the defense trial attorney and the reality of defense attorneys engaged in plea bargaining and exchange relations;

12.   the role of the defense attorney as client-counselor and agent-mediator, and the environment of criminal defense work;

13.   the characteristics and weaknesses of the three systems for indigent defense: assigned counsel, contract counsel, and public defender

14.   the issue of attorney competence and standards for assessing the ineffective assistance of counsel.

15.   the impact of local legal culture on the courts; the development and impact of courtroom workgroups

CHAPTER SUMMARY

The United States has a dual court system consisting of state and federal courts that are organized into separate hierarchies. Trial courts and appellate courts have different jurisdictions and functions. Despite resistance from local judges and political interests, reformers have sought to improve state court systems through centralized administration, state funding, and a separate personnel system. The judge, is a key figure in the criminal justice process, who assumes the roles of adjudicator, negotiator, and administrator. State judges are selected through various methods, including partisan elections, nonpartisan elections, gubernatorial appointment, and merit selection. Merit selection methods for choosing judges have gradually spread to many states. Such methods normally use a screening committee to make recommendations of potential appointees who will, if placed on the bench by the governor, go before the voters for approval or disapproval of their performance in office.

American prosecutors at all levels have considerable discretion to determine how to handle criminal cases. There is no higher authority over most prosecutors that can overrule a decision to decline to prosecute (*nolle prosequi*) or to pursue multiple counts against a defendant. The prosecutor can play a variety of roles, including trial counsel for the police, house counsel for the police, representative of the court, and elected official. Prosecutors' decisions and actions are affected by their exchange relationships with many other important actors and groups, including police, judges, victims and witnesses, and the public. Three primary models of prosecutors' decision-making policies are legal sufficiency, system efficiency, and trial sufficiency. The image of defense attorneys portrayed in the media as courtroom advocates is often vastly different from the reality of pressured, busy negotiators constantly involved in bargaining with the prosecutor over guilty plea agreements. Relatively few private defense attorneys make significant incomes from criminal work, but larger numbers of private attorneys accept court appointments to handle indigent defendants' cases quickly for relatively low fees. Three primary methods for providing attorneys to represent indigent defendants are appointed counsel, contract counsel, and public defenders. Defense attorneys must often wrestle with difficult working conditions and uncooperative clients as they seek to provide representation, usually in the plea negotiation process. The quality of representation provided to criminal defendants is a matter of significant concern, but U.S. Supreme Court rulings have made it difficult for convicted offenders to prove that their attorneys did not provide a competent defense.

The outcomes in criminal cases are largely influenced by a court's local legal culture, which defines the "going rates" of punishment for various offenses. Courtroom workgroups composed of judges, prosecutors, and defense attorneys who work together to handle cases through cooperative plea bargaining processes. Most convictions are obtained through plea bargains, a process that exists because it fulfills the self-interest of prosecutors, judges, defense attorneys, and defendants. Plea bargaining is facilitated by exchange relations between prosecutors and defense attorneys. In many courthouses, there is little actual bargaining, as outcomes are determined through the implicit bargaining process of settling the facts and assessing the "going rate" of punishment according to the standards of the local legal culture.

CHAPTER OUTLINE
I.   INTRODUCTION
        Clara Harris was found guilty of murder for driving over her husband with her Mercedes Benz after she
        had caught her husband in an affair with another woman. As Harris entered the court system, her fate in
        large part was determined by the decisions of judges, prosecutors, and defense attorneys. Her punishment of
        20 years in prison and a $10,000 fine resulted from the strategies and arrangements of the prosecutor and
        defense attorney as well as decisions made by the judge and jury.

II.   THE STRUCTURE OF AMERICAN COURTS

A.   "Dual court system" includes state and federal courts. Both have trial and appellate courts. American trial
        courts are strikingly decentralized. Except for a few states with centralized court systems, courts operate
        under the state penal code but are staffed and funded by county or city government. Leads to local political
        influence and community values shaping courts and their decisions. There are also Native American tribal
        courts. **Jurisdiction** is the geographic or legal boundaries within which control may be exercised by a court
        of law

B.   Both the federal and state court systems have trial and appellate courts. There are three levels of courts:
        1.   **Trial courts of limited jurisdiction**: limited to hearing formal charges against accused persons,
                holding preliminary hearings, and perhaps trials for minor offenses. At the federal level, there are
                no trial courts of limited jurisdiction.
        2.   **Trial courts of general jurisdiction**: trials in all cases, criminal and civil. Often referred to as
                felony courts. This is where jury trials take place and judges impose punishment. All federal cases
                begin in the general jurisdiction trial courts, the U. S. District Courts.
        3.   **Appellate courts** (courts of last resort and in most states intermediate appellate courts): appeals
                from the lower courts. Intermediate appellate courts often lack discretion to decline to hear cases
                and usually sit in panels of three judges. Further appeals may be filed with state supreme courts or
                the U. S. Supreme Court at the federal level.

C.   TECHNOLOGY ISSUES IN CRIMINAL JUSTICE: The Electronic Courtroom- Increasingly, courtrooms
        in the U. S are using technology for hearings and conferences. PowerPoint presentations and internet access
        are provided for attorneys. Some critics question whether this technology could be used to distort the
        perceptions of jurors.

III.   TO BE A JUDGE

A.   Introduction
        1.   Judges perceived to be most powerful actor [although prosecutor arguably really more powerful];
                judges not just involved in trials, also a presence in a range of activities: signing warrants, setting
                bail, arraignments, accepting guilty pleas, scheduling cases.
        2.   Judge is the person in the system who is expected to *embody* justice; specific expectations about
                judge's manner and demeanor; judges frequently function as lawgivers as other actors involved in
                fact-finding; judges are believed to be removed from the social context of the courtroom
                participants and to base their decisions on their objective interpretation of the law after thoughtful
                consideration of the issues.

B.   Who Becomes a Judge?
        Judges enjoy high status and salaries well above the rates for most American workers, yet lower than pay
        for partners at large law firms.
        1.   Judges overwhelmingly white and male.
        2.   In many cities, political factors dictate that judges be drawn from specific racial, religious, and
                ethnic groups -- black and Hispanic still underrepresented: affects symbolic aspect of justice when
                contrasted with demographic composition of defendants in urban centers.
        3.   Criminal court judges frequently have lowest status on judicial hierarchy; get less respect and
                prestige from public; many judges seek to move to civil or appellate judgeships.

C.   Functions of the Judge
    1.   Adjudicators: play role as neutral actor between prosecution and defense in making decisions on bail, pleas, sentencing, motions. Must avoid any appearance of bias.
    2.   Negotiators: because most case dispositions determined by negotiation, judges spend much of their time talking to prosecutors, defense attorneys, etc. Judges may even provide informal advice to defense attorney or even defendant about what is likely to happen. Court rules in some states forbid judicial participation in plea bargaining -- although participate behind the scenes in many others.
    3.   Administrators: seldom-recognized function is the administration of the courthouse. In urban areas, there may be a professional court administrator. Judges, however, will still be responsible for administration of their courtroom and staff. In rural areas, administrative burdens on judges may be more substantial.

D.   How to Become a Judge
    Quality of courts and justice depends on having judges with proper skills and qualities. Public confidence in courts diminished by poor or impolite performance.
    1.   CLOSE-UP: Improper Judicial Behavior-What happens when judges make inappropriate comments to defendants?
    2.   Debates exist about whether higher quality judges would emerge from selection processes that de-emphasize politics or, alternatively, whether voters in a democracy should be able to choose their public officials, including their judges.
    3.   Methods of Selection:
        a.   Gubernatorial appointment-judges appointed by the governor of a state
        b.   Legislative selection-judges appointed by the state legislature
        c.   **Merit selection**-a reform plan by which judges are nominated by a commission and appointed by a governor for a given period.
        d.   **Nonpartisan election**- an election in which candidates' party affiliations are not listed on the ballot
        e.   **Partisan election**- an election in which candidates are openly endorsed by political parties

    IDEAS IN PRACTICE: Can campaign fundraising in judicial elections make judges indebted to interest groups?

    4.   Election Systems:
        a.   Campaigns for judgeships are generally low-key, low-visibility contests marked by little controversy; and usually only a small portion of the voters participate in the election. Candidates are constrained by ethical requirements from discussing issues. State supreme courts may produce highly visible campaigns.
        b.   In many cities, judgeships are fuel for the political machine as a means to reward party loyalists; in addition, the judgeships captured by a political party may permit the appointment of other loyalists to a variety of courthouse positions (clerks, bailiffs, etc.)
    5.   **Merit Selection**
    First initiated in Missouri in 1940 and now has spread to other states.
        a.   When a vacancy occurs, a nominating commission of lawyers and citizens sends the governor a list of three recommended names and the governor chooses one of them be the new judge. After one year, the citizens vote in a retention election on whether to approve the judge's continued service.
        b.   Process still contains politics within the legal profession and selection process can favor elite lawyers with ties to corporations.
    6.   WHAT AMERICANS THINK. Public opinion data show that Americans express concern about the influence of politics on judges.

IV.   THE PROSECUTORIAL SYSTEM
      Prosecuting attorneys make discretionary decisions about whether to pursue criminal charges, which charges to make, and what sentence to recommend.

A.   Introduction
     1.   **U. S. Attorney**: federal prosecutor, appointed by the President in each of 94 districts around the country; responsible for prosecuting federal crimes.
     2.   **State Attorney General**: elected in most states; in Alaska, Delaware, and Rhode Island, they direct all local prosecutions as well as state prosecutions.
     3.   County Prosecutors: 2,341 offices in country; primary location of prosecutions; elected except in Connecticut and New Jersey and therefore heavily involved in local politics.
          a.   Number of assistant prosecutors will vary by size of office -- all the way up to 500 in Los Angeles; assistants usually young attorneys who use position to gain trial experience.

B.   Politics and Prosecution
     1.   In most states, prosecutors are elected. The process and organization of prosecution is inescapably political. For example:
          a.   Appointment of assistant prosecutors may serve the political party's purposes
          b.   Decision about whether or not to prosecute may include consideration of prosecutor's or political party's electoral interests.
          c.   Historically, some groups (e.g., racial minorities) received harsher treatment when prosecutors used their discretion to pursue their cases while not pursuing others' cases.

C.   The Prosecutor's Influence
     1.   Prosecutors have great influence because they are involved in all stages of the criminal justice process and they are linked throughout the process with other actors in the system-police, defense attorneys, and judges.
     2.   Prosecutors also gain power from the fact that their decisions and actions are hidden from public view. **Prosecutor's complex** is the idea that prosecutors may view themselves as instruments of law enforcement and they strive to close each case with a conviction.

D.   The Prosecutor's Roles
     1.   As lawyers for the state, they are expected to do everything in their power to win the public's case, but as officers of the court and members of the local legal profession, they are also obligated to see that justice is done.
     2.   Four role conceptions found among prosecutors involves a different view of the prosecutor's "clients":
          a.   Trial counsel for the police: crime-fighter stance and follow police department policies.
          b.   House counsel for the police: give legal advice so that arrests will stand up in court.
          c.   Representative of the court: enforce rules of due process to ensure that police act in accordance with law and respect rights of defendants.
          d.   Elected official: make decisions that are responsive to local public opinion -- but this creates risks of partisan political influence on decision making.

E.   Discretion of the Prosecutor
     1.   Autonomy, lack of supervision, and low visibility of decisions give prosecutors broad discretionary authority to make decisions at each step of the criminal justice process.
     2.   A QUESTION OF ETHICS: Case of prosecutor determining robbery charges when the evidence is not crystal clear.
     3.   Prosecutors determine number of **counts** to be pursued.
     4.   **Discovery**: Legal requirement that information be made available to the defense attorney, part of prosecutor's obligation to act impartially in seeking justice rather than in seeking only convictions on behalf of the state.
     5.   Prosecutor may reduce charge in exchange for a plea bargain.
     6.   Prosecutor may drop charge (**nolle prosequi** or nol. pros.) completely according to discretionary judgment without providing any reason to anyone.

F.   Key Relationships of the Prosecutor
The decisions made by the prosecuting attorney's office are not based solely on formal policies and role conceptions. They are also influenced by relationships with other actors in the justice system. Precise decisions and procedures will vary with each environment: e.g., prosecutors may make actual charging decisions or they may merely rubber stamp police decisions.
      1.   Police
            a.   Prosecutors are dependent on the police to bring them the evidence with which they must achieve their goals -- solid cases.
            b.   Prosecutors depend on the police for investigations; prosecutors' success can depend on the quality of police investigations.
            c.   Prosecutors can affect police by returning cases for further investigation or by refusing to approve arrest warrants.

      2.   Victims and Witnesses
            a.   The relationship of the victim to the accused can create problems for prosecutors: complaining witnesses may refuse to cooperate because they know or have a continuing relationship with the perpetrator. Studies show significantly higher conviction rates in stranger crimes than in nonstranger crimes in which the victim may decide not to cooperate with the prosecution. May lead prosecutor to dismiss cases.
            b.   Prosecutors may also drop cases when they think the victims will be unreliable or will not be believed as witnesses.
      3.   Judges and Courts
            a.   Sentencing history of each judge may influence prosecutors' decisions about which charges to file and whether or not to prosecute.
      4.   The Community
            a.   Like other elected officials, prosecutors cannot remain unresponsive to public opinion. Otherwise they may risk losing their jobs.
            b.   Prosecutors' decisions are also affected by relationships with news media, state and federal officials, legislators, and political party officials.
            CLOSE-UP: **Community Prosecution** involves bringing prosecutors into close contact with citizens in an effort to reduce crime and increase the effectiveness of the criminal justice system.

G.   Decision-Making Policies
      1.   Pretrial phase involved with screening cases to remove those that do not meet legal standard for probable cause, to divert eligible cases to other agencies, and to prepare appropriate charges for remaining cases.
      2.   Patterns vary among offices: screening emphasized by some prosecutors, generating quickly negotiated guilty pleas emphasized by others, and delaying pleas to build pressure on defendant up to trial date used by others.
      3.   The **accusatory process** consists of the series of activities that take place from the moment of arrest and booking through the formal charging (either information or indictment). This process involves activities of police, grand jury, bail agency, and court linked with the activities of the prosecuting attorney.

VII. **DEFENSE ATTORNEY**: IMAGE AND REALITY

A.   Introduction
      1.   Television shows have made defense lawyers familiar figures in the minds of the public as outspoken courtroom advocates.
      2.   In reality, defense attorneys are involved in interactions outside of public view that lead to plea bargains and dismissals.

B.   Role of the Defense Attorney
1.   Criminal defense lawyers are essential advocates on behalf of defendants through the application of pretrial investigative skills, verbal skills in plea negotiations and courtroom proceedings, and ability to creatively question prosecution witnesses.
2.   The defense attorney plays an important role in protecting the defendant's constitutional rights.
3.   In addition to advocacy functions, defense counsel provide psychological support to the defendant and the defendant's family.
4.   An effective defense requires respect, openness, and trust between attorney and client.

C.   The Realities of the Defense Attorney's Job
1.   If defense attorneys are inexperienced or uncaring, they may not present an effective defense.
2.   The provision of defense counsel does not automatically create the adversarialness assumed by the due process model. Defense attorneys' actual behavior will depend on exchange relations and organizational setting of the court.
3.   Effective defense attorneys seek to understand the facts of the case and the nature of the prosecution's evidence before deciding on the best course of action for the client, whether it is a plea bargain or a trial.
4.   Neither the public nor defendants understand the defense attorney's responsibilities for protecting people's rights and working, often in a cooperative fashion with the prosecution, to secure the most favorable outcome for the client.

D.   The Environment of Criminal Practice
1.   Much of the service provided by defense counsel involves preparing clients for the likelihood of conviction and punishment.
2.   Defense counsel's "guilty knowledge" may be psychological burden; defense counsel is only judicial actor to view the defendant in the context of social environment and family ties.
3.   Defense counsel interact continuously with lower class clients and with police, social workers, and minor political appointees. They may be required to visit jails at all hours of day or night. Even if they prevail in the case, they may be unable to collect their fees from their clients.
4.   The low pay for such work is a key factor in the environment: defense attorneys must make every effort to obtain payment ahead of time, including trying to get payment from defendant's relatives if defendant does not   pay. Leads to handling a multitude of cases for very modest fees. Creates incentives to negotiate quick pleas, since they may pay the same as a three-day trial.
5.   Defense counsel must adjust to burden of losing most of their cases.

WORK PERSPECTIVE: Lisa Peebles (Federal Public Defender) Syracuse, New York

E.   Counsel for Indigents
1.   Supreme Court requirement that counsel be appointed early in criminal process for all defendants facing incarceration has drastically raised the percentage of defendants relying on publicly supported criminal defense lawyers. In some jurisdictions, 90 percent of accused must be provided with counsel.
2.   Major Supreme Court Rulings on Right to Counsel
3.   The quality of representation for the poor is often questioned. Appointed counsel and public defenders have few incentives to fight each case vigorously.
4.   Frequently the image of the zealous defense lawyer is contradicted by the reality of a lawyer appointed in the courtroom who speaks briefly with the client before entering a quick guilty plea.
5.   Ways of Providing Indigents With Counsel
    a.   **Assigned Counsel:** court appoints a private practice attorney to represent indigent. Widely used in small cities and rural areas, but also used in some urban areas, including those that use public defenders for most cases. *Ad Hoc System*: judge selects lawyers at random from a prepared list or appoints lawyers who are present in the courtroom. Coordinated System: court administrator oversees the appointment of counsel. Attorney competence is sometimes questionable. Lawyers seeking appointments may be recent law school grads who need income or else attorneys who were not successful in more lucrative areas of legal practice. Fee schedules may be so low as to lead assigned counsel

to encourage their clients to plead guilty; spares attorney from prospect of working hard on a case for very little money. Profitability comes from doing a large number of cases as quickly as possible.

  b. **Contract System:** the government enters into a contract with a law firm, individual attorney, or non-profit organization that will provide representation for all indigent defendants.

  c. **Public Defender**: Public defenders are salaried government employees who handle indigents' criminal cases. Public defender systems predominate in large cities. Public defenders often viewed as superior to assigned counsel because attorneys are full-time specialists in criminal law. Public defenders also regarded as more efficient because they are less inclined to create delays. Public defenders face overwhelming caseloads. Because public defenders are government employees, it may be difficult for them to gain the trust and cooperation of their clients

WHAT AMERICANS THINK: Few American trust criminal defendant attorneys "a lot." Most trust criminal defense attorneys "somewhat" or a "little."

 6. A QUESTION OF ETHICS: Attorneys sometimes need to build a relationship with a judge in order to get court appointments

 7. Attorney Effectiveness and Competence

  a. Right to counsel is of little value if attorneys are not competent and effective.

  b. U. S. Supreme Court has made it hard for defendants to prove that they were denied effective counsel. They must identify specific errors that affected the result of the case and made the case decisions unfair.

VII. THE COURTROOM: HOW IT FUNCTIONS

 1. **Local Legal Culture**-The shared beliefs, attitudes, and norms of a court community – great influence over what happens. Can be used to explain why courts operate differently even though they have the same formal rules and procedures. Shared norms serve to:

  a. Help participants distinguish between "our" court and other jurisdictions (e.g., judges and prosecutors talk about how "we" do a better job than neighboring courts).

  b. Stipulate how members should treat one another. For example, strongly adversarial defense actions may not be in keeping with expected local behavior -- attorneys expected to not "rock the boat" by challenging local customary practices.

  c. Describe how cases *should* be processed. Most importantly, affect the "**going rate**" -- the local view of the appropriate sentence given the offense and defendant's prior record and other characteristics. Also affects attitudes about proper plea negotiations, **continuances** (an adjournment of a scheduled case until a later date) and eligibility for appointed counsel or public defender.

 2. **workgroup-** cases processed and decisions made through interactions and reciprocal relationships of prosecutor, defense attorney, judge, and perhaps others (bailiff, court clerk, etc.). Workgroup concept seems especially important in urban courts. There must be interaction of the members of the group. The members have the same attitudes about one or more motives or goals that determine the direction in which the group will move. The members develop a set of norms that determine the boundaries within which interpersonal relations may be established and activity carried out. If interaction continues, a set of roles becomes stabilized and the group differentiates itself from other groups. A network of interpersonal relationships develops on the basis of the members' likes and dislikes for one another.

REVIEW OF KEY TERMS

Fill in the appropriate term from the list for each statement below

appellate courts
 jurisdiction
trial courts of general jurisdiction
trial courts of limited jurisdiction
nonpartisan election
partisan election
merit selection
United States attorneys
prosecuting attorney
state attorney general
prosecution complex
count
discovery
nolle prosequi
accusatory process
defense attorney
assigned counsel
community prosecution
public defender
contract counsel
local legal culture
going rate
continuance
courtroom workgroup

1.   A(n) _____ is an adjournment of a scheduled case until a later date as requested by attorneys and granted (or denied) by the trial judge.

2.   _____ is a collection of individuals who interact in the workplace on a continuing basis, share goals, and develop norms about how activities should be carried out.

3.   _____ is the shared norms and values by members within a court community that helps to shape how cases should be handled and how a participant should behave in the judicial process.

4.   _____ is an attorney employed on a full-time salaried basis by a public or private non profit organization to represent indigents.

5.   _____ is the lawyer who represents the accused in the criminal justice process.

6.   _____ is a private attorney among a list of attorneys appointed by the government to represent an indigent defendant for a relatively small fee.

7.   _____ is an attorney in private practice who successfully submits a bid to the government to represent all indigent defendants in a county during a set period of time and for a specified dollar amount.

8.   _____ is the prosecutor responsible for federal crimes in each federal district court.

9.   _____ is the series of activities from arrest through the filing formal charges with the court.

10.   _____ is a separate offense of which a person is accused in an indictment or information.

11.   _____ is the discretionary decision to decline to initiate a prosecution.

12.   Each state has an elected _____ who usually has power to bring prosecutions in certain cases such as statewide consumer fraud..

13.   _____ is the prosecutor's pretrial disclosure to the defense of facts and evidence to be introduced at trial.

14.   _____ is a biased orientation that may detract from a prosecutor's responsibilities as an officer of the court.

15.   _____ is regarded as the most powerful figure in the criminal justice system.

16.   _____ is a judicial selection method in which the selection of candidates is controlled by the political parties.

17.   _____ is the trial court that has jurisdiction of misdemeanor cases.

18.   A court's _____ defines the legal boundaries within which control may be exercised.

19.   _____ is a method of selecting judges where a commission nominates and a governor appoints for a given period.

20.   _____ is the level of the judicial hierarchy that looks for errors by police or the trial court.

21.   _____ is the local court officials' shared view of the appropriate sentence.

22.   _____ is the trial court that handles felony cases.

23.   _____ is a method of selecting judges by election in which candidates' party affiliations are not listed on the ballot.

24.   _____ is an initiative to reduce crime and increase the effectiveness of the criminal justice system by bringing prosecutors into closer contact with citizens.

REVIEW OF KEY PEOPLE
Fill in the appropriate person from the list for each statement below
Clara Harris
Madelyne Gorman Toogood
Ally McBeal
Johnnie Cochran
Robert Shapiro

1.   _____ and _____ were attorneys whose efforts helped acquit O. J. Simpson of murder charges in 1995.

2.   _____ made national news when she was captured on videotape slapping and punching her four-year old daughter.

3.   _____ was prosecuted for murdering her husband when she repeatedly ran over him with her Mercedes Benz.

4.   Most Americans obtain their image of attorneys through television shows such as _____.

SELF-TEST SECTION

Multiple Choice Questions

8.1. Which of the following are court systems within the U. S.?

a) federal

b) state

c) tribal

d) all of the above

e) a and b

8.2. Which of the following is NOT a reason to become a judge?

a) perform public service

b) gain political power

c) gain prestige

d) gain wealth

e) all of the above

8.3. Which of the following is a seldom-recognized function of most judges?

a) negotiating

b) managing the courthouse

c) adjudicating

d) all of the above

e) none of the above

8.4. Which statement best describes U. S. election campaigns for lower court judgeships?

a) low-key contests with great controversy

b) high-profile contests with little controversy

c) high-profile contests with great controversy

d) low-key contests with little controversy

e) there are no elections for lower court judgeships in the United States

8.5. In Europe, how does a person become a judge?

a) special training in law school

b) elected to office

c) judicial lottery

d) appointed by the old boys network

e) inherit a judgeship

8.6. The vast majority of criminal cases are handled in...

a) city level offices of the prosecuting attorney

b) state level offices of the prosecuting attorney

c) township level offices of the prosecuting attorney

d) county level offices of the prosecuting attorney

e) federal offices of the prosecuting attorney

8.7. How does each state obtain an attorney general?

a) gubernatorial appointment

b) state legislative appointment

c) state bar appointment

d) state supreme court appointment

e) election by the voters

8.8. Which of the following best describes the role of prosecutors within the criminal justice system?
a) prosecutors are involved in every aspect of the criminal justice system
b) prosecutors are only involved with adjudication
c) prosecutors are concerned with pre-trial processes and adjudication
d) prosecutors define their own roles for themselves
e) state law defines the role of a prosecutor

8.9. Which of the following traits of a victim will affect whether a prosecutor pursues charges?
a) criminal record of the victim
b) victim's role in his or her own victimization
c) credibility of the victim
d) all of the above
e) none of the above

8.10.Which of the followings is NOT a basic duty of the defense attorney?
a) to save criminals from punishment
b) to protect constitutional rights
c) keep the prosecution honest in preparing and presenting cases
d) prevent innocent people from being convicted
e) all of the above are basic duties

8.11. Most criminal defense attorneys interact with...
a) upper class clients
b) middle class clients
c) lower class clients
d) upper and middle class clients
e) upper and lower class clients

8.12. The right to an attorney is found in the _____ Amendment.
a) First
b) Second
c) Fourth
d) Fifth
e) Sixth

8.13. When does the U. S. Supreme Court require that attorneys be appointed to defend suspects?
a) early in the criminal justice process
b) immediately prior to jury selection
c) immediately prior to a trial
d) immediately prior to sentencing
e) the Court has no such requirement

8.14. Which of the following is (are) a court(s) of last resort?
a) state supreme courts
b) U. S. Supreme Court
c) U. S. Circuit Courts of Appeals
d) a and b
e) none of the above

8.15. Which of the following is an appellate court?
a) trial court of limited jurisdiction
b) U. S. Supreme Court
c) U. S. Circuit Courts of Appeals
d) all of the above
e) b and c

8.16. Prior to the 1960s, a vast majority of judges were…
a) white men with strong political connections
b) white men with weak political connections
c) white men with no political connections
d) white women with strong political connections
e) white women with weak political connections

8.17. Which of the following is TRUE about lawyers when they are first elected to serve as judges?
a) lawyers are well-prepared because they have received specialized training
b) lawyers are especially well-prepared to supervise courthouse operations
c) lawyers must learn on the job because they have no prior experience
d) all of the above are true
e) all of the above are false

8.18. What level of the U. S. government has prosecutors?
a) cities
b) federal
c) state
d) county
e) all of the above

8.19. For every felony conviction in federal courts, there are more than ___ felony convictions in state courts.
a) 5
b) 20
c) 50
d) 100
e) 1000

8.20. Prosecutors are most successful when a defendant has committed a crime against a(n)…
a) family member
b) friend
c) stranger
d) acquaintance
e) prosecutors are successful regardless of the victim

8.21. Which of the following represents the initiative of community prosecution?
a) community prosecution will bring prosecutors closer to the citizens
b) community prosecution will reduce crime
c) community prosecution will increase the effectiveness of the criminal justice system
d) all of the above
e) none of the above

8.22. Which of the following television dramas provides a realistic view of defense attorneys?
a) Law and Order
b) Ally McBeal
c) The Practice
d) all of the above
e) none of the above

8.23. What is a continuance?
a) a continuance is an adjournment of a scheduled case until a later date
b) a continuance is a case that will continue on appeal
c) a continuance is a closing argument by an attorney that spans more than one day
d) a continuance is a lawyer's request to continue a trial past the regular working hours
e) a continuance is a judge's request to force the jury to continue their deliberations to verdict

8.24. Which of the following actor(s) participate in a courtroom workgroup?
a) judges
b) prosecutors
c) media
d) a and b
e) a and c

8.25. Which of the following is TRUE about federal and state prosecutors' handling of criminal cases?
a) federal and state prosecutors have little discretion
b) federal prosecutors have significant discretion but state prosecutors have little discretion
c) federal prosecutors have little discretion but state prosecutors have significant discretion
d) federal and state prosecutors have significant discretion
e) federal and state prosecutors have no discretion at all

True and False Questions

_____8.1. Most criminal cases are heard at the state level.

_____8.2. Native Americans have their own court systems in the United States.

_____8.3. State court systems do not have appellate courts.

_____8.4. The United States Supreme Court is the court of last resort in the federal system.

_____8.5. Judges can control their work schedules better than private practice attorneys.

_____8.6. All prosecutors are selected by governors in all 50 states.

_____8.7. Prosecutors serve a variety of "clients" such as the police and the public.

_____8.8. A prosecutor is NOT required to disclose facts and evidence to the defense during the pretrial phase.

_____8.9. Community prosecution is an idea that has NOT been tested in the U. S.

_____8.10. Most defense attorneys are nationally known and charge large fees.

_____8.11. The right to counsel has required the government to provide attorneys to indigent defendants since the ratification of the Constitution in 1789.

_____8.12. A small percentage of Americans who were surveyed have a lot of trust in criminal defense attorneys.

_____8.13. The American trial courts are centralized.

_____8.14. The work of a judge is limited to presiding at trials.

_____8.15. Some judges are responsible for managing the administrative affairs at their courthouses.

_____8.16. The selection process of judges is nonpolitical.

_____8.17. Courts apply rules and procedures in exactly the same way across the nation.

_____8.18. Researchers do NOT consider judges to be part of the local legal culture.

_____8.19. Television shows, such as *Law and Order*, provide a realistic view of the courtroom.

_____8.20. In a workgroup, each participant has a specified role.

WORKSHEET 8.1: JUDICIAL SELECTION

Respond to the following questions in light of the text's discussion of the importance of judicial selection methods. Think about the implications and consequences of each selection methods (Gubernatorial Appointment, Legislative Appointment, Partisan Election, Nonpartisan Election, Merit Selection)

1. What are the four most important qualities that we should look for in the people we select to be judges?

_____

_____

_____

_____

2. How do we know which people possess these qualities?

_____

_____

_____

3. Which judicial selection method would provide the best means to identify and select the people who possess these qualities?

_____

_____

_____

_____

4. What are the drawbacks to this judicial selection method?

_____

_____

_____

_____

_____

5. Which judicial selection method is used in the state where you live or go to school? Why do you think that this state uses this selection method instead of one of the other methods?

_____

_____

_____

WORKSHEET 8.2: COUNSEL FOR INDIGENTS

If you were given the responsibility for selecting the method of providing counsel for indigent defendants within your local courthouse, which method would you choose? For each method listed below, state whether you would select that method and explain why or why not?

ASSIGNED COUNSEL_____

_____

_____

_____

_____

_____

CONTRACT COUNSEL_____

_____

_____

_____

_____

_____

PUBLIC DEFENDER_____

_____

_____

_____

_____

Is there some other feasible
alternative?_____

_____

_____

_____

_____

_____

WORKSHEET 8.3. COURTROOM WORKGROUP

A newly elected prosecutor has hired you as a consultant. She wants to know whether she should assign assistant prosecutors to single courtrooms to handle all cases before a specific judge or, alternatively, rotate assistant prosecutors to different courtrooms and other assignments every week. She says, "I've heard that these 'courtroom workgroups,' whatever they are, form if you keep assistant prosecutors in one courtroom. What should I do?"

1. Define the concept of "courtroom workgroup."

_____

_____

_____

2. Describe how courtrooms will work if an assistant prosecutor is permanently assigned to one courtroom. What are the consequences?

_____

_____

_____

_____

_____

_____

3. How will courtrooms work if assistant prosecutors are rotated? What are the consequences?

_____

_____

_____

_____

_____

_____

4. Which approach do you recommend? Why?

_____

_____

_____

_____

_____

CHAPTER 9

PRETRIAL PROCEDURES, PLEA BARGAINING, AND THE CRIMINAL TRIAL

LEARNING OBJECTIVES

After covering the material in this chapter, students should understand:

1. the underlying purposes of bail;

2. the actors who influence the bail decision;

3. the consequences of being detained, especially for poor defendants, and the debate over preventive detention;

4. mechanisms utilized to reform the bail system or as alternatives to money bail;

5. the central role of plea bargaining and prosecutor' discretion in determining the outcomes of 90 percent of criminal cases;

6. the difference between implicit and explicit plea bargaining;

7. the role of exchange relationships in plea bargaining, the actors who influence plea negotiations, and the tactics used by those actors;

8. the justifications for and criticisms of plea bargaining.

9. the stages of the trial process;

10. the nature and prevalence of jury trials; the functions of the jury; the selection of juries and the experience of being a juror;

11. the appellate process evaluated.

CHAPTER SUMMARY

Pretrial processes determine the fates of nearly all defendants through case dismissals, decisions defining the charges, and plea bargains that affect more than 90 percent of cases. Defense attorneys use motions to their advantage to gain information and delay proceedings to benefit their clients. The bail process provides opportunities for many defendants to gain pretrial release, but poor defendants may be disadvantaged by their inability to come up with the money or property needed to secure release. Preventive detention statutes may permit judges to hold defendants considered dangerous or likely to flee. Bail bondsmen are private businesspeople who provide money for defendants' pretrial release for a fee. Their activities create risks of corruption and discrimination in the bail process, but they may help the system by reminding defendants about court dates and tracking down defendants who disappear. Although judges bear primary responsibility for setting bail, prosecutors are especially influential in recommending amounts and conditions for pretrial release. Initiatives to reform the bail process include release on own recognizance (ROR), police-issued citations, and bail guidelines. Pretrial detainees, despite the presumption of innocence, are held in difficult conditions in jails containing mixed populations of convicted offenders, detainees, and troubled people. The shock of being jailed creates risks of suicide and depression.

Most convictions are obtained through plea bargains, a process that exists because it fulfills the self-interest of prosecutors, judges, defense attorneys, and defendants. Plea bargaining is facilitated by exchange relations between prosecutors and defense attorneys. In many courthouses, there is little actual bargaining, as outcomes are determined through the implicit bargaining process of settling the facts and assessing the "going rate" of punishment according to the standards of the local legal culture. The U.S. Supreme Court has endorsed plea bargaining and addressed legal issues concerning the voluntariness of pleas and the obligation of prosecutors and defendants to uphold agreements. Plea bargaining has been criticized for pressuring defendants to surrender their rights and reducing the sentences imposed on offenders. Through the dramatic courtroom battle of prosecutors and defense attorneys, trials are presumed to provide the best way to discover the truth about a criminal case. Less than 10 percent of cases go to trial, and half of those are typically bench trials in front of a judge, not jury trials. Cases typically go to trial because they involve defendants who are wealthy enough to pay attorneys to fight to the very end, they involve charges that are too serious to create incentives for plea bargaining. The U.S. Supreme Court has ruled that juries need not be made up of twelve members, and twelve-member juries can, if permitted by state law, convict defendants by a majority vote instead of a unanimous vote. Juries serve vital functions for society by preventing arbitrary action by prosecutors and judges, educating citizens about the justice system, symbolizing the rule of law, and involving citizens from diverse segments of the community in judicial decision making. The jury selection process, especially in the formation of the jury pool and the exercise of peremptory challenges, often creates juries that do not fully represent all segments of a community. The trial process consists of a series of steps: jury selection, opening statements, presentation of prosecution's evidence, presentation of defense evidence, presentation of rebuttal witnesses, closing arguments, judge's jury instructions, and the jury's decision. Rules of evidence dictate what kinds of information may be presented in court for consideration by the jury. Types of evidence include are real evidence, demonstrative evidence, testimony, direct evidence, and circumstantial evidence. Convicted offenders have the opportunity to appeal, although defendants who plead guilty--unlike those convicted through a trial--often have few grounds for an appeal.

Appeals focus on claimed errors of law or procedure in the investigation by police and prosecutors or the decisions by trial judges. Relatively few offenders win their appeals, and most of those simply gain an opportunity for a new trial, not release from jail or prison. After convicted offenders have used all of their appeals, they may file a habeas corpus petition to seek federal judicial review of claimed constitutional rights violations in their cases. Very few petitions are successful.

CHAPTER OUTLINE
I.   INTRODUCTION
        The arrest of film actor, **Robert Blake**, on charges that he murdered his wife, **Bonny Bakley**, demonstrated that during the decision on bail criminal defendants are deprived of liberty despite the presumption of innocence in the American criminal justice system. Judges often times set bail at a very high amount such that it is impossible for defendants to meet or judges might not set bail at all if there is a risk that the defendant will flee or if he or she is deemed a danger to the community. Bail, plea bargaining, and trials are processes that have great influence over whether people will lose their freedom or receive punishment.

II.   FROM ARREST TO TRIAL OR PLEA
A.   Introduction
        1.   After arrest, the suspect is taken to the station for booking, including photographs and fingerprints. For warrantless arrests, a probable cause hearing must be held within forty-eight hours.
        2.   At the subsequent **arraignment**, the formal charges are read and the defendant enters a plea. Prosecutors evaluate the evidence to make discretionary determinations about what charges to pursue or whether the charges should be dropped.
        3.   Decisions to drop charges may be influenced by the defendant's age, prior record, seriousness of offense, or jail overcrowding. Sudden decisions may also be influenced by bias based on race or some other factor.
        4.   Large numbers of cases are filtered out of the court system through prosecutor's discretionary decisions. Various factors influence how and when cases are filtered out of the system before trial.
        5.   Most cases pass through a process that operates somewhat like an assembly line. The defense attempts to use motions to its advantage by, for example, seeking to suppress evidence or to learn about the prosecutor's case. Filed in only about 10 percent of felony cases and 1 percent of misdemeanor cases.
        6.   **Motion** defined: a motion is an application to a court requesting an order be issued to bring about a specified action. A court hearing may be held on the motion with the opposing attorneys presenting arguments about the legality of the procedures used in police arrests and investigations, the sufficiency of the evidence, or the exclusion of evidence.

III.   BAIL: PRETRIAL RELEASE
A.   Introduction
    1.   WHAT AMERICANS THINK: Members of the public are less concerned than lawyers about a suspected criminal being deprived of their freedom without being charged with a crime.
    2.   **Bail** is a sum of money or property specified by the judge that will be posted by the defendant as a condition of pretrial release and that will be forfeited if the defendant does not appear in court for scheduled hearings. Bail is a mechanism to permit presumptively innocent defendants to avoid loss of liberty pending the outcome of the case. The Eighth Amendment to the U.S. Constitution forbids excessive bail but does not establish a right to bail. Congress and some states have reformed bail's underlying purpose (i.e., return of the defendant) to allow preventive detention in order to permit holding some defendants in jail without bail, especially if they might pose a danger to the community upon release

B.   The Reality of the Bail System
    1.   Issue of bail may arise at the police station, during an initial court appearance (misdemeanor), or at the arraignment (felony).
    2.   Amount of bail normally based on judge's perception of the seriousness of the crime and the defendant's record. Because bail is set within 24 to 48 hours after arrest, there is little time to seek background information about the defendant. Within particular localities, judges develop, in effect, standard rates for particular offenses.
    3.   To post bail, prisoner must give the court some form of monetary surety, usually cash, property, or bond from a bonding company. For lesser offenses, may be released on their own recognizance (ROR).
    4.   Bail system favors affluent defendants who have enough money for bail and disadvantages poor defendants who may end up stuck in jail.
    5.   Study of the most populous counties in the U. S. showed that nearly two-thirds of felon defendants released prior to disposition of their cases.
IDEAS IN PRACTICE: Is it fair to set bail at an extraordinary amount because someone has wealth and property? Is this fair?

C.   Bail Bondsmen
    1.   Bondsmen are central figures, available to those who need to produce sufficient cash to gain release. Using their own assets , they will provide the surety for a fee ranging from 5 to 10 percent.
        a.   They are licensed by the state and choose their own clients, and may set their own collateral requirements.
        b.   They may track down and return bail jumpers without extradition and by force if necessary.
    2.   Bondsmen exert influence on the court through their ability to cooperate with police officers who recommend their services rather than those of other bondsmen. In return, bondsmen may refuse to provide bail for defendants whom the police would like to keep in jail. Bondsmen are private, profit-seeking actors with no official connection to the court who can, in effect, nullify a judge's decision that a defendant is eligible for release on bail.
    3.   Positive impact of bondsmen is to maintain social control over defendant during the pretrial period; remind clients about court dates; put pressure on defendant's friends and family to make sure defendant appears for court; bondsmen may help prepare defendants for ultimate outcome and may encourage and facilitate guilty pleas by using their experience to accurately predict how specific judges will sentence for particular crimes; help to relieve pressure on overcrowded jails by assisting with release of some defendants.
    4.   Any potential benefits provided by bondsmen might be provided as well or better if courts had effective pretrial services offices.

D.   Setting Bail
    1.   For minor offenses, bail generally set by a police officer according to a set schedule.
    2.   Judges use discretion to set bail by taking account of severity of offense, defendant's characteristics, and concern for community protection.

3.   When a judge sets bail, the amount of bail and conditions of release result from interactions among the judge, prosecutor, and defense attorney.

4.   Study of Hispanic arrestees shows that those who could afford their own attorneys were seven times more likely to gain pretrial release than indigent defendants.

E.   Reforming the Bail System

    1.   Critics of the bail system focus on the judicial discretion in setting bail amounts, the fact that poor defendants being deprived of their freedom while better-off citizens can afford bail, the perceived unsavory role of bondsmen, and bad jail conditions imposed on those detained while awaiting trial.

    2. Alternatives to Bail:

        a.   **Citation**: citation or summons issued by police officer; avoids booking, arrest, bail, and jailing; in some jurisdictions, fewer than five percent of those issued citations failed to appear; bailbondsmen have opposed this method as a threat to their livelihood.

        b.   **Release on Own Recognizance (ROR):** pioneered by Vera Institute of Justice in New York City. Court personnel talk to defendants about their family ties and roots in the community (i.e., job, family, prior record, length of time in local area), then recommend ROR if sufficient contacts exist. In first three years, 3,500 of 10,000 defendants released on ROR, only 1.5 percent failed to appear -- a rate three times better than regular bail.

        c.   **Ten Percentage Cash Bail:** many judges are unwilling to use ROR, so some states have instituted policy in which defendants deposit a percent of bail as collateral -- when they return to court, they receive 90 percent of this back. Program assists release; does not enrich bondsmen.

        d.   Bail Guidelines: guidelines developed to establish criteria that will produce more consistency in bail decisions.

        e.   **Preventive Detention**: called a basic threat to liberties by civil libertarians, but approved by Congress for federal court in Bail Reform Act of 1984. Judges can consider whether defendant poses a danger to community and decide not to set bail. Decision is made at hearing at which prosecution contends there is risk of flight, risk that defendant will obstruct justice by threatening a witness or juror, and defendant accused of crime of violence, or one punishable by life imprisonment or death. Supreme Court upheld preventive detention (e.g., **U.S. v. Salerno and Cafero**).

        f.   CLOSEUP: Preventive Detention: Two Sides of an Issue. Two stories illustrate the problems associated with preventive detention (a person can lose his/her job and family if bail is denied while an innocent person awaits trial) and also problems associated with not using preventive detention (i.e. a person commits more serious crimes while out on bail)

III. PRETRIAL DETENTION

A.   Jail

    1.   American jails hold almost 500,000 people in jail at any one day and half are in pretrial detention while the other half are serving short sentences; nearly all are poor.

    2.   Initial time after arrest often moments of panic and crisis: vulnerability, helplessness, fright, and ominous threat of loss of freedom produce high stress and most jail suicides occur within the first six to ten hours of detention, and most psychotic episodes occur during or just after intake.

    3.   Crisis can be exacerbated when arrested person is intoxicated or under the influence of drugs; for young offenders, the threat of victimization by violence can produce debilitating depression.

IV. **PLEA BARGAINING**

A.   Introduction

    1.   The most important stage in the criminal justice process: a vast majority of cases involve guilty pleas.

    2.   In **Santobello v. New York (1971)**, Supreme Court has ruled that plea bargaining is legal; prosecutors and judges call it necessary; defense attorneys call it advantageous to their clients.

    3.   Supreme Court in Blackledge v. Allison (1976) acknowledged the mutuality of advantage to defendants and prosecutors from the process.

4. Plea bargaining defined: defendant's agreement to plead guilty to a criminal charge with the reasonable expectation of receiving some consideration from the state for doing so.

5. In the case of **John Walker Lindh,** the 21 year-old American captured while fighting for the Taliban in Afghanistan, plea bargaining was an attractive option for the prosecutors and the defendant because it ensured a conviction and the government received information about the Taliban and the al Qaeda network in exchange for a reduced sentence.

6. When plea bargaining was barred in California's felony court, it did not disappear. It simply moved to the arraignment stage in the lower court.

7. CLOSE UP: Banning Plea Bargaining in Tennessee. Effort by D.A. to ban plea bargaining for serious charges.

B. Exchange Relationships in Plea Bargaining
1. Defense attorney, prosecutor, defendant, and sometimes judge participate. All have particular objectives and all can gain from the process (defense attorney gets fee quicker for less work; prosecutor gets sure conviction; defendant gets less than maximum possible sentence; judge gets quick disposition of case without time-consuming trial)

C. Tactics of Prosecutor and Defense: ritual in which friendliness and joking may mask antagonistic views. Each side tries to impress the other with confidence in the strength of its case; little effort to conceal information because standard practice seems to be that confidences shared in negotiations will not be used in court -- defense attorneys who violate this norm may not receive favorable bargains in future cases; defense attorneys seek to "humanize" the defendant so prosecutor will not treat as just another case.
1. Prosecutors' tactic is the multi-count indictment -- even when cannot prove all charges; puts greater pressure on defendant to plead guilty; gives prosecutor more items to negotiate away.
2. Defense attorneys may threaten to move ahead with jury trial; defense attorneys may threaten delays, during which witnesses' memories may fade -- but other defense attorneys feel more effective bargaining on friendly basis rather than trying to pin down or threaten the prosecutor.

D. Pleas Without Bargaining
1. Guilty pleas may not result from formal negotiations. In some courthouses, prosecutor, defense attorney, and sometimes judge talk simply to settle the facts in the case. (i.e., was it really an assault or just a pushing and shoving match?); when they agree on what kind of crime it was, then the local "going rate" punishment for such crimes is clear to all actors and the defense attorney can know what the punishment will be upon entering a guilty plea.
2. Both prosecutor and defense attorney may be members of the same local legal culture with shared values and understandings about the punishments for particular offenses.
3. Implicit plea bargaining may be less likely to occur when there is personnel turnover in a court community that inhibits recognition of shared values.
4. Process may differ from courthouse to courthouse; some courts may use "slow plea of guilty" as defendant pleads to lesser charge as case progresses through trial; prosecutors may use diversion or dropping cases to reduce caseload in other courts.

E. Legal Issues in Plea Bargaining
1. Questions exist concerning the voluntariness and sanctity of plea bargains. Many judges now more open about admitting in court that they are aware of plea bargains struck in particular cases.
2. **Boykin v. Alabama (1969):** defendant must make affirmative statement that plea was voluntary before judge accepts the plea. Thus courts have created standardized list of questions for judges to read to defendants when entering guilty pleas to ensure no coercion was used against defendant.
3. **Alford v. North Carolina (1970):** court can accept guilty plea entered by a defendant who still maintains he was innocent but is willing to accept punishment for lesser charge to avoid risk of maximum penalty.
4. *Ricketts v. Adamson* (1987): defendants must keep their part of the bargain if they agree to testify against others as part of the plea bargain.
5. **Bordenkircher v. Hayes (1978):** prosecutors can threaten defendants with additional charges if they do not agree to plead guilty. Supreme Court regards this as part of the "give and take" of plea bargaining but critics regard it as coercion.

6. A QUESTION OF ETHICS: Guilty plea ceremony reveals that defendant believes that promises have been made.

F. Criticisms of Plea Bargaining
    Practice has been criticized.
    1. Due process considerations: plea bargaining does not provide procedural fairness because defendants forfeit the constitutional rights designed to protect them -- argument by civil libertarians
    2. Sentencing policy: society's interest in applying appropriate punishments for crimes is diminished by plea bargaining; in overcrowded urban courts, harried prosecutors and judges make concessions for the sake of administrative expediency -- argument by law and order advocates.
    3. Low Visibility: plea bargaining hidden from judicial scrutiny; judge has little information about the crime or defendant when decisions primarily made by prosecutor and defense attorney; judge cannot check on how much pressure applied to the defendant; result is "bargain justice" in which the judge, public, and even defendant cannot know for sure who got what from whom in exchange for what -- because prosecutor and defense attorney's self-interest and exchange relationship is not visible to others in the process.
    4. Inconsistent with the espoused values of the adversarial system; makes the criminal justice process look like a "game" in the eyes of the criminal offenders and therefore no different than the other forms of unprincipled deal making occurring elsewhere in society, including deals among criminals.
    5. Unjust to penalize people for asserting their right to have a trial; based on findings that more people go to prison when they demand a trial than when they plea bargain.
    6. Concern that innocent people will be pressured to plead guilty out of fear of what might happen to them if they happened to be convicted at trial. Innocent people who lack faith in the justice system may plead guilty because they do not want to take the chance of being convicted of something more serious.

V. TRIAL: THE EXCEPTIONAL CASE

A. Introduction
    1. Seriousness of the charge is the most important factor influencing the decision to go to trial. When the penalty is harsh, defendants will risk a jury trial.
    2. Fewer than ten percent of felony cases go to trials. Of these, only one half are trials by jury, the rest are **bench trials** presided over by a judge without a jury
    3. Trials are very costly in terms of time and resources.

B. Jury Trial
    1. Trials are based on the idea that the adversarial process and laws of criminal procedure and evidence will produce the truth.
        a. The judge must make sure that rules are followed, and the jury must impartially evaluate the evidence and reflect the community's interests. The **jury** is the sole evaluator of the facts in the case.
    2. Juries perform six vital functions in the criminal justice system:
        a. Prevent government oppression by safeguarding citizens against arbitrary law enforcement.
        b. Determine whether the accused is guilty on the basis of the evidence presented.
        c. Represent diverse community interests so that no one set of values or biases dominates decision making.
        d. Serves as a buffer between the accused and the accuser.
        e. Educates citizens selected for jury duty about the criminal justice system.
        f. Symbolizes the rule of law and the community that supports the criminal justice system.
    3. Juries provide the element of direct democracy in the judicial process through citizens' participation in decision making in a branch of government controlled by lawyers and judges.

4.	In the United States, a jury in a criminal trial traditionally consists of twelve citizens but some states now allow as few as six persons. This reform was recommended as a way to modernize court procedures and reduce expenses.
	a.	Smaller jury size was upheld by the Supreme Court in **Williams v. Florida (1970).** For a jury of six, a unanimous vote is required (Burch v. Louisiana, 1979) but with larger verdicts a majority vote is enough for conviction.
	b.	Twelve-person juries are generally used for capital cases.

C.	The Trial Process
	After jury selection, the trial proceeds through stages of attorneys' statements, presentation of witnesses and evidence, closing arguments, and decisions.
	1.	Jury Selection
		a.	Jury Pool: when jurors are drawn from registered voters, then nonwhites, the poor, and young people are underrepresented.
		b.	Underrepresentation of people from different backgrounds can affect decisions because it limits the presence of alternative experiences and values among the decision makers.
		c.	Jury unrepresentativeness can best be attacked by the use of comprehensive list from which citizens are randomly selected for duty. Supplementary pools: drivers' license lists, utility customers, taxpayers--would add names to the roster.
		d.	Only about 15 percent of the American adult population have ever served on juries.
		e.	As a result, retired people, housewives with grown children and the unemployed tend to be overrepresented on juries.
		f.	**Voir dire** is the process of examining (i.e., questioning) potential jurors to ensure a fair trial. Attorneys for both sides and the judge may question each juror about background, knowledge of the case, or acquaintance with people involved in the case.
		g.	If a juror says something to indicate that he or she may be unable to make a fair decision, then he or she may be **challenged for cause**. The judge must rule on the challenge and whether or not the juror will be excluded from the pool. There is usually no limit on the number of challenges for cause.
		h.	**Peremptory challenge** is the attorneys' power to exclude a juror without giving any reason. Each side is given a limited number of peremptory challenges and they can use hunches to exclude potential jurors whom they believe may be sympathetic to the opposing side.
			Some attorneys hire "jury experts" -- social scientists who can advise on how to use peremptory challenges in order to gain sympathetic demographic groups of jurors.
		i.	Although the Supreme Court has said that peremptory challenges cannot be based on the race or gender of potential jurors, the Court also permits trial judges to accept flimsy excuses when it appears that race or gender is being improperly applied.
	2.	Opening Statements: statements by attorneys are not evidence, so judges try to keep each side from making inflammatory or prejudicial remarks. Lawyers use this opportunity to establish themselves with the jurors and to emphasize points they intend to make during the trial.
	3.	Presentation of the Prosecution's Evidence: the prosecution bears the burden of providing proof beyond a reasonable doubt because the American system has a formal presumption of innocence that the prosecutor must overcome.
		a.	**Real evidence**: objects, weapons, records, fingerprints, or stolen property.
		b.	**Demonstrative evidence:** maps, x-rays, photographs, and diagrams. These are things that the jurors can see for themselves. Real evidence is one kind of demonstrative evidence.
		c.	Testimony: witnesses must be legally competent: have the intelligence and memory capacity to remember events and tell the truth; witnesses may be cross-examined by opposing counsel.
		d.	**Direct evidence:** eyewitness accounts.
		e.	**Circumstantial evidence**: requires that the jury infer a fact from witness observation.
		f.	Rules of evidence govern what judge will either exclude from presentation or permit the attorneys to put into evidence.

4. Presentation of Defense's Evidence: evidence usually presented for one or more of the following purposes:
   a. Rebut or cast doubt on state's case.
   b. Offer an alibi.
   c. Affirmative defense is presented (e.g., self-defense, insanity, etc.) to claim that defendant cannot be held responsible under the law.
   d. Defense also must consider whether or not the defendant will take the stand and thereby be subject to impeachment and cross-examination.
   e. TECHNOLOGY ISSUES IN CRIMINAL JUSTICE: Policy Computer Simulations in the Courtroom-In recent years, attorneys have attempted to use computer technology to present clearer images of events. Just as computer programmers have developed realistic games for computers, similar realism has now been developed in computer-generated recreations of crime scenes.
5. Presentation of Rebuttal Witnesses: prosecution witnesses to rebut the defense's case.
6. Closing Arguments by Each Side: opportunity to tie case together and to make impassioned, persuasive presentation to the judge or jury.
7. Judge's Instructions to the Jury: judge determines the law and instructs jury on the manner in which the law bears on their decision.
   a. Judge may discuss standard of proof (beyond a **reasonable doubt**), the necessity of the prosecution proving all of the elements of a crime, and the rights of the defendant (e.g., not required to testify and no inference should be drawn regarding the defendant's silence).
   b. Judge will explain the charges and the possible verdicts. Instructions may be an ordeal for jurors and it may be difficult for them to understand and retain instructions since instructions may last more than an hour or two.
8. Decision by the Jury: jurors deliberate in private room; may request that judge reread to them portions of the instructions, or they may ask for additional instructions, or for portions of the trial transcript.
   a. If the jury becomes deadlocked and cannot reach a verdict, the trial may end with a hung jury -- and the prosecution can choose to retry the case with a different jury.
   b. When the jury reaches a verdict, the prosecutor, defense attorney, and judge assemble in the courtroom to hear it; the prosecutor or defense lawyer can request that the jury be polled: each member of the jury must state their decision in open court. This procedure presumably ensures that there is no pressure on a juror by other members of the jury.
   c. If it is a guilty verdict, the judge may continue bail or incarcerate the defendant while awaiting the presentence report: a report prepared by a probation officer on the defendant's background and record which will be used by the judge in determining the sentence.

WORK PERSPECTIVE: The Honorable James G. Carr, United States District Judge in Toledo, Ohio

E. Evaluating the Jury System
   1. Studies indicate that juries' behavior is consistent with theories of group behavior; participation and influence in the process are related to social status: men were found to be more active than women; whites more than minority members; better educated more than less well educated.
   2. Much of jurors' discussion does not concern the testimony and evidence, but instead the court procedures, opinions about witnesses, and personal reminiscences.
   3. 30 percent of cases, a vote taken soon after sequestration was the only one necessary to reach a verdict; in the rest of cases, the majority on the first ballot eventually won out 90 percent of the time. Because of group pressures, only rarely did a lone juror produce a hung jury; recent research has reconfirmed the importance of group pressures on decision making.

VI.   APPEALS
A.   <u>Basis for Appeals</u>
    Appeals are based on the contention that one or more errors were made during the criminal justice process.
    1.   A case originating in state court is usually appealed through the state appellate courts. f there is a federal constitutional question, then the case may subsequently enter the federal court system and perhaps ultimately be considered by the U.S. Supreme Court.
    2.   Study found that eighty percent of appeals unsuccessful because the appellate court affirmed the trial court decision.

B.   **Habeas Corpus**
    1.   The "great writ" is a command by a court to a person holding a prisoner in custody requiring that the prisoner be brought before the judge. This procedure permits the judge to determine whether the person is legally held. Federal courts can review whether or not there are any constitutional violations affecting the convictions of federal *and* state prisoners.
    2.   There has been a tremendous increase in habeas corpus petitions although only about one   percent are successful; this causes an increase in caseloads for federal judges; many federal courts cope with caseload burdens by assigning such cases to law clerks or to U.S. magistrate judges.
    3.   There is no right to counsel for habeas corpus petitions, so most prisoners must attempt to present their own cases. They generally lack sufficient knowledge to identify and raise constitutional issues effectively.
    4.   Since the 1980s, the Supreme Court has made decisions imposing more difficult procedural requirements on prisoners seeking to file habeas corpus petitions. In 1996, Congress created further restrictions on petitions by passing a new statute affecting habeas corpus procedures.

C.   <u>Evaluating the Appellate Process</u>
    1.   Some conservatives argue that appeals should be limited; appeals are regarded as a burden on the system and an impediment to swift punishment of convicted offenders. However, since 90 percent of accused persons plead guilty and relatively few of these people have any basis for appeal, the actual number of appeals (as a percentage of total cases) seems less significant.
    2.   Appeals can serve the important function of righting wrongs.

KEY TERMS AND PEOPLE
<u>Fill in the appropriate term from the list for each statement below</u>
Santobello v. New York (1971)
jury
bench trial
Bordenkircher v. Hayes (1978)
Boykin v. Alabama (1969)
North Carolina v. Alford (1970)
plea bargaining
circumstantial evidence
demonstrative evidence
direct evidence
peremptory challenge
real evidence
Williams v. Florida (1970)
challenge for cause
reasonable doubt
voir dire
appeals
arraignment
bail
motion
citation
percentage bail

preventive detention
release on recognizance (ROR)
United States v. Salerno and Cafero (1987)
habeas corpus

1.   In the case of _____, the Supreme Court ruled that when a guilty plea rests on a promise of a prosecutor, the promise must be fulfilled.

2.   _____ permits defense attorneys and prosecutors to remove jurors without providing a reason.

3.   _____ evidence provided by a witness from which a jury must infer a fact.

4.   _____ is also known as negotiating a settlement and is the most important step in the criminal justice process.

5.   _____ is evidence that is NOT based on witness testimony but that demonstrates information relevant to a crime, such as maps, X-rays and photographs.

6.   _____ are requests to a higher court that it review actions taken in a completed trial.

7.   _____ is when a judge presides over a trial without a jury.

8.   In the case of _____, the Supreme Court ruled that a plea of guilty by a defendant who maintains his or her innocence may be accepted for the purpose of a lesser sentence.

9.   _____ is the process of questioning of prospective jurors to screen out persons the attorneys think may be biased.

10.   _____ a writ or judicial order requesting the release of a person from a jail, prison, or mental hospital. It provides the basis for persons in prison to challenge the legal basis for their incarceration.

11.   In the case of _____, the Supreme Court ruled that a defendant's rights were not violated by a prosecutor who warned that refusing to enter a guilty plea would result in a harsher sentence.

12.   _____ permits, with the judge's approval, the removal of a prospective juror who demonstrates a particular bias or some other legal disability.

13.   _____ is the representative of the community in the criminal trial that finds facts and decides whether the defendant is guilty.

14.   _____ is the standard used by a jury in criminal cases to decide if the prosecution has provided enough evidence for a conviction.

15.   In the case of _____, the Supreme Court ruled that juries of fewer than twelve members are constitutional.

16.   _____ is presented by the prosecutor and includes concrete objects, such as fingerprints and stolen property.

17.   In the case of _____, the Supreme Court ruled that defendants must state that they are voluntarily making a plea of guilty.

18.   _____ includes eye witness accounts of what happened.

19.   A(n) _____ is a panel of citizens selected according to law and sworn to determine matters of fact in a criminal case and to deliver a verdict of guilty or not guilty.

20. _____ is the stage in the criminal justice process in which formal charges are read in court and the accused pleads guilty or not guilty.

21. _____ is an application to a court requesting that an order be issued to bring about a specific action.

22. _____ is a sum of money or property, specified by a judge, that will be presented to the court by the defendant as a condition of pretrial release.

23. _____ a written order or summons, issued by a law enforcement officer, directing an alleged offender to appear in court. It is a method of summoning defendants to return to court without using the system's resources for arrests and jailing.

24. _____ is a mechanism where defendants may deposit a percentage (usually ten percent) of the full bail with the court.

25. _____ pretrial release granted without paying bail if the defendant promises to appear in court.

26. _____ results when bail is not set and a defendant remains in jail because he or she has been determined to be a danger to any other person and the community.

27. In the case of _____, the Supreme Court ruled that preventive detention was constitutional and a legitimate use of government power designed to prevent people from committing crimes while on bail.

KEY PERSONS
Fill in the appropriate person from the list for each statement below
Hernando Williams
Potter Stewart
John Walker Lindh
Robert Blake
Ricardo Armstrong

1. _____, a 21-year old American captured while fighting for the Taliban in Afghanistan, received a 20 year sentence for pleading guilty to felony charges, including conspiring to kill Americans.

2. _____, wrote in his opinion for the Supreme Court in *Blackledge v. Allison (1976)* that plea bargaining "can benefit all concerned" in a criminal case.

3. _____, a well-known actor, was arrested for allegedly murdering his wife on May 4, 2001.

4. _____ was one of the first defendants held under the Bail Reform Act of 1984. The 28-year-old janitor, who had a prior burglary conviction, was denied bail after being charged with robbing two Ohio banks.

5. Prosecutors point to the release of _____ as the classic example of the need for preventive detention. As he drove to court to face charges of raping and beating a woman he abducted at a shopping mall, another woman lay trapped inside his car trunk.

SELF-TEST SECTION

Multiple Choice Questions

9.1. How often are decisions made quickly about bail?
a) never
b) not very often
c) often
d) almost always
e) always

9.2. Which of the following is a TRUE statement about courts in the United States?
a) courts are under pressure to limit the number of cases going to trial
b) courts are under pressure to limit the number of plea bargains
c) courts are under pressure to limit the number of persons releases on bail
d) all of the above are TRUE
e) all of the above are FALSE

9.3. What was the name of well-known actor who was arrested for murdering his wife in May of 2001?
a) Marlon Brando
b) Robert Blake
c) David Duchovny
d) Robert Downey Jr.
e) Tom Cruise

9.4. What is the rate of conviction for arrests that a prosecutor decides to pursue?
a) very low rate of conviction
b) average rate of conviction
c) low rate of conviction
d) high rate of conviction
e) 100% rate of conviction

9.5. Which of the following is NOT a purpose of bail?
a) to ensure that the defendant appears in court for trial
b) to protect the community from further crimes that some defendants may commit while out on bail
c) to punish the defendant
d) all of the above are purposes of bail
e) none of the above are purposes of bail

9.6. When does the question of bail arise?
a) at the police station
b) at the initial court appearance
c) at the arraignment
d) all of the above
e) none of the above

9.7. When does the question of bail arise in most misdemeanor cases?
a) at the scene of the arrest
b) at the initial court appearance
c) at the arraignment
d) at the opening arguments of the trial
e) in chambers between the attorney and the judge

9.8. When does the question of bail arise in most felony cases?
a) at the police station
b) at the initial court appearance
c) at the arraignment
d) at the opening arguments of the trial
e) in chambers between the attorney and the judge

9.9. Who usually sets bail for serious offenses?
a) police officer
b) prosecutor
c) public defender
d) judge
e) jury

9.10. Who usually sets bail for minor offenses?
a) police officer
b) prosecutor
c) public defender
d) judge
e) jury

9.11. Where is the right to representation by an attorney at bail hearings found in the Bill of Rights?
a) Fourth Amendment
b) Fifth Amendment
c) Seventh Amendment
d) Eighth Amendment
e) there is no constitutional right to representation by an attorney at bail hearings

9.12. In a 2001 study of the most populous counties in the U. S., what percent of felony suspects were unable to make bail?
a) 0%
b) 5%
c) 15%
d) 29%
e) 56%

9.13. What is the usual fee charged by a bail bondsperson?
a) 1 percent of the bail amount
b) 5 to 10 percent of the bail amount
c) 20 to 30 percent of the bail amount
d) 40 to 50 percent of the bail amount
e) 90 percent of the bail amount

9.14. . In the 2001 study of the most populous counties in the U. S., what percent of felony suspects were detained without bail?
a) 7%
b) 25%
c) 45%
d) 69%
e) 86%

9.15. Which of the following is NOT true about bail bondspersons?
a) they usually act in their own self-interest
b) they usually have close relationships with police and correctional officials
c) they slow the processing of cases
d) they are required to be licensed by the state
e) all of the above are TRUE

9.16. What determines the amount of bail set by the judge?
a) the interactions of the judge, prosecutor, and defense attorney
b) the interactions of the bailiff, jury, and defense attorney
c) the interactions of the judge, clerk, and defendant
d) the interactions of the judge, court reporter, and defense attorney
e) the interactions of the judge, probation officer, and bail bondsperson

9.17. What did the Supreme Court hold concerning six person juries in *Burch v. Louisiana (1979)*?
a) six person juries are unconstitutional
b) six person juries must deliver at least a five to one vote to convict a defendant
c) six person juries must deliver at least a four to two vote to convict a defendant
d) six person juries must deliver at least a unanimous vote to convict a defendant
e) six person juries must contain at least one minority juror in cases with a minority defendant.

9.18. Which of the following is true about the trial process?
a) the selection of the jury occurs after the opening statements by the prosecution and the defense
b) the defense presents evidence and witnesses before the prosecution
c) the judge offers instructions to the jury after a decision is reached in a case
d) the selection of jurors is never bias toward the defendant
e) retired persons and homemakers with grown children are overrepresented on juries

9.19. The courtroom process of questioning prospective jurors in order to screen out those who might be incapable of being fair is called...
a) mala in se
b) habeas corpus
c) voir dire
d) ex post facto
e) demonstrative evidence

9.20. In the elimination of jurors from the jury pool, what is the difference between a peremptory challenge and challenge for cause?
a) peremptory challenges cannot be used in felony cases
b) challenge for cause cannot be used in felony cases
c) a judge must rule on a peremptory challenge, but attorneys control a challenge for cause
d) a judge must rule on a challenge for cause, but attorneys generally control a peremptory challenge
e) peremptory challenges and challenge for cause are the same

9.21. The prosecution must prove that a defendant is guilty beyond a...
a) probable cause
b) 100% doubt
c) reasonable doubt
d) preponderance of the evidence
e) questionable suspicion

9.22. In a trial, fingerprints submitted as evidence would be considered...
a) circumstantial evidence
b) reasonable evidence
c) real evidence
d) direct evidence
e) probable evidence

9.23. In a trial, eyewitness accounts submitted as evidence would be considered...
a) circumstantial evidence
b) reasonable evidence
c) real evidence
d) direct evidence
e) probable evidence

9.24. In a trial, what type of evidence requires the jury to infer a fact from what a witness observed?
a) circumstantial evidence
b) reasonable evidence
c) real evidence
d) direct evidence
e) probable evidence

9.25. Which of the following is TRUE concerning appeals and the right to attorney?
a) defendants are NOT guaranteed a right to attorney during the appellate process
b) defendants are guaranteed a right to attorney during the first appeal only
c) defendants are guaranteed a right to attorney for two appeals
d) defendants are guaranteed a right to attorney for three appeals
e) defendants are guaranteed a right to attorney during the entire appellate process, or for an unlimited number of appeals

True and False Questions

_____9.1. The bail bondsperson does NOT profit from his position.

_____9.2. In the interest of justice, a prosecutor will often spend time and resources on a case where the evidence against a defendant is weak.

_____9.3. A person cannot be denied bail.

_____9.4. The bail bondsperson is a private businessman.

_____9.5. Bail is always set by a judge.

_____9.6. Most bail for violent offenders is set under $5,000.

_____9.7. Juries in the United States must always be comprised of twelve members.

_____9.8. The prosecution presents evidence and witnesses before the defense presents its case.

_____9.9. Among all occupational groups, lawyers are mostly likely to be chosen to serve on juries because of their knowledge about law.

_____9.10. A judge has a final ruling on all peremptory challenges made by attorneys.

_____9.11. Racial discrimination has been a problem in lawyers' use of peremptory challenges.

_____9.12. A defendant who wins an appeal must be set free and cannot be tried again.

_____9.13. Plea bargaining reduces the time that people must spend in jail.

_____9.14. Most public order offenses have bail set under $5,000.

_____9.15. Robert Blake was wrongfully charged with murdering his wife and was released in October 2003.

_____9.16. The Supreme Court ruled that preventive detention was unconstitutional because it violated the presumption of innocent until proven guilty in a court of law.

_____9.17. Many people are arrested for offenses that they commit under the influence of alcohol or some other substance.

_____9.18. John Walker Lindh, a U. S. citizen who fought for the Taliban in Afghanistan, was acquitted on charges of serving as a soldier for the Taliban.

_____9.19. Prosecutors can force defendants into a plea bargain.

_____9.20. Most Americans think that Terry Nichols was as responsible as Timothy McVeigh for the Oklahoma City bombing.

WORKSHEET 9.1: BAIL

Imagine that you are a judge responsible for setting bail. For each of the following cases, indicate whether you would order Release on Own Recognizance (ROR), set bail at some specific amount [state the amount], or deny bail and order preventive detention. Provide brief comments that explain each decision.

1. Jane Williams is a new assistant professor of literature at the local university. She is twenty-six years old. She has no relatives in the area and her family lives 500 miles away in the city where she went to college for the eight years it took to earn her undergraduate and graduate degrees. She is charged with fraud in obtaining $50,000 in student loans during the previous three years by lying about her income and assets on student loan application forms. Seven years earlier she pleaded guilty in her home town to a misdemeanor charge of underage drinking.

_____

_____

_____

_____

_____

2. Karl Schmidt is charged with attempted rape. He is accused of attacking a woman in his car while giving her a ride home from the bar where he met her. He is a twenty-two year old, rookie police officer [now suspended from the force] who has lived in the city for his entire life and has no prior record.

_____

_____

_____

_____

_____

3. Susan Claussen is charged with theft for ordering and eating dinner at an expensive restaurant, and then leaving without paying the bill. She has been charged with and entered guilty pleas to the offense on five previous occasions over the past three years. She has been placed on probation several times and served one thirty-day jail sentence. She is unemployed and a life-long resident of the city. She lives with her parents.

_____

_____

WORKSHEET 9.2: PLEA BARGAINING

Imagine that you are the prosecutor who has been responsible for investigating and prosecuting the case of a suspected serial killer. Over the span of a few years, eight hunters, fishermen, and joggers have been found dead in isolated areas of a three-county rural area. Each one had been shot by a sniper from a great distance. Two bits of evidence led you to arrest a suspect. First, among the many tips you received about possible suspects, one informant described the employee of a nearby city water department who owned many guns and frequently drove out into the country to shoot at random animals he encountered, including farmers' cows and pet dogs. Second, you knew that one of the victims was shot with a rifle that was made in Sweden and was not commonly available in local gun stores. You learned from a second informant that the city employee sold one of these unusual Swedish rifles to another gun enthusiast shortly after the time that a hunter was killed by a shot from such a rifle. You located the gun and ballistics tests indicated a high probability that it was the weapon used in that particular murder. You charged the suspect with five of the eight murders and you scrambled to find evidence to link him with these and the remaining three murders. You have spoken publicly about seeking the death penalty. Now, after months of heavy publicity about the case, you announce that the defendant will plead guilty to one count of murder and be sentenced to life in prison. (Based on a real case in Canton, Ohio).

When giving a guest lecture in a criminal justice course at a nearby university, a student asks you to explain how the plea bargain in this case can be viewed as a "good" or "fair" result in light of the number of victims and the fact that you could have pursued the death penalty. Whether or not you personally agree with the plea bargain, in your role as the prosecutor, how would you explain the benefits of the plea bargain with respect to various interested actors and constituents listed below.

BRIEFLY EXPLAIN IF AND HOW THE PLEA BARGAIN BENEFITS THE:

PROSECUTOR_____

_____

JUDGE_____

_____

COURT SYSTEM_____

_____

DEFENSE ATTORNEY_____

_____

DEFENDANT_____

_____

SOCIETY_____

VICTIMS' FAMILIES_____

WORKSHEET 9.3: JURY SELECTION

Imagine that a thirty-year-old African-American woman is facing trial for the murder of her Hispanic husband. He was shot while standing in the doorway of the house soon after he returned home from work. There are no eyewitnesses. The murder weapon had the wife's fingerprints on it. On the advice of her lawyer, she never answered any questions from the police. Several defense witnesses will testify that the deceased husband used to beat his wife frequently.

1. If you are the prosecutor in this case, what is the demographic profile of your ideal juror? (e.g., age, race, education, occupation, gender, political party affiliation, religion, etc.) Why?

_____

_____

_____

_____

2. If you are the defense attorney in this case, what is the demographic profile of your ideal juror? Why?

_____

_____

_____

_____

_____

3. If you were the prosecutor, what questions would you want to ask the potential jurors during *voir dire*? Why?

_____

_____

_____

_____

_____

4. If you were the defense attorney, what questions would you want to ask the potential jurors during *voir dire*?

_____

_____

_____

WORKSHEET 9.4: JURY PROCESSES

There are many debates about changing the jury system How would you address the following issues?

1. Should peremptory challenges be abolished? What would be the consequences of excluding potential jurors only for cause and not through attorneys' discretionary decisions?

_____

_____

_____

_____

_____

_____

_____

2. Should juries have twelve members or should we use six-member juries for criminal cases? What are the consequences of using small juries?

_____

_____

_____

_____

_____

_____

_____

3. Should guilty verdicts be unanimous? What would be the consequences of permitting people to be convicted of crimes by non-unanimous jury decisions?

_____

_____

_____

_____

_____

_____

CHAPTER 10

PUNISHMENT AND SENTENCING

LEARNING OBJECTIVES

After completing the material in this chapter, students should understand:

1.   the philosophical basis for criminal punishment;

2.   the goals and weaknesses of retribution;

3.   the goals and weaknesses of deterrence;

4.   the goals and weaknesses of incapacitation;

5.   the goals and weaknesses of rehabilitation;

6.   the nature and extent of the various forms of criminal sanctions, including incarceration, intermediate sanctions, probation, and death;

7.   the constitutional and policy debates concerning the application of capital punishment;

8.   the influences on sentencing, including administrative context, attitudes and values of judges, presentence report, and sentencing guidelines;

9.   the debates about who receives the harshest punishment.

CHAPTER SUMMARY

The four goals of the criminal punishment in the United States are 1) retribution, 2) deterrence, 3) incapacitation, and 4) rehabilitation. The U. S. system is experimenting with restoration is a new approach to punishment. These goals are carried out through a variety of punishments such as incarceration, intermediate sanctions, probation, and death. Penal codes vary as to whether the permitted sentences are indeterminate, determinate, or mandatory. Each type of sentence makes certain assumptions about the goals of the criminal sanction. Good time allows correctional administrators to reduce the sentence of prisoners who live according to the rules and participate in various vocational, educational, and treatment programs. The death penalty is allowed as a form of punishment by the U.S. Supreme Court if the judge and jury are allowed to take into consideration mitigating and aggravating circumstances. The death penalty can be used by the states against juveniles, but not against the mentally retarded or the mentally insane. The U. S. Supreme Court led by Chief Justice William Rehnquist (1986-present) is attempting to limit the number of appeals for defendants on death row in multiple courts within the United States criminal justice system. Judges have considerable discretion in handing down sentences. Judges consider such factors as the seriousness of the crime, the offender's prior record, and mitigating and aggravating circumstances. The sentencing process is influenced by the administrative context of the courts, the attitudes and values of the judges, and the presentence report. Since the 1980s, sentencing guidelines have been formulated in federal courts and seventeen states as a way of reducing disparity among the sentences given offenders in similar situations. Severe or unjust punishments may result from racial discrimination or wrongful convictions.

CHAPTER OUTLINE

I.   INTRODUCTION
        Sentencing of **Marjorie Knoller** for involuntary manslaughter in the fatal dog mauling of her neighbor, Diane Whipple. Knoller, her husband, and adopted son had been raising attack dogs and allowed the dogs

to roam freely knowing that the dogs were dangerous and uncontrollable. Knoller was convicted of involuntary manslaughter and received the four maximum sentence from the judge because she showed a lack of remorse and her repeated lies on the witness stand. Sentencing is a crucial point in the criminal justice system. After guilt is determined, a decision must be made about what to do with the defendant.

II.   THE GOALS OF PUNISHMENT

A.   <u>Introduction</u>
    1.   In America, punishment has always been shaped by the values of fairness and justice. The ultimate purpose of the criminal sanction is assumed to be the maintenance of social order. However, the justice sought by crime victims often conflicts with fairness to offenders.
    2.   Criminal sanction in the United States have four main goals:
        a.   Retribution (deserved punishment).
        b.   Deterrence.
        c.   Incapacitation.
        d.   Rehabilitation.
    3.   In the twenty-first century, some are calling for a fifth goal of restorative justice.

B.   **Retribution**-<u>Deserved Punishment</u>
    1.   Idea that those who do wrong should be punished alike, in proportion to the gravity of the offense or to the extent to which others have been made to suffer ("an eye for an eye").
    2.   Some claim that retribution is a basic human emotion and that the community may express its revulsion at offensive acts by taking the law into their own hands if the state does not impose retribution on offenders: Retribution is thus an expression of the community's disapproval of crime.
    3.   Risk of chaos may not exist for failure to punish all crimes, such as an adult smoking marijuana.
    4.   Resurgence of interest in retribution among scholars and observers of criminal justice in recent years. Scholars have argued that punishment should be applied only for the wrong inflicted and not primarily to achieve utilitarian benefits (deterrence, incapacitation, rehabilitation). Offenders should be penalized for their wrongful acts because fairness and justice dictate that they deserve punishment.
    WHAT AMERICANS THINK: A majority of Americans (53%) think that retribution is the most important purpose in sentencing adults.

C.   <u>Deterrence</u>
    1.   **Jeremy Bentham**, leader of the 18th and 19th century utilitarians, found retribution to be pointless. Benthamites saw human behavior as governed by individual calculations about the degree of pleasure over pain to be derived from an act. Advocated seeking "good" results from punishment: namely deter potential criminals by the example of sanctions laid on the guilty.
    2.   **General deterrence:** idea that the general population will be dissuaded from criminal behavior by observing that punishment will necessarily follow commission of a crime and that the pain will be greater than the benefits that may stem from the illegal act. The punishment must be severe enough so that all will be impressed by the consequences.
        a.   For general deterrence to be effective, the public must be informed of the equation and continually reminded of it by the punishments of the convicted (e.g., public hanging thought to be a general deterrent).
    3.   **Special deterrence** (often called specific or individual deterrence): concerned with changes in the behavior of the convicted. It is individualized in that the amount and kind of punishment are calculated to deter the criminal from repeating the offense.
    4.   Problems with deterrence
        a.   Deterrence presumes that people act rationally, but many people commit crimes while under the influence of alcohol and drugs.
        b.   Problem of obtaining proof of the effectiveness of deterrence. General deterrence suffers because social science is unable to measure its effects; only those who are *not* deterred come to the attention of criminal justice researchers.

      c.   Not clear how the criminal justice system influences the effect of deterrence through the speed, certainty, and severity of the allocated punishment. Low probability of being caught for some crimes defeats the goal of deterrence.

D. **Incapacitation**

  1.   The assumption of incapacitation is that a crime may be prevented if criminals are physically restrained.

  2.   Prison is the typical mode of incapacitation, since offenders can be kept under control so that they cannot violate the rules of society. Capital punishment is the ultimate method of incapacitation.

  3.   Incapacitative sanction is different from these other goals in that it is future-oriented (unlike retribution); is based on personal characteristics of the offender, not on characteristics of the crime (unlike general deterrence); and is not intended to reform the criminal.

  4.   Problems of incapacitation:

      a.   Undue severity. Offenders are not released until the state is reasonably sure that they will no longer commit crimes; length of sentence not necessarily dependent on seriousness of offense. Under incapacitation theory, a one-time impulse killer could get less punishment than a habitual shoplifter.

      b.   Flawed predictions: not able to predict accurately which offenders will commit future offenses.

  5.   **Selective incapacitation** of great interest in recent years because of research suggesting that a relatively small number of offenders are responsible for a large number of violent and property crimes (e.g., burglars tend to commit many offenses before they are caught).

      a.   Such policies can impose significant costs because the costs of incarceration are so high.

E. **Rehabilitation**

  1.   The most appealing modern justification for use of the criminal sanction: the offender should be treated and resocialized while under the care of the state.

  2.   Assumes that techniques are available to identify and treat the causes of the offender's behavior.

  3.   Because rehabilitation is oriented solely toward the offender, no relationship can be maintained between the severity of the punishment and the gravity of the crime.

  4.   According to the concept of rehabilitation, offenders are not being punished, they are being treated and will return to society when they are well.

      a.   Leads to indeterminate sentences with maximum and minimum terms, as well as discretion for the parole board to decide when the offender is ready for release.

  5.   From the 1940s until the 1970s, the rehabilitative ideal was so widely shared that it was almost assumed that matters of treatment and reform of the offender were the only questions worthy of serious attention in the whole field of criminal justice and corrections. Since then, however, the model has come under closer scrutiny and in some quarters has been discredited. Some social scientists have wondered whether the causes of crime can be diagnosed and treated.

  6.   There is still support for the idea of rehabilitation in public opinion polls and among prison wardens.

F. A New Approach to Punishment: Restorative Justice

  1.   **Restorative Justice**: Crime violates sense of community as well as the individual victim. Use mediation to devise ways to restore victim and community.

  2.   This new approach means that losses suffered by the victim are restored, the threat to local safety is removed, and the offender again becomes a fully participating member of the community.

  3.   CLOSE UP: RESTORATIVE JUSTICE IN VERMONT. Community sentencing boards instead of judges to tailor penalties to lesser crimes. Sanctions are often more severe than probation but there are questions about whether penalties are applied equally and fairly.

III.   FORMS OF THE CRIMINAL SANCTION

A.   Introduction

  1.   The U. S. does not have a single, uniform set of sentencing laws. The punishments are specified in the criminal code of each of the states and of the federal government. Each code differs in terms of

severity of the punishment for specific crimes and in the discretion given to judges to tailor a sanction to an individual offender.

B.   Incarceration
1.   Most visible penalty imposed by U.S. courts although less than 30 percent of persons under correctional supervision are in prisons and jails.
2.   Believed to have high deterrent value, but expensive and may hamper offender's reintegration into society.
3.   **Indeterminate Sentences**: in accord with the goal of rehabilitation, state legislatures also adopted indeterminate (often termed indefinite) sentences. Based on idea that correctional personnel must be given the discretion to make a release decision on the grounds of successful treatment, penal codes with indeterminate sentences stipulate a minimum and maximum amount of time to be served in prison.
     a.   **"Good time"** may be subtracted from either the minimum or maximum; "good time" is earned through good behavior in prison.
4.   **Determinate Sentences**: Growing dissatisfaction with the rehabilitative goal led to efforts in support of determinate sentences based on the assumption of deserved punishment. A convicted offender is given a specific length of time to be served and at the end of this term (minus credited "good time") the prisoner is automatically freed (there is no parole board).
     a.   Release is not tied to participation in any treatment program or the judgment of the parole board about the future recidivism of the offender.
     b.   Many states have moved toward setting a specific term in prison for each crime category; tends to reduce judges' discretion (**"presumptive sentence"**).
5.   **Mandatory Sentences**: criticisms of excessive leniency and early releases have led legislatures to adopt mandatory sentences, stipulating some minimum period of incarceration that must be served by persons convicted of selected crimes. No regard may be given to the circumstances of the offense or the background of the individual; the judge has no discretion and is not allowed to suspend the sentence.
     a.   Examples include "three strikes and you're out" life sentences.
     b.   Mandatory prison terms are most often specified for violent crimes, drug violations, habitual offenders, or crimes where a firearm was used. Plea bargaining can undercut the intentions of the legislature by negotiating for a different charge. For example, such actions have undercut the Massachusetts law mandating one-year sentences for possessing an unregistered firearm.
     c.   WHAT AMERICANS THINK: A large majority of Americans (82%) favor a law requiring mandatory life imprisonment for anyone convicted of a violent felony for the third time.
6.   Three Strikes Law: impact on nonviolent crimes and increase in imprisonment costs.
7.   Sentence versus Actual Time Served: in all but four states, days are subtracted from prisoners' minimum or maximum term for good behavior or for participation in various types of vocational, educational, and treatment programs ("good time"). Service also shortened by release to the community on parole.
     a.   Correctional officials consider these sentence-reduction policies necessary for the maintenance of institutional order and as a mechanism to reduce overcrowding.
     b.   Good time is also taken into consideration by prosecutors and defense attorneys during plea bargaining.
8.   **"Truth in Sentencing"**: requirement that offenders serve a substantial portion of their sentences before release on parole usually must serve 85 percent of sentence for a violent crime. Policy can increase imprisonment costs.

C. **Intermediate Sanctions**
    1. Punishments such as fines, home confinement, intensive probation supervision, restitution and community service, boot camp, and forfeiture are among the sentencing forms that fit this category that is expanding in response to the expense and overcrowding of prisons.
    2. Morris and Tonry stipulate that these sanctions not be used in isolation from each other but that they be combined to reflect the severity of the offense, the characteristics of the offender, and the needs of the community.
    3. For effective use of intermediate punishments it is recommended that they be enforced by mechanisms that take seriously any breach of the conditions of the sentence. Too often criminal justice agencies have put few resources into the enforcement of non-incarcerative sentences.

D. **Probation**
    1. Nearly 60 percent of adults under correctional supervision are on probation; designed as a means of simultaneously maintaining control and assisting offenders while permitting them to live in the community under supervision; if conditions violated, probation may be revoked and the sentence may be served in prison.
    2. The sanction is often tied to incarceration. Judges may set a prison term but suspend it upon successful completion of a period of probation.
    3. In some jurisdictions the court is authorized to modify an offender's prison sentence after a portion is served by changing it to probation. This is often referred to as "**shock probation**" (called "split probation" in California).
    4. Probation is generally advocated as a way of rehabilitating offenders with less serious offenses or clean prior records. It is less expensive than prison and may avoid prison's embittering effects on young offenders.

E. Death
    1. Other Western democracies have abolished the death penalty but the United States continues to use it.
    2. History: Prior to the 1960s, capital punishment was used regularly in the United States; in recent years critics have questioned how capital punishment fits with the Eighth Amendment's prohibition against cruel and unusual punishment.
        a. The number of persons under sentence of death has increased dramatically in the past decade. About 3,700 incarcerated persons were awaiting execution in thirty-seven death penalty states as of January 1, 2003; two-thirds of those on death row were in the South, with the greatest number in that area concentrated in Florida, Georgia, Alabama, and Texas.
        b. About 200 people are added to death row each year.
    3. The Death Penalty and the Constitution: capital cases conducted according to higher standards of fairness and due process
        a. **Furman v. Georgia (1972):** the Supreme Court ruled that the death penalty, as administered, constituted cruel and unusual punishment, thereby voiding the laws of thirty-nine states and the District of Columbia. Only two of the justices argued that capital punishment per se was cruel and unusual, in violation of the Eighth Amendment.
        b. **Gregg v. Georgia (1976):** thirty-five states had enacted new legislation designed to eliminate the faults cited in Furman v. Georgia. The Court upheld those laws that required the sentencing judge or jury to take into account specific aggravating and mitigating factors in deciding which convicted murderers should be sentenced to death. Capital cases two-part process: first trial to determine guilt and second hearing focused solely on punishment.
        c. *McCleskey v. Kemp* **(1987):** McCleskey's attorneys cited research that showed disparity in the imposition of the death sentence in Georgia based on the race of the murder victim and, to a lesser extent, the race of the defendant. By a 5-4 vote the justices rejected McCleskey's assertion. Justice Lewis Powell, for the majority, said that the appeal challenged the discretionary aspects of the criminal justice system, especially with regard to prosecutors, judges, and juries. McCleskey would have to prove that the decision

makers in his case had acted with a discriminatory purpose by producing evidence specific to the case and not the generalized statistical study.

    d.   Execution of the Retarded: In **Atkins v. Virginia (2002),** Justice John Paul Stevens wrote for the majority in a ground-breaking decision that ruled the execution of the mentally retarded is unconstitutional.

    e.   In Ring v. Arizona (2002), the U. S. Supreme Court ruled that juries, rather than judges, must make the crucial factual decisions as to whether a convicted murderer should receive the death penalty.

    f.   WHAT AMERICANS THINK: A majority of Americans (68%) favor the death penalty for women but a majority of Americans oppose the death penalty for the mentally ill (75%), the mentally retarded (82%) and for juveniles (69%).

    4.   Continuing Legal Issues:

Legal issues related to the death penalty occupied the attention of jurists and activists during recent years. Supreme Court said in Ford v. Wainwright that states cannot execute the insane. In *Ford v. Wainwright (1986),* **Justice Thurgood Marshall** wrote for the majority in ruling that the Eighth Amendment prohibited the state from executing the insane.

    a.   However, are problems with defining and identifying insanity.

    b.   Execution of Juveniles: twenty three of the thirty-eight death penalty states allow for the execution of juveniles. **Justice Thurgood Marshall** wrote opinions arguing against the death penalty in general but for juveniles as well during his years on the Court.

        i.   Thompson v. Oklahoma (1988): the court narrowly decided offender who was fifteen years old when he committed murder should not be executed.

        ii.   Stanford v. Kentucky (1989) and Wilkins v. Missouri (1989): the justices upheld the convictions and death sentences of offenders who were 16 and 17 years old at the time of their crime.

        iii.   The Supreme Court has sanctioned executions of juveniles under some circumstances. As of January 1, 2003, there were 83 men on death row under the age of 18 in the U. S.

    c.   Effective Counsel: Issues about the adequacy of defense lawyers' efforts. In Strickland, v. Washington (1984), the Supreme Court ruled that defendants in capital cases had the right to representation that meets an "objective standard of reasonableness."

    d.   Death-Qualified Juries: Should people who are opposed to the death penalty be excluded from juries in capital cases?

    e.   Appeals: During this time sentences are reviewed by the state courts and through the writ of habeas corpus by the federal courts. Appellate review is time-consuming and expensive process, but it also has an impact. Dozens of death row inmates have been released when their innocence was later discovered.

    f.   Death: A Continuing Controversy. **Governor George Ryan** of Illinois issued a moratorium on the death penalty because the process from fraught with errors. More than 200 new death sentences are now being given out each year yet the number of executions remain low. Is this situation the result of a complicated appeals process or of lack of will on the part of both political leaders and a society that is perhaps uncertain about the taking of human life?

        i.   WHAT AMERICANS THINK: A majority of Americans (72%) favor the death penalty for a person convicted of murder.

IV. THE SENTENCING PROCESS

A.   <u>Introduction</u>: Judges have responsibility for sentencing after conviction, whether the conviction was by judge, jury, or plea bargain. Initial definitions of punishments are defined by legislatures. There may be room under the law for judges to use discretion in shaping individuals sentences.

        WHAT AMERICANS THINK: Americans are relatively split on whether a person convicted of murder should be given a punishment of life in prison without parole (45%) or the death penalty (49%).

B.   The Administrative Context of the Courts
    1.   Misdemeanor Courts: Assembly Line Justice-limited jurisdiction courts have limits on the punishments that can be meted out for specific offenses, usually maximum of one year in jail. These courts handle over 90 percent of criminal cases for arraignment and preliminary hearing before referring case to a general jurisdiction trial court or for completion through dismissal or sentence.
        a.   Most lower courts are overloaded and the time allotted for each case is minimal. Judicial decisions are mass produced because the actors in the system work together on the basis of three assumptions:
            i.   There is a high probability that anyone brought to court is guilty and doubtful cases will be filtered out beforehand by the prosecutor and police.
            ii.   The vast majority of defendants will plead guilty.
            iii.   Those charged with minor offenses will be processed in volume: normally a guilty plea is entered and a sentence is pronounced immediately after the charges are read.
        b.   Even those who are not convicted, experience punishment from being drawn into the system. People who are arrested and detained suffer psychic and social costs that range from losing jobs to being stigmatized.
            i.   These costs can also encourage rapid, perfunctory practices in the courtroom and guilty pleas. This helps to explain why so many people waive their right to a jury trial and plead guilty. Better to take the punishment (probably probation) than to remain in jail, incurring more personal costs, and risking that a more serious punishment may ultimately be applied.
    2.   Felony Court: in courts of general jurisdiction, sentencing influenced by organizational considerations and community norms, including interactions and relationships between judges, prosecutors, and defense attorneys.

THE POLICY DEBATE: Should the death penalty to be abolished? The moratorium imposed by **Governor George Ryan** of Illinois in 2000 renewed debate about the death penalty. Arguments for the death penalty include social retribution, deterrence, and less expensive that allowing offenders to live in prison. Arguments against the death penalty include the idea that it violates the human dignity in the U. S. Constitution, it is not a deterrent, innocent persons are executed, it is a financial burden of the legal system because it involves millions of dollars in legal fees, and it is applied largely to the poor and minorities.

TECHNOLOGY ISSUES IN CRIMINAL JUSTICE-Sentencing By Computer: In Michigan, private computer companies have developed software that will do sentencing calculations quickly for judges and for the probation officers who write presentence reports.

B.   Attitudes and Values of Judges
    1.   Sentencing differences among judges can be ascribed to a number of factors:
        a.   Conflicting goals of criminal justice.
        b.   The fact that judges are the products of different backgrounds and have different social values.
        c.   The administrative pressures on the judge.
        d.   The influence of community values on the system.
        e.   The particular judge's attitude toward law, toward a particular crime, and toward a particular type of offender.
        f.   the protection of the community
        g.   the practical implications of the sentence
WORK PERSPECTIVE: The Honorable Kirk Daily, District Associate Judge, Ottumwa, Iowa
        h.   WHAT AMERICANS THINK: A large majority of Americans (66%) think the courts do not deal harshly enough with criminals.

C.   The **Presentence Report**
1.   An important ingredient in sentencing; the report is based on the investigation of the probation officer. In some states, the probation officer makes an actual recommendation; in others, the probation officer merely provides information. Report can be based on hearsay.
2.   The language of the report is crucial in conveying an impression. It may be written in a neutral style or it may suggest something negative about the offender's attitude.
3.   A Question of Ethics: Sentencing of two co-defendants. Should there be a different sentence for an offender convicted at trial as compared to one who enters a guilty plea?
4.   The presentence report helps judges to ease the strain of decision making; helps to shift responsibility to the probation department.
5.   CLOSE-UP: Sample Presentence Report. An example of a presentence report from the Corrections Department in New Mexico containing an evaluation and recommendation.

D.   **Sentencing Guidelines**
Guidelines have emerged in the federal system and some state systems as a means to limit the discretion of judges and to reduce sentencing disparities for offenders convicted of the same offense. Sentencing ranges in the guidelines are based on seriousness of offense and criminal history of the offender.
1.   Guidelines appear in a grid constructed on the basis of two scores, seriousness of offense and offender's history/prior record or other offender characteristics. The grid provides an offender score which indicates the sentencing range for the particular offender who commits a specific offense. Judges are expected to provide a written explanation if they depart from the guidelines/grid.

A QUESTION OF ETHICS: Should a judge sentence a defendant more harshly if he or she plead guilty in exchange for leniency?

E.   Who Gets the Harshest Punishment?
1.   Racial Disparities: Research on racial disparities is inconclusive. Some studies have shown that members of racial minorities and the poor are treated more harshly by the system. Other studies show no clear link between harshness of sentence and the offender's race or social status.
2.   **Wrongful Convictions**: While much public concern is expressed over those who "beat the system" and go free, comparatively little attention is paid to those who are innocent, yet convicted. Each year several such cases of persons convicted but innocent come to national attention.

IDEAS IN PRACTICE: Using Table 10.4 (Minnesota guidelines), you must determine the sentence of a convicted felon.

V. PROSECUTION, ADJUDICATION, AND SENTENCING: Inside the Criminal Justice System and Beyond: One Man's Journey, written by Chuck Terry

KEY TERMS AND PEOPLE
Fill in the appropriate term from the list for each statement below
determinate sentence
general deterrence
selective incapacitation
incapacitation
indeterminate sentence
intermediate sanctions
mandatory sentence
presentence report
presumptive sentence
probation
rehabilitation
retribution
restorative justice

sentencing guidelines
shock probation
specific deterrence
truth-in-sentencing
Atkins v. Virginia (2002)
Furman v. Georgia (1972)
Gregg v. Georgia (1976)
McCleskey v. Kemp (1987)
Witherspoon v. Illinois (1968)
good time
wrongful conviction

1. _____ is making the best use of expensive and limited prison space by targeting for incarceration those individuals whose incapacity will do the most to reduce crime in society.

2. _____ is a term of incarceration based on a minimum and maximum amount of time to be served in prison.

3. _____ is punishment inflicted on criminals with the intent to discourage them from committing any future crimes.

4. _____ is a sentence in which the offender is released after a short incarceration and placed in the community under supervision.

5. _____ is punishment designed to repair the damage done to the victim and community by an offender's act.

6. _____ is a sentence for which the legislature or a commission sets a minimum and maximum range of months or years.

7. _____ is a type of sentence determined by statutes which require that a certain penalty shall be imposed and executed upon certain convicted offenders.

8. _____ is the Supreme Court case which reactivated capital punishment after states revised their death penalty decision-making procedures.

9. _____ refers to laws that require offenders to serve a substantial proportion of their sentence before being released on parole.

10. _____ is a variety of punishments that are more restrictive than traditional probation but less stringent and costly than incarceration.

11. _____ is a punishment involving conditional release under supervision.

12. _____ is the underlying goal of punishment in which the offender is considered deserving of punishment and the punishment fits the seriousness of the crime.

13. _____ is the Supreme Court case that approved the execution of offenders who committed capital offenses at age sixteen.

14. _____ is the deprivation of the ability to commit crimes against society, usually through means of detention in prison.

15. _____ is a case in which the Supreme Court rejected a claim that systematic racial discrimination made the death penalty unconstitutional.

16. _____ is a sentence that fixes the term of imprisonment at a specific period.

17. _____ are a reform designed to reduce the disparities in sentences for people who have committed the same or similar crimes.

18. _____ is the goal of restoring a convicted offender to a constructive place in society.

19. _____ is the credit awarded to prisoners in most states which permits them to earn days off of their sentences through proper behavior.

20. _____ is the Supreme Court case that temporarily halted executions in the United States.

21. _____ is the punishment of criminals that is intended to serve as an example to the public and discourage others from committing crimes.

22. _____ is submitted by the probation officer to the judge.

23. In the case of _____, the Supreme Court ruled that the execution of the mentally retarded is unconstitutional.

24. _____ occur when people are falsely convicted and sentenced.

25. In the case of _____, the Supreme Court held that potential jurors who have general objections to the death penalty or whose religious convictions oppose its use cannot be automatically excluded from jury service.

REVIEW OF KEY PEOPLE
Fill in the appropriate person(s) from the list for each statement below
Napoleon Beasley
Jeremy Bentham
Majorie Knoller
George Ryan
Michael Tonry
Thurgood Marshall
Norval Morris

1. _____ and _____ stipulate that intermediate sanctions should not be used in isolation, but rather in combination to reflect the severity of the offense, the characteristics of the offender, and the needs of the community.

2. In 2000, Governor _____ of Illinois called for a moratorium on the death penalty in his state.

3. In *Ford v. Wainwright (1986)*, Justice _____ wrote for the majority in ruling that the Eighth Amendment prohibited the state from executing the insane.

4. The deterrence approach has its roots in eighteenth-century England and the social philosopher named _____.

5. _____ was put to death in Texas on may 28, 2002 for a murder committed when he was 17 years old during a botched car jacking.

6. _____ was convicted of involuntary manslaughter in the fatal dog mauling death of her neighbor.

Multiple Choice Questions

10.1. What did the U. S. Supreme Court rule in *McClesky v. Kemp (1987)*?
a) the Supreme Court declared that the death penalty is illegal in cases involving the mentally retarded
b) the Supreme Court ruled that juries, rather than judges, must make the crucial factual decisions as to whether a convicted murderer should receive the death penalty
c) the Supreme Court ruled that under a hate crime statute a higher sentence may be imposed if the judge found that a crime was committed with a biased motive
d) the Supreme Court ruled that the Eighth Amendment prohibited the state from executing the insane
e) Supreme Court declared that the death penalty did NOT violate the Constitution through imposition in a racially discriminatory manner

10.2. Which of the following is TRUE concerning the appeal process for death penalty cases?
a) the appeal process is quick and inexpensive
b) the appeal process is quick but expensive
c) the appeal process is time-consuming and expensive
d) the appeal process is time-consuming but inexpensive
e) there is no appeal process for death penalty cases

10.3. Punishments that are less severe and costly than prison, but more restrictive than traditional probation, are called...
a) indeterminate sentences
b) mandatory sentences
c) "good time" sentences
d) presumptive sentences
e) intermediate sanctions

10.4. Which is the most frequently applied criminal sanction?
a) probation
b) the death penalty
c) life in prison
d) indeterminate sentences
e) presumptive sentences

10.5. . What did the U. S. Supreme Court rule in *Atkins v. Virginia (2002)*?
a) the Supreme Court declared that the death penalty is illegal in cases involving the mentally retarded
b) the Supreme Court ruled that juries, rather than judges, must make the crucial factual decisions as to whether a convicted murderer should receive the death penalty
c) the Supreme Court ruled that under a hate crime statute a higher sentence may be imposed if the judge found that a crime was committed with a biased motive
d) the Supreme Court ruled that the Eighth Amendment prohibited the state from executing the insane
e) Supreme Court declared that the death penalty did not violate the Constitution through imposition in a racially discriminatory manner

10.6. What did the U. S. Supreme Court rule in *Ring v. Arizona (2002)*?
a) the Supreme Court declared that the death penalty is illegal in cases involving the mentally retarded
b) the Supreme Court ruled that juries, rather than judges, must make the crucial factual decisions as to whether a convicted murderer should receive the death penalty
c) the Supreme Court ruled that under a hate crime statute a higher sentence may be imposed if the judge found that a crime was committed with a biased motive
d) the Supreme Court ruled that the Eighth Amendment prohibited the state from executing the insane
e) Supreme Court declared that the death penalty did not violate the Constitution through imposition in a racially discriminatory manner

10.7. What did the U. S. Supreme Court rule in *Stanford v. Kentucky (1989)*?
a) the Supreme Court declared that the death penalty is illegal in cases involving the mentally retarded
b) the Supreme Court ruled that juries, rather than judges, must make the crucial factual decisions as to whether a convicted murderer should receive the death penalty
c) the Supreme Court ruled that under a hate crime statute a higher sentence may be imposed if the judge found that a crime was committed with a biased motive
d) the Supreme Court ruled that the Eighth Amendment did NOT prohibit a state from executing juveniles
e) Supreme Court declared that the Eighth Amendment prohibited a state from executing the insane

10.8. What did the U. S. Supreme Court rule in *Ford v. Wainwright (1986)*?
a) the Supreme Court declared that the death penalty is illegal in cases involving the mentally retarded
b) the Supreme Court ruled that juries, rather than judges, must make the crucial factual decisions as to whether a convicted murderer should receive the death penalty
c) the Supreme Court ruled that under a hate crime statute a higher sentence may be imposed if the judge found that a crime was committed with a biased motive
d) the Supreme Court ruled that the Eighth Amendment prohibited the state from executing juveniles
e) Supreme Court declared that the Eighth Amendment prohibited the state from executing the insane

10.9. Why did Marjorie Knoller receive a four year sentence for involuntary manslaughter in the fatal dog mauling death of her neighbor, Diane Whipple?
a) the four year sentence was a determinate sentence and the judge had no discretion
b) the four year sentence was a maximum sentence and the judge imposed it because Knoller did not show any remorse
c) the four year sentence was a minimum sentence and the judge imposed it because Whipple had aggravated the dog on several occasions
d) Knoller was released because of her cooperation with authorities and the four year sentence was for time served
e) Knoller plea bargained because she was facing a life sentence

10.10. Which of the following purpose(s) justifies the use of the death penalty?
a) incapacitation
b) retribution
c) deterrence
d) all of the above
e) none of the above

10.11. What area of the U. S. has the greatest number of persons on death row?
a) West
b) South
c) Northeast
d) Midwest
e) all of the above areas have the same proportion of persons on death row

10.12. What did the U. S. Supreme Court rule in *Furman v. Georgia (1972)*?
a) the Supreme Court declared that the death penalty as administered constituted cruel and unusual punishment
b) the Supreme Court ruled that juries, rather than judges, must make the crucial factual decisions as to whether a convicted murderer should receive the death penalty
c) the Supreme Court ruled that under a hate crime statute a higher sentence may be imposed if the judge found that a crime was committed with a biased motive
d) the Supreme Court ruled that the Eighth Amendment prohibited the state from executing juveniles
e) Supreme Court declared that the Eighth Amendment prohibited the state from executing the insane

10.13. What did the U. S. Supreme Court rule in *Strickland v. Washington (1984)?*
a) the Supreme Court ruled that juries, rather than judges, must make the crucial factual decisions as to whether a convicted murderer should receive the death penalty
b) the Supreme Court ruled that under a hate crime statute a higher sentence may be imposed if the judge found that a crime was committed with a biased motive
c) the Supreme Court ruled that the Eighth Amendment prohibited the state from executing juveniles
d) Supreme Court declared that the Eighth Amendment prohibited the state from executing the insane
e) the Supreme Court ruled that defendants in capital cases had the right to representation that meets an "objective standard of reasonableness"

10.14. What did the U. S. Supreme Court rule in *Witherspoon v. Illinois (1968)*?
a) the Supreme Court hold that potential jurors who have general objections to the death penalty cannot be automatically excluded from jury service in capital cases
b) the Supreme Court ruled that juries, rather than judges, must make the crucial factual decisions as to whether a convicted murderer should receive the death penalty
c) the Supreme Court ruled that under a hate crime statute a higher sentence may be imposed if the judge found that a crime was committed with a biased motive
d) the Supreme Court ruled that the Eighth Amendment prohibited the state from executing juveniles
e) Supreme Court declared that the Eighth Amendment prohibited the state from executing the insane

10.15. What is the average amount of time spent on death row according to the Bureau of Justice Statistics in 2001?
a) six months
b) one years
c) eleven years
d) twenty-one years
e) thirty years

10.16. Which branch(es) of government established the penal codes that set forth the sentences judges can impose?
a) executive
b) judicial
c) legislature
d) executive and the legislature
e) executive and the judicial

10.17. Which of the following is a problem associated with the concept of deterrence?
a) social scientists have several measurements for the effects of general deterrence
b) sentencing policies based upon deterrence never achieve their objectives
c) deterrence assumes that all people think before they act
d) all of the above
e) none of the above

10.18. What type of jurisdiction do misdemeanor, or lower courts, maintain in the American system?
a) general
b) limited
c) intermediate
d) all of the above
e) none of the above

10.19. What type of jurisdiction do felony courts, maintain in the American system?
a) general
b) limited
c) intermediate
d) all of the above
e) none of the above

10.20. Punishment designed to repair the damage done to the victim and the community by an offender's criminal act is called...
a) rehabilitation
b) general deterrence
c) restorative justice
d) specific deterrence
e) retribution

10.21. Who is usually responsible for investigating the convicted person's background for the presentence report?
a) judge
b) police
c) clerk
d) probation officer
e) prosecutor

10.22. Which goal of punishment is illustrated if a judge imposes a sentence "because the offender's punishment will serve as an example to others"?
a) retribution
b) deterrence
c) incapacitation
d) rehabilitation
e) restorative justice

10.23. How many states have the "three strikes and you're out" laws?
a) roughly one-tenth
b) roughly one-quarter
c) roughly one-half
d) roughly three-fourths
e) all fifty states

10.24. The three strikes and you're out law is an example of a(n)...
a) probation
b) good time sentencing
c) indeterminate sentencing
d) intermediate sentencing
e) mandatory sentencing

10.25. Which of the following is a goal of punishment in the American system of criminal justice?
a) retribution
b) deterrence
c) incapacitation
d) rehabilitation
e) all of the above

True and False Questions

_____10.1. Virtually all states and the federal government have some types of mandatory sentences.

_____10.2. It is legal for states to execute the mentally retarded.

_____10.3. "Good time" refers to the amount of a time that a judge allows a jury to deliberate a decision.

_____10.4. Imprisonment is the least visible penalty imposed by U. S. courts.

_____10.5. Intermediate sanctions are punishments that are less severe and financially burdensome than prison.
_____10.6. The most frequently employed criminal sanction is probation.

_____10.7. Jeremy Bentham supported the deterrence approach toward punishment.

_____10.8. In recent years less attention has been paid to the concept of selective incapacitation, whereby offenders who repeat certain kinds of crimes are sentenced to long prison terms.

_____10.9. At sentencing, judges rarely give reasons for the punishments imposed.

_____10.10. Rehabilitation is focused upon the victim of a crime.

_____10.11. Wrongful convictions include those cases where the conviction of a truly guilty person is overturned on appeal because of due process errors.

_____10.12. About 99% of death row inmates are male.

_____10.13. Truth-in-sentencing refers to laws that require offenders to serve a large proportion of their prison sentence before being released on parole.

_____10.14. Most states do not use the death penalty as punishment in the United States.

_____10.15. It is illegal to execute juveniles.

_____10.16. Offenders can have their prison sentence reduced by earning good time for good behavior.

_____10.17. Felony cases are processed and offenders are sentenced in courts of limited jurisdiction.

_____10.18. Presentence reports are compiled by prosecutors.

_____10.19. Since the 1940s sentencing guidelines have been established in the federal courts and in all fifty states.

_____10.20. Sentencing guidelines are constructed on the basis of past sentences.

WORKSHEET 10.1   FORMS OF THE CRIMINAL SANCTION

Discuss whether and how the underlying purposes of the criminal sanction fit with various forms of punishment. Ask yourself: Does this form of punishment effectively advance any or all of the underlying purposes? For each punishment, comment on the pros and cons of all of the following: rehabilitation, deterrence, incapacitation, retribution.

1. INCARCERATION:_____

_____

_____

_____

_____

2. PROBATION:

_____

_____

_____

_____

_____

3. FINES: _____

_____

_____

_____

_____

4. CAPITAL PUNISHMENT:_____

_____

_____

_____

_____

5. COMMUNITY SERVICE:_____

_____

_____

WORKSHEET 10.2   SENTENCING

Imagine that you are a judge deciding on sentences for individuals who have entered guilty pleas in the following situations. What sentence would you impose?

1. A nineteen-year-old high school dropout pleads guilty to burglary. He broke into a home and was caught carrying a VCR out the window when the homeowners awoke from the noise of someone in their living room. He has one previous felony conviction for burglary.

SENTENCE:_____

2. A college senior who was caught copying copyrighted computer software from a university computer system onto his own diskette without permission. The value of the software was $700. The student entered a guilty plea to a simple theft charge with an agreement that the prosecutor would recommend leniency. The student has been suspended from college for one year by the school's disciplinary board.

SENTENCE:_____

3. A man who recently completed a prison sentence for armed robbery killed a man during an argument at a bar. The defendant claimed that the victim owed him money so he went to the bar with a knife in order to scare the victim. A confrontation between the two developed into a fight and the victim was stabbed to death. The defendant entered a guilty plea to the charge of second-degree murder. He has served prior prison terms for two armed robbery convictions.

SENTENCE:_____

Now look at the Minnesota sentencing guidelines in the chapter. What would be the sentence for each offender under the guidelines?

1. _____

2. _____

3. _____

Do you think the guidelines are too harsh, too lenient, or just right? Explain.

_____

_____

_____

_____

_____

_____

CHAPTER 11

CORRECTIONS

LEARNING OBJECTIVES

After covering the material in this chapter, students should understand:

1. the history of corrections, from the development of the penitentiary to reformatories to the rise and fall of rehabilitation, including the Pennsylvania and New York systems and community corrections;

2. the nature of prisons by classification and the fragmented organization of corrections nationally;

3. the nature of and problems facing local jails;

4. institutions for women and private prisons;

5. constitutional rights of prisoners, probationers, and parolees;

6. Laws and regulations that define the relationships between correctional administrators and their staff such as civil service laws and liability of correctional personnel

7. Correctional policy trends for prisoners, probationers, and parolees

CHAPTER SUMMARY

From the colonial days to the present, the methods of criminal punishments that are considered appropriate have variety. The development of the penitentiary ended corporal punishment. The Pennsylvania and New York systems competed with different ideas about the penitentiary. In 1870, the Declaration of Principles was written in Cincinnati and it contained critical ideas about reform and rehabilitation for prisoners. The administration of corrections in the U. S. is decentralized and scattered across all levels of government. Jails are distinct from prisons and usually to hold persons awaiting trial and persons who have been sentenced for misdemeanors to terms of less than one year. Since the 1960s, the prisoners' rights movement, through lawsuits in the federal courts, has brought many changes to the administration and conditions of American prisons. Paroleos and probationers also have been recognized by the federal courts in regard to constitutional protections. Two important aspects of correctional work: civil service laws and liability of correctional personnel. Civil service laws set procedures for hiring, promoting, assigning, disciplining, and firing public employees. These laws protect employees from arbitrary actions by supervisors. Also, as noted above, the Supreme Court ruled that prisoners can bring lawsuits against correctional officials. Finally, prison populations have increased dramatically during the last ten years and there has also been a great increase in facilities and staff to administer them.

CHAPTER OUTLINE

I. INTRODUCTION
A. The United States has the highest incarceration rate in the entire world.
B. **Corrections** refers to the great number of programs, services, facilities, and organizations responsible for the management of people accused or convicted of criminal offenses, Corrections includes prisons, probation, parole, work camps, Salvation Army facilities, medical facilities, and other contexts.
C. More than 6.5 million adults and juveniles are given correctional supervision by more than 700,000 administrators, psychologists, officers, counselors, social workers, and others. One of every 20 men and one out of every 100 women in America either is being supervised in the community (on probation or parole) or is incarcerated.
D. Corrections is a system authorized by all levels of government, administered by both public and private organizations, and with a total cost of over $50 billion yearly.

II.   DEVELOPMENT OF CORRECTIONS

A.   The Invention of the Penitentiary
1.   18th century scholars and social reformers in Europe and America engaged in an almost complete rethinking of the nature of society and the place of the individual in it. The **Enlightenment**, as the philosophical movement was called, challenged traditional assumptions by emphasizing the individual, the limitations on government, and rationalism.
2.   The period following the French Revolution led to the elimination of torture as a public spectacle and the adoption of "modern" penal codes that emphasized selecting and modifying punishment to fit the individual offender.
3.   Punishment moved away from the infliction of pain; instead, correctional intervention was to change the individual and set him or her on the right path.
4.   **John Howard** (1726-1790), sheriff of Bedfordshire, England, wrote *The State of Prisons in England and Wales* (1777) which led to the development of the *penitentiary*.
   a.   Howard described horrible prison conditions; led to creation by Parliament of house of hard labor. The institution would be based on four principles:
      i.   a secure and sanitary building;
      ii.   systematic inspection;
      iii. the abolition of fees; and
      iv.   a reformatory regime.
   b.   Prisoners were to be confined to solitary cells during the night, and to labor silently in common rooms during the day. The regimen was to be strict and ordered.
   c.   Howard believed that the new institution (**penitentiary**) was to give criminals an opportunity for penitence (sorrow and shame for their wrongs) and repentance (willingness to change their ways), its purpose was to punish and reform.

B.   Reform in the United States
1.   From 1776-1830, emphasis shifted from the assumption that deviance was part of human nature to a belief that crime was a result of forces operating in the environment. If the humane and optimistic ideals of the new nation were to be realized, it must be possible to reform the criminal element of society.
2.   In the first decades of the nineteenth century, the creation of penitentiaries in Pennsylvania and New York attracted the attention of legislators in other states and also investigators from Europe.
3.   Visitors from abroad made it a point to include a penitentiary visit on their itinerary.
4.   The Pennsylvania System
   a.   The Philadelphia Society for Alleviating the Miseries of Public Prisons, formed in 1787 under the leadership of Dr. Benjamin Rush included a large number of Quakers. It urged replacement of capital and corporal (bodily) punishment by incarceration. The Quakers believed that criminals could best be reformed if they were placed in solitary confinement so that, alone in their cells, they could consider their deviant acts, repent, and reform themselves.
   b.   Walnut Street Jail in Philadelphia (1790): provided for solitary confinement; each cell held one inmate and was small and dark (only six feet by eight feet, and nine feet high). No communications of any kind were allowed. It was from this limited beginning that the Pennsylvania system of **separate confinement** evolved based on premise of rehabilitation.
   c.   Eastern Penitentiary near Philadelphia (1829) isolated inmates not only from the community but also from one another. In each cell was a fold-up steel bedstead, a simple toilet, a wooden stool, a workbench, and eating utensils. Light came from an eight-inch window in the ceiling. Solitary labor, Bible reading, and reflection were regarded as the keys to the moral rehabilitation.
      i.   The only human voice the prisoner heard would be that of a clergyman who would visit on Sundays.
   d.   However, the Eastern Penitentiary soon proved unworkable because investigators noted that the goal of separate confinement was not fully observed, physical punishments were

used to maintain discipline, and prisoners suffered mental breakdowns from isolation. However, it was not abolished until 1913.

5. The New York System
   a. Auburn penitentiary (1819): Under the Auburn system, prisoners were kept in individual cells at night but congregated in workshops during the day. In this **congregate system,** however, inmates were forbidden to talk to one another or even to exchange glances while on the job or at meals.
   b. Auburn's warden, **Elam Llynds,** instituted a reign of discipline that included the lockstep and the wearing of prison stripes. He also started a contract labor system under which inmates' labor was sold on a contractual basis to private employers who provided the machinery and raw materials which inmates made salarable products in the institution.
   c. American reformers saw the New York approach as a great advance in penology, and it was copied throughout the Northeast
   d. Advocates of both systems agreed that the prisoner must be isolated from society and placed on a disciplined routine. They believed that deviancy was a result of corruption pervading the community.

6. Prisons in the South and the West
   a. Scholars neglect the development of the prisons in the South and the West.
   b. In the South, the **lease system** was developed. This allowed businesses in need of workers to negotiate with the state for the labor and care of prisoners. Prisoners were leased to firms that used them in milling, logging, cotton picking, mining, and railroad construction.
   c. Except in California, the prison ideologies of the East did not greatly influence penology in the West. Prior to statehood, prisoners were held in territorial facilities or federal military posts and prisons.

C. The Reformatory Movement
   1. By the middle of the nineteenth century, reformers had become disillusioned with the penitentiary. The Pennsylvania and New York systems had not achieved rehabilitation or deterrence and prisons had become overcrowded and understaffed. Discipline, brutality, and corruption were common as, for example, in Sing Sing Prison in New York.
   2. In 1870 the newly formed National Prison Association (predecessor of today's American Correctional Association) met in Cincinnati and issued a **Declaration of Principles,** which sounded the trumpet for a new round of penal reform. Progressive penologists advocated a new design for penology.
   3. The Declaration of Principles asserted that prisons should be operated in accordance with a philosophy of inmate change that would reward reformation with release. Fixed sentences should be replaced by sentences of indeterminate length, and proof of reformation should replace the "mere lapse of time" in bringing about the prisoner's freedom.
   4. Elmira Reformatory (1876) under **Zebulon Brockway,** the superintendent, regarded education a the key to reform and rehabilitation. The **reformatory** was an institution for young offenders that emphasizes training, a mark system of classification, indeterminate sentences, and parole.
      a. Brockway's approach at Elmira Reformatory provided for indeterminate sentences, permitting the reformatory to release inmates on parole when their reform had been assured.
      b. Elmira used the "mark" system of classification in which prisoners earned their way up (or down) by following rules.
   5. Difficulties with reformatory movement: institutions frequently emphasized punishment rather than education and rehabilitation, and difficult to judge whether or not a prisoner had been reformed.

D. Improving Prison Conditions for Women
   1. Until the beginning of the nineteenth century, women offenders in North America and Europe were treated no differently than men. Both men and women were incarcerated together.
   2. An English Quaker, **Elizabeth Fry,** led reform efforts in England after visiting London's Newgate Prison in 1813.

3.   Women's Prison Association formed in New York in 1944. Elizabeth Farnham, head matron at Sing Sing Prison's women's wing sought to implement Fry's ideas in the United States. Her efforts were blocked by male supervisors and legislators.

4.   Cincinnati's Declaration of Principles did not address the issue of women offenders.

5.   Although the House of Shelter, a women's reformatory, was founded in Detroit after the Civil War, it was not until 1873 that the first independent female-run prison opened in Indiana. Within fifty years, thirteen other states had followed this lead.

6.   Three principles guided female prison reform during this period:
   a.   the separation of women prisoners from men;
   b.   the provision of care in keeping with the needs of women;
   c.   the management of women's prisons by female staff.

7.   Shortly after the establishment of the first federal prison for women (Alderson, West Virginia with **Mary Belle Harris** as warden), the reform movement had run its course and largely achieved its objective of establishing separate prisons.

E.   <u>Rehabilitation Model</u>

1.   Early twentieth century belief in state action to deal with the social problems of slums, vice, and crime. The Progressives believed that with the concepts of the social and behavioral sciences, rather than religious or moral precepts, they could rehabilitate criminals.

2.   The new activists relied on the developments of modern criminology associated with a scientific approach to crime and human behavior known as the positivist school, which focused on the behavior of the offender.

3.   Progressives emphasized two strategies:
   a.   The need to improve conditions in the environments they believed to be breeding grounds of crime.
   b.   Emphasize ways to rehabilitate the individual offender.

4.   Progressives instituted the presentence report, with its extensive personal history, as a means to enable judges and correctional officials to analyze the individual's problem and to take action toward rehabilitation.

5.   By the 1920s, probation, indeterminate sentence and parole, and treatment programs were being espoused by reform penologists as the instruments of this more scientific approach to criminality.

6.   In 1930s, attempts were made to implement fully what became known as the *rehabilitation model* of corrections. Penologists using the newly prestigious social and behavioral sciences helped shift the emphasis of the postconviction sanction to treatment of criminals, whose social, intellectual, or biological deficiencies were seen as the causes of their illegal activities.

7.   The essential structural elements of parole, probation, and the indeterminate sentence were already in place in most states. Therefore, incorporating the rehabilitation model required only the addition of classification systems to diagnose offenders and treatment programs that would rehabilitate them.

8.   Because they compared their correctional methods to those used by physicians in hospitals, this approach was often referred to as the **medical model**. Under this approach, correctional institutions were to be staffed with persons who could diagnose the causes of an individual's criminal behavior, prescribe a treatment program, and determine when a cure had been effected so that the offender could be released to the community.

9.   After World War II, group therapy, behavior modification, counseling, and numerous other approaches all became part of the "new penology" emphasizing rehabilitation.

10.   Allocation of state budgets maintained a gap between the rhetoric of the rehabilitation model and the reality that institutions were still being run with custody as an overriding goal.

11.   The failure of these new techniques to stem crime, the changes in the characteristics of the prison population, and the misuse of the discretion required by the model prompted another cycle of correctional reform, so that by 1970s rehabilitation as a goal had become discredited.

F.   Community Model
       1.   **Community corrections** was based on the assumption that the goal of the criminal justice system should be to reintegrate the offender into the community. Arose from sense of social disorder in turbulent 1960s and 1970s.
       2.   It was argued that corrections should turn away from an emphasis upon psychological treatment to programs that would increase the opportunities for offenders to be successful citizens, e.g., vocational and educational programs.
       3.   Programs attempted to help offenders find jobs and remain connected to their families. Correctional workers served as advocates for offenders.
       4.   The community corrections model dominated corrections until the 1970s, when it gave way to a new punitiveness in criminal justice in conjunction with the rebirth of determinate sentences.

G.   **Crime Control Model**
       1.   Legislators, judges and corrections officials responded in the 1980s and 1990s with a renewed emphasis upon incarceration as a way to solve the crime problem.
       2.   Policy attacks were mounted against certain structures of rehabilitation including indeterminate sentences, treatment programs, and discretionary release on parole.
       3.   States created **"supermax" prisons** and limited prisoners' activities. Some states banned weightlifting and college courses. Other places reinstituted chain gangs.

III.   ORGANIZATION OF CORRECTIONS IN THE UNITED STATES

A.   Introduction
       1.   Each level of government has some responsibility for corrections, and often one level exercises little supervision over another. The federal government, the fifty states, the District of Columbia, the 3,047 counties, and most cities each have at least one facility and many programs. State and local governments pay about 95 percent of the cost of all correctional activities in the nation.

B.   Federal Corrections Systems
       1.   The Federal Bureau of Prisons was created by Congress in 1930. Facilities and inmates are classified in a security-level system ranging from Level 1 (the least secure, camp-type settings such as the Federal Prison Camp at Tyndall, Florida) through Level 6 (the most secure, such as the U.S. Penitentiary, Florence, Colorado).
       2.   Probation and parole supervision for federal offenders are provided by the Division of Probation, a branch of the Administrative Office of the United States Courts. Officers are appointed by the federal judiciary and serve at the pleasure of the court.

C.   State Corrections Systems- Every state has a centralized department of the executive branch that administers corrections, but the extent of these departments' responsibility for programs varies.
       1.   Community Corrections
              a.   Probation, intermediate sanctions, and parole are the three major ways that offenders are punished in the community.
              b.   In many states probation and intermediate sanctions are administered by the judiciary, often by county and municipal governments.
              c.   By contrast, parole is handled by state government. Parole boards are either part of the department of corrections or an independent agency. Parole supervision is handled by a state agency in each community.
       2.   State Prison Systems
              a.   Wide variation exists in the way correctional responsibilities are divided between the state and local governments.
              b.   State correctional institutions for men include a great range of facilities usually classified by level of security: maximum, medium and minimum. Such programs, including prisons, reformatories, industrial institutions, prison farms, conservation camps, forestry camps, and halfway houses. This variety does not exist for women.
              c.   Thirty-eight states have created prisons that exceed maximum security. An estimated 20,000 men are currently kept in these "supermax" prisons.

d. The maximum security prison (where 35 percent of state inmates are confined) is built like a fortress, surrounded by stone walls with guard towers and designed to prevent escape.

e. The medium security prison (holding 47 percent of state inmates) resembles the maximum security prison in appearance, but is less rigid and tense. Prisoners have more privileges, and contact with the outside world through visitors, mail, and freer access to radio and television. Greater emphasis on rehabilitative programs.

f. The minimum security prison (with 18 percent of state inmates) houses least violent offenders, principally white-collar criminals. The minimum security prison does not have the guard towers and walls usually associated with correctional institutions. Prisoners may live dormitory style or even in small private rooms rather than barred cells. There is a relatively high level of personal freedom: inmates may have television sets, choose their own clothes, and move about casually within the buildings. May be greater emphasis on treatment programs, work release, and opportunities for education.

3. State Institutions for Women

a. Only 6.8 percent of the incarcerated population are women. Thus there are relatively few institutions for women.

b. A higher proportion of women defendants are sentenced to probation and intermediate punishments, partly as a result of males' more frequent commission of violent crimes.

c. Institutions for women are often more pleasant than similar institutions for men.

d. Because there may only be one prison in a state, women are often isolated from their families and communities.

e. TECHNOLOGY ISSUES IN CRIMINAL JUSTICE: Remote-controlled Stun Belt- a controversial new type of control could affect prisoners at all levels. The stun belts could prove to be deadly if a prisoner's heart rhythm is susceptible to disruption.

D. Private Prisons

1. Idea that private businesses can run prisons effectively and inexpensively. Has long been used for specific services but only recently for entire prisons.

2. The $1 billion per year private prison business is dominated by Corrections Corporation of America and Wackenhut.

3. Cost comparisons between public and private facilities often do not include "true costs," such as fringe benefits. In regard to flexibility, it is argued that because correctional space requirements rise and fall, private entrepreneurs can provide additional space when it is needed, and their contracts can go unrenewed when space is in oversupply. In Texas, the state pays the private companies about $30 a day on average for each prisoner, compared with $39.50 per day state prisons.

4. Political, fiscal, and administrative issues remain:

a. Ethical questions of the propriety of delegating social-control functions to persons other than the state--may be the most difficult to overcome.

b. Contractors might use their political influence to continue programs not in the public interest.

c. Labor unions have pointed out that the salaries, benefits, and pensions of workers in private prisons are lower than those of their public counterparts.

d. Questions remain about quality of services, accountability of service providers to corrections officials, and problems related to contract supervision.

5. Competition from private sector might be beneficial during era of financial constraints on government units that need new prison space.

E. Jails: Local Correctional Facilities

1. Introduction

a. Most people do not distinguish between jails and prisons. Prisons are at the federal or state level and house inmates with sentences of one year or more. Jails are local facilities for person awaiting trial.

      b.   There are 3,365 locally administered jails in the United States, 2, 700 have county-level jurisdiction, and most are administered by an elected sheriff. An additional 600 or so are municipal jails

      c.   The capacity of jails varies greatly. The Los Angeles County Men's Central Jail holds more than six thousand inmates. Most jails, are much smaller: 67 percent hold fewer than fifty persons.

           i.   Small jails are becoming less numerous because of new construction and new regional, multi-county facilities.

2.   Who Is in Jail?

      a.   There are an estimated 11 million jail admissions every year. Nationally, over 630,000 people are in any given day. Many people are held for less than twenty-four hours, others may reside in jail as sentenced inmates for up to one year, a few may await their trials for more than a year.

      b.   Jail are disproportionately inhabited by men, minorities, the poorly educated, and those with low income.

3.   Managing Jails

      a.   Jail administrators face several problems:

           i.   Role of the Jail: Traditionally jails have been run by law enforcement agencies. Sheriffs think of jail as merely an extension of law enforcement activities, but many serve corrections functions because half of jail inmates are sentenced offenders under correctional authority. The primary function of jails is to hold persons awaiting trial and persons who have been sentenced as misdemeanants to terms of no more than one year.

           ii.   Inmate Characteristics: The mixture of offenders of widely diverse ages and criminal histories is another often cited problem in U.S. jails. Because most inmates are viewed as temporary residents, little attempt is made to classify them for either security or treatment purposes. Horror stories of the mistreatment of young offenders by older, stronger, and more violent inmates occasionally come to public attention. Increasingly jails are housing sentenced felony offenders for whom space is lacking at the state prison. Others held in jail are persons awaiting transportation to prison, and persons convicted of parole or probation violations. Because of the great turnover and because local control provides an incentive to keep costs down, correctional services (i.e., recreation, medical, education, vocational) are usually absent or minimal. Idleness may contribute to high levels of violence and suicides.

           iii.   Fiscal Problems: Jails help to control crime but also drain local revenues.

IDEAS IN PRACTICE: Many jurisdictions are using direct supervision which has a particular design and set of programs to use the physical plant to improve a staff's ability to interact with the inmate population and to provide services.

V. THE LAW OF CORRECTIONS

A.   Introduction

      1.   Until the 1960s, the courts, with few exceptions, took the position that the internal administration of prisons was an executive, not a judicial, function. Judges maintained a **hands-off policy.**

           a.   Judges accepted the view that they should not interfere with in the operational agencies dealing with probation, prison, and parole.

      2.   Since the 1960s, the courts have taken a larger role in protecting the constitutional rights of prisoners.

B.   Constitutional Rights of Prisoners

      1.   In 1964, the Supreme Court ruled in **Cooper v. Pate (1964)** that prisoners may sue state officials over the conditions of their confinement such as brutality by guards, inadequate nutritional and medical care, theft of personal property, and the denial of basic rights. These changes had the effect of decreasing the custodian's power and the prisoners' isolation from the larger society. This

case activated the use by prisoners of civil rights lawsuits under the Civil Rights Act of 1871 referred to as Section 1983 of the U.S. Code.

2. The first successful cases concerning prisoner rights involved the most excessive of prison abuses: brutality and inhuman physical conditions. Gradually, however, prison litigation has focused more directly on the daily activities of the institution, especially on the administrative rules that regulate inmates' conduct.

   a. **First Amendment**: Prisoner litigation has been most successful with respect to many of the restrictions of prison life--access to reading materials, censorship of mail, and some religious practices--have been successfully challenged by prisoners in the courts. For example, in 1974 the Court said that censorship of mail could be allowed only when there is a substantial governmental interest in maintaining security. The result has been a notable increase in communication between inmates and the outside world. However, in 1987 (*Turner v. Safley*), the Court upheld a Missouri ban on correspondence between inmates by saying that such regulation was reasonably related to legitimate penological interests. Challenges concerning the free exercise of religion have caused the judiciary some problems, especially when the practice may interfere with prison routine.
   The arrival in the 1960s of the Black Muslim religion in prisons holding large numbers of urban blacks set the stage for litigation demanding that this group be granted the same privileges as other faiths (special diets, access to clergy and religious publications, opportunities for group worship). Attorneys for Muslims were successful in winning several important cases that helped establish for prisoners the right to free exercise of religion.

   b. **Fourth Amendment**: The Fourth Amendment prohibits "unreasonable" searches and seizures and the courts have not been active in extending these protections to prisoners. Thus regulations viewed as reasonable in light of the institutions' needs for security and order may be justified. **Hudson v. Palmer (1984)** upheld the right of officials to search cells and confiscate any materials found. Decisions strike a fine balance between the right to privacy and institutional goals. Body searches have been harder for administrators to justify than cell searches, for example, but they have been upheld when they are part of a clear policy demonstrably related to an identifiable legitimate institutional need and when they are not intended to humiliate or degrade.

   c. **Eighth Amendment**: Eighth Amendment's prohibition of cruel and unusual punishments leads to claims involving the failure of prison administrators to provide minimal conditions necessary for health, to furnish reasonable levels of medical care, and to protect inmates from assault by other prisoners.
      i.   Three principal tests were initially applied by courts to determine whether conditions violate the protection of the Eighth Amendment: Whether the punishment shocks the general conscience of a civilized society, Whether the punishment is unnecessarily cruel, Whether the punishment goes beyond legitimate penal aims.
      ii. The "*totality of conditions*" may be such that life in the institution may constitute cruel and unusual punishment. Specific institutions in some states and the entire prison system in other states have been declared to violate the Constitution.

   d. **Fourteenth Amendment**:
      i.   One word and two clauses of the Fourteenth Amendment are relevant to the question of prisoners' rights The relevant word is state and the two clauses are those requiring (*procedural*) *due process* and *equal protection*.
      ii. Due Process in Prison Discipline: Administrative discretion in determining disciplinary procedures can usually be exercised within the prison walls without challenge.
      iii. Yet in a series of decisions in the 1970s the Supreme Court began to insist that procedural fairness be included in the most sensitive of institutional decisions: the process by which inmates are sent to solitary confinement and the method by which "good time" credit may be lost because of misconduct. For example, in **Wolff v. McDonnell (1974),** the Court extended certain procedural rights to inmates: to receive notice of the complaint, to have a fair hearing, to confront

witnesses, to be assisted in preparing for the hearing, and to be given a written statement of the decision. Yet the Court also said that there is no right to counsel at a disciplinary hearing. Most prisons have established rules that provide some elements of due process in disciplinary proceedings. In many institutions, a disciplinary committee receives the charges, conducts hearings, and decides guilt and punishment.

     iv.   Equal Protection: Institutional practices or conditions that discriminate against prisoners on the basis of race or religion have been held unconstitutional. In *Lee v. Washington (1968)*, the Supreme Court firmly established that racial discrimination may not be official policy within prison walls. Racial segregation is justified only as a temporary expedient during periods when violence between the races is demonstrably imminent. The most recent Equal protection claims have involved issues concerning female offenders but the Supreme Court has yet to rule on this matter.

  e. Impact of the Prisoners' Rights Movement

     i.   The prisoners' rights movement led to concrete improvements in institutional living conditions and administrative practices. Law libraries and legal assistance are now generally available; communication with the outside is easier; religious practices are protected; inmate complaint procedures have been developed; and due process requirements are emphasized.

C.   <u>Law and Community Corrections</u>

  1.   Two-thirds of adults under supervision live in the community on probation or parole. Court have addressed issues concerning due process and searches and seizures. Conditions of parole may interfere with their constitutional rights.

  2.   In *Mempa v. Rhay* (1967), the Supreme Court determined that a state probationer had the right to counsel at a revocation proceeding, but nowhere in the opinion did the Court refer to any requirement for a hearing.

  3.   In *Morrisey v. Brewer* (1972), the Court ruled that due process rights require prompt, informal, two –part inquiry before an impartial hearing officer before parole is revoked. The parolee may present relevant information and confront witnesses.

  4.   In *Gagnon v. Scarpelli* (1973), the Supreme Court ruled that revocation of probation and parole requires a preliminary and a final hearing.

    a.   At these hearings the probationer has the right to cross-examine witnesses and to be given notice of the alleged violations and a written report of the proceedings.

    b.   The Supreme Court ruled that although there is no automatic right to counsel this decision is to be made on a case-by-case basis. It is then that the judge decides upon incarceration and its length. If the violation has been minor, the judge may simply continue probation, but with greater restrictions.

D.   <u>Law and Correctional Personnel</u>

  1.   Laws and regulations define the relationships between correctional administrators and their staff.

  2.   Two important aspects of correctional work: civil service laws and liability of correctional personnel

    a.   Civil service laws set procedures for hiring, promoting, assigning, disciplining, and firing public employees. These laws protect employees from arbitrary actions by supervisors. Civil Rights Act of 1964 prohibits discrimination based on race, gender, national origin, and religion.

    b.   The Supreme Court ruled that Prisoners can bring lawsuits against correctional officials in *Cooper v. Pate* (1964). Public employees and their agencies may be sued when a person's civil rights are violated by the agency's "customs and usages."-*Monell v. Dept. of Social Services for the City of New York* (1978)

VIII. CORRECTIONAL POLICY TRENDS

A.   Introduction
      1.   Since the mid 1970s, the size of the prison population has risen dramatically. This has meant a 500 percent increase in budgets, more than 3.8 million persons on probation, 750,000 under parole supervision and 2 million persons in prison and jails.

B.   Community Corrections
      1.   Escalating prison grown has captured the public's attention, yet the number of person's on probation and parole has grown dramatically. Why? Because of more arrests, successful prosecutions and the lower costs of probation compared to incarceration.
      2.   POLICY DEBATE: Is there a Prison-Commercial Complex? Are corporations expanding their domain by working with legislators who are getting "tough on crime?" or Is prison expansion simply related to the need for increased space to house more serious offenders?
      3.   Probation
            a.   People on probation make up over seventy percent of the correctional population but resources such as money and staff have not risen accordingly.
      4.   Parole
            a.   The number of persons on parole has also grown rapidly. Over one-half million felons are released from prison each year and allowed to live within a community under supervision.

C.   Incarceration
      1.   Since 1973, the incarceration rate has quadrupled but crime levels have stayed the same. In 2001, the nation's prison population rose only one percent which is the lowest since 1979. It is difficult to predict if this trend will continue. There are some regional differences in increases in prison populations.
      2.   Five reasons often given to account for the growth of the American prison population:
            a.   Increased Arrests and More Likely Incarceration
            b.   Tougher Sentences: hypothesis is a hardening of public attitudes toward criminals during the past decade reflected in longer sentences, in a smaller proportion of those convicted being granted probation, and in fewer being released at the time of the first parole hearing. Move toward determinate sentencing in many states means that many offenders are now spending more time in prison.
            c.   Prison Construction: the increased rate of incarceration may be related to the creation of additional space in the nation's prisons. Again, public attitudes in favor of more punitive sentencing policies may have influenced legislators to build more prisons. If serious offenses are less common, judges will be inclined to use prison space for less harmful offenders.
      CLOSE-UP: Connecticut: Trying to Build Its Way Out. The State of Connecticut launched a massive $1 billion program to build prisons to deal with the problem of overcrowded prisons.
            d.   War on Drugs: Crusades against illegal narcotics have produced stiff mandatory sentences by federal government and states.
            e.   State Politics: Election of "law and Order" governors associated with increases in prison populations even in states with lower crime rates than neighboring states.
            f.   Because of public attitudes, crime rates, and the expansion of prison space, incarceration rates are likely to remain high. A policy shift may occur if taxpayers begin to object to the high costs.
      WHAT AMERICANS THINK: Given the attitudes of a majority of Americans toward crime and punishment, fear of crime, and the expansion of prison space, incarceration rates will likely remain high.

REVIEW OF KEY TERMS

Fill in the appropriate term for each statement

penitentiary
community corrections
congregate system
corrections
crime control model of corrections
Enlightenment
medical model
reformatory
rehabilitation model
separate confinement
lease system
Cincinnati Declaration of Principles
supermax prisons
hands-off policy
Cooper v. Pate (1964)
First Amendment
Fourth Amendment
Eighth Amendment
Fourteenth Amendment
Hudson v. Palmer (1984)
Wolff v. McDonnell (1974)

1. _____ refers to the great number of programs, services, facilities, and organizations responsible for the management of people accused or convicted of criminal offenses.

2. _____ is where inmates were released to contractors who provided prisoners with food and clothing in exchange for their labor.

3. _____ is an institution for young offenders that emphasizes training, a mark system of classification, indeterminate sentences, and parole.

4. _____ advocated a new design for penology: that prisons should operate according to a philosophy of inmate change, with reformation rewarded by release.

5. _____ was a philosophical movement that emphasized the individual limitations on government, and rationalism.

6. _____ was based upon the assumption that criminal behavior is caused by biological or psychological conditions that require treatment.

7. _____ is a model of corrections based on the assumption that criminal behavior can be controlled by more use of incarceration and other forms of strict supervision.

8. _____ are designed to hold the most disruptive, violent, and corrigible offenders.

9. _____ is a penitentiary system developed in New York in which prisoners worked together silently during the day before being held in isolation at night.

10. _____ is an institution intended to punish criminals by isolating them from society and from one another so that they could reflect on their misdeeds and repent.

11. _____ is a penitentiary system developed in Pennsylvania by the Quakers involving isolation in individual cells.

12. _____ s a model of corrections based on the assumption that the reintegration of the offender into society should be the goal of the criminal justice system.

13. _____ is a model based on behavioral and social sciences that emphasized the need to restore a convicted offender to a constructive place in society through some form of vocational or educational training or therapy.

14. _____ is the orientation that judges had toward prisoners' rights prior to the 1960s.

15. In the case of _____, the Supreme Court declared that officials may search cells without a warrant and seize materials found there.

16. In the case of _____, the Supreme Court declared that prisoners are entitled to file civil rights lawsuits against government officials.

17. In the case of_____, the Supreme Court declared that the basic elements of procedural due process must be present when decisions are made concerning the discipline of an inmate.

18. The _____ contains the due process clause that limits state power.

19. The _____ prohibits unreasonable searches and seizures.

20. The _____ prevents Congress from making laws respecting the establishment of religion or prohibiting its free exercise.

21. The _____ has been tied to prisoners' need for decent treatment and minimum health standards.

REVIEW OF KEY PEOPLE
Fill in the appropriate person for each statement
John Howard
Mary Belle Harris
Elizabeth Fry
Elam Llynds
Charles Williams
Zebulon Brockway

1. _____ was the first prisoner in the Eastern Penitentiary near Philadelphia in 1829.

2. Under the New York System, the warden at Auburn penitentiary, _____, was convinced that convicts were incorrigible and that industrial efficiency should be the overriding purpose of the prison.

3. _____ was the English reformer who is associated with sparking reform for women offenders.

4. _____ was the English reformer whose investigation of prison conditions led Parliament to enact reforms and sparked reform movements in England and the United States.

5. The first reformatory took shape in 1876 at Elmira, New York when _____ was appointed superintendent.

6. The first federal prison for women opened in Alderson, West Virginia with _____ as the warden.

SELF-TEST SECTION

Multiple Choice Questions

11.1.How many adults are under some form of correctional control in The United States?
a) roughly 1 million
b) roughly 3.5 million
c) roughly 6.5 million
d) roughly 10.9 million
e) roughly 20 million

11.2. What is the ratio of men under correctional control to the entire population of men ?
a) 1 out of every 5
b) 1 out of every 10
c) 1 out of every 20
d) 1 out of every 50
e) 1 out of every 100

11.3. What is the ratio of women under correctional control to the entire population of women ?
a) 1 out of every 5
b) 1 out of every 10
c) 1 out of every 20
d) 1 out of every 50
e) 1 out of every 100

11.4. What percent of persons under correctional supervision are living in the community on probation or parole?
a) 5 percent
b) 25 percent
c) 45 percent
d) 70 percent
e) 90 percent

11.5. What has happened to the prison population over the past three decade in the U. S.?
a) the prison population has stayed the same
b) the prison population has double
c) the prison population has quadrupled
d) the prison population has been cut in half
e) the prison population has been cut 75 percent

11.6. At what level of government is corrections found in the U. S.?
a) federal
b) state
c) city
d) county
e) all of the above

11.7. Prior to 1800, who did Americans copy in using physical punishment as the main criminal sanction?
a) Europeans
b) Japanese
c) Africans
d) Mexicans
e) Chinese

175

11.8. As sheriff of Bedfordshire, England, who was especially influential in promoting the reform of corrections?
a) John Howard
b) Michel Foucault
c) Zebulon Brockway
d) Benjamin Rush
e) Elizabeth Fry

11.9. Who inspired the Philadelphia Society for Alleviating the Miseries of Public Prisons which formed in 1787?
a) John Howard
b) Michel Foucault
c) Zebulon Brockway
d) Benjamin Rush
e) Elizabeth Fry

11.10. What was the first penitentiary created by the Pennsylvania legislature in 1790?
a) Philadelphia Jail Institute
b) Pittsburgh Prison House
c) Auburn House
d) Walnut Street Jail
e) Sing Sing Prison

11.11. Who was the warden at the Auburn Penitentiary who was convinced that convicts were incorrigible and that industrial efficiency should be the overriding purpose of the prison?
a) John Williams
b) John Howard
c) Elizabeth Fry
d) Benjamin Rush
e) Elam Llynds

11.12. Which system rented prisoners to firms that used them in milling, logging, cotton picking, mining and railroad construction?
a) New York system
b) Pennsylvania system
c) lease system
d) Auburn system
e) loan system

11.13. The prison ideologies of the East did not greatly influence penology in the West, except for the state of…
a) Arizona
b) California
c) New Mexico
d) Oregon
e) Nevada

11.14. Which law passed by Congress restricted the employment of federal prisoners?
a) Federal Bureau of Prisons Act of 1930
b) Anticontract Law of 1887
c) Hatch Act of 1940
d) Pendleton Act of 1883
e) The Prisoners Services Act of 1982

11.15. What system based prisoner release on performance through voluntary labor, participation in educational and religious programs, and good behavior?
a) enlightenment system
b) congregate system
c) lease system
d) mark system
e) Walnut Jail system

11.16. When did the reformatory system start to decline?
a) by the outbreak of the Civil War
b) by the outbreak World War I
c) by the outbreak of World War II
d) during the Korean conflict
e) during the Vietnam conflict

11.17. When and where was the Women's Prison Association was formed?
a) 1804 in Boston
b) 1844 in New York
c) 1903 in Cleveland
d) 1925 in Kansas City
e) 1987 in Las Vegas

11.18. Who was the head matron of the women's wing at Sing Sing (1844 to 1848), sought to implement Elizabeth's Fry's ideas but was thwarted by the male overseers and legislators and was forced to resign?
a) John Williams
b) John Howard
c) Elizabeth Farnham
d) Benjamin Rush
e) Zebulon Brockway

11.19. What was NOT addressed in the Cincinnati Declaration of Principles?
a) rewarding reformed prisoners with release
b) fixed sentences should be replaced with indeterminate sentences
c) classification of prisoners on the basis of character and improvement
d) the problems of female offenders
e) all of the above were addressed

11.20. When and where was the first independent female-run prison opened?
a) 1809 in Massachusetts
b) 1824 in New Jersey
c) 1873 in Indiana
d) 1953 in Missouri
e) 1976 in California

11.21. Who was the warden of the first federal prison for women which opened in Alderson, West Virginia in 1927?
a) Mary Belle Harris
b) John Howard
c) Elizabeth Farnham
d) Benjamin Rush
e) Elizabeth Fry

11.22. What did the U. S. Supreme Court rule in *Hudson v. Palmer (1984)*?
a) the Court upheld the right of officials to search cells and confiscate any materials
b) the Court ordered the Texas prison system to address a series of unconstitutional conditions
c) the Court firmly established that racial discrimination may not be official policy within prison walls
d) the Court ruled that because of differences and needs, identical treatment is not required for men and women
e) the Court ruled that prisoners do NOT have rights

11.23. What did the U. S. Supreme Court rule in *Pargo v. Elliott (1995)*?
a) the Court upheld the right of officials to search cells and confiscate any materials
b) the Court ordered the Texas prison system to address a series of unconstitutional conditions
c) the Court firmly established that racial discrimination may not be official policy within prison walls
d) the Court ruled that because of differences and needs, identical treatment is not required for men and women
e) the Court ruled that prisoners do NOT have rights

11.24. What did the U. S. Supreme Court rule in *Pernnsylvania Board of Pardons and Parole v. Scott (1998)*?
a) the Court upheld the right of officials to search the homes of inmates who had been paroled
b) the Court ordered the Pennsylvania prison system to address a series of unconstitutional conditions
c) the Court established that evidence that would be barred from use in a criminal trial can be used in parole revocation hearings
d) the Court ruled that identical treatment is not required for men and women at parole hearings
e) the Court ruled that prisoners do NOT have rights at parole hearings

11.25. Which of the following measures to reduce prison overcrowding is favored by ninety percent of the American population favor?
a)shorter sentences
b)early release for prisoners for good behavior
c)local program to keep non-violent and first time offenders active in the community
d)giving the parole board more authority to release offenders
e)increasing taxes to build more prisons

True and False Questions

_____11.1. The U. S. and Canada have roughly the same population of prisoners.

_____11.2. Elam Llynds started a contract labor system.

_____11.3. The mark system of classification placed the prisoner's fate in his own hands.

_____11.4. Group therapy became part of rehabilitation after World War II.

_____11.5. John Howard was the first prisoner executed at Sing Sing prison.

_____11.6. From 1776 to around 1830, the emphasis shifted to a belief that crime was a result of forces operating in the environment.

_____11.7. The United States now has the highest incarceration rate in the developed world.

_____11.8. The Enlightenment focused upon increasing the powers of government, group behavior, and irrationalism.

_____11.9. The crime control model of corrections emphasized incarceration as a way to solve the crime problem.

_____11.10. The U. S. Bureau of Prisons was created by executive order in 1860 by Abraham Lincoln.

_____11.11. Community corrections focuses on reintegrating the offender into society.

_____11.12. Prisoners have the First Amendment right to free exercise of religion.

_____11.13. Women comprise roughly 35 percent of the incarcerated population.

_____11.14. Private run prisons do not exist anymore in the U. S.

_____11.15. Private prisons provide better security than government-operated prisons.

_____11.16. The crime control model of corrections is less punitive than the community model.

_____11.17. There is no difference between prisons or jails.

_____11.18. Prisoners do NOT have a right against cruel and unusual punishment.

_____11.19. The primary function of jails is to hold persons awaiting trial and persons who have been sentenced for misdemeanors to terms of less than one year.

_____11.20. Most jails are at the county level.

WORKSHEET 11.1: HISTORY OF CORRECTIONS

Imagine that you are the head of a state department of corrections during several eras of American history. Describe each of the following approaches to corrections as you would implement them to make them work as well as they could. Then describe the drawbacks of each approach.

Separate Confinement (Pennsylvania) _____

_____

_____

_____

Drawbacks:_____

_____

_____

Congregate System (New York)_____

_____

_____

_____

Drawbacks:_____

_____

_____

Rehabilitation Model_____

_____

_____

_____

Drawbacks:_____

_____

_____

Community Model_____

_____

_____

Drawbacks:_____

_____

WORKSHEET 11.2 : PRISONERS' RIGHTS: YOU ARE THE JUDGE

Corrections officers at the main gate receive a report that a fight involving twelve prisoners has broken out in Cellblock C and that the corrections officers in Cellblock C are unable to break up the fight. Seven corrections officers run down the corridor from the main gate toward Cellblock C. As they round a corner, they practically run into inmate Joe Cottrell who is mopping and waxing the corridor floor. One officer grabs Cottrell by the shoulders and throws him aside while saying, "Get out of the way!" Cottrell falls into a wall, dislocates his shoulder, and later files a lawsuit against the officer by claiming that the rough treatment and resulting injury violated his Eighth Amendment right against cruel and unusual punishment. Were his Eighth Amendment rights violated? Explain.

_____

_____

_____

_____

_____

_____

A prison chapel is used every Sunday for Christian services. A small group of prisoners reserve the chapel for each Tuesday evening where they meet to study an ancient religion from Asia that they claim to follow. For two years, they use the chapel every Tuesday to meditate and discuss books about their religion, and they do not cause any trouble. Then, one year Christmas falls on a Wednesday, and the Asian religion group is told that they cannot have their meeting because the chapel is needed for a Christian Christmas eve service. They file a lawsuit claiming that their First Amendment right to free exercise of religion is being violated because they cannot use the chapel on Christmas eve. Are their rights being violated? Explain.

_____

_____

_____

_____

_____

_____

_____

WORKSHEET 11.3: CAUSES OF RISING PRISON POPULATIONS

Describe each of the theories used to explain the increase in imprisonment of offenders.

Tougher Sentencing_____

_____

_____

_____

Increased Arrests and More Likely Incarceration_____

_____

_____

_____

State Politics_____

_____

_____

_____

Construction_____

_____

_____

_____

War on Drugs_____

_____

_____

_____

Which theory do you believe provides the best explanation? Explain why.

_____

_____

_____

_____

CHAPTER 12

COMMUNITY CORRECTIONS: PROBATION AND INTERMEDIATE SANCTIONS

LEARNING OBJECTIVES

After covering the material in this chapter, students should understand:

1.   the assumptions underlying community corrections;

2.   the evolution of probation, the nature of probation services, and probation revocation;

3.   intermediate sanctions including fines, restitution, forfeiture, home confinement, community service, intensive probation, and boot camps;

4.   the difficulties in implementing intermediate sanctions;

5.   the future of community corrections.

CHAPTER SUMMARY
Community supervision through probation and intermediate sanctions are a growing part of the criminal justice system. Probation is imposed on more than half of offenders. Persons with this sentence live in the community according to conditions set by the judge and under the supervision of a probation officer. Intermediate sanctions are designed as punishments that are more restrictive than probation and less restrictive than prison. The range of intermediate sanctions allows judges to design sentences that incorporate one or more of the punishments. Some intermediate sanctions are implemented by courts (fines, restitution, forfeiture), others in the community (home confinement, community service, day reporting centers, intensive supervision probation) and in institutions and the community (boot camps). The use of community corrections is expected to grow in the twenty-first century, despite the implementation problems.

CHAPTER OUTLINE
I. CASE EXAMPLE: Actress **Winona Ryder** attempted to leave a Saks Fifth Avenue store without paying for items. Her bag was allegedly found to contain nearly $5,000 worth of merchandise as well as unauthorized prescription painkillers. Ryder was charged with second-degree burglary, grand theft, and possession of a controlled substance, all felonies. She faced the possibility of three years in prison. However, Ryder was sentenced to three years probation plus community service, counseling, and restitution. Is justice well served by a community sentence in this case? During the nineteenth-century reform period, it was recognized that supervision in the community was a more appropriate means to bring about the desired change in some offenders. Although probation developed in the 1840s, many states still relied more on incarceration than on probation, and it was not until the 1960s that a variety of community alternatives was developed. Tough sentences of incarceration imposed during the 1980s and the "war on drugs" produced high costs for state governments. In the late 1980s with prison crowding becoming a major national problem, there was new interest in creating a set of intermediate sanctions--intensive probation supervision, home confinement, and electronic monitoring.

II.   COMMUNITY CORRECTIONS: ASSUMPTIONS

      A.   **Community corrections** aims at building ties that can reintegrate the offender into the community: assumes that the offender must change, but it also recognizes that factors within the community that might encourage criminal behavior (unemployment, for example) must change, too. Four factors are usually cited in support of community corrections:
            1.   Some offenders' background characteristics or crimes are not serious enough to warrant incarceration.
            2.   Community supervision is cheaper than incarceration.

3. If rehabilitation is measured by recidivism, or returning to crime, prison is no more effective than community supervision. In fact, some studies show that just being in prison raises the offender's potential for **recidivism**, when a person commits repeat offenses.

4. Ex-inmates require both support and supervision as they try to remake their lives in the community.

B. Central to the community corrections approach is a belief in the "least restrictive alternative," the notion that the criminal sanction should be applied only to the minimum extent necessary to meet the community's need for protection, the gravity of the offense, and society's need for deserved punishment.

C. "WHAT AMERICANS THINK"- Surveys have found there is support for community-based punishments for some type of offenders.

III. PROBATION: CORRECTION WITHOUT INCARCERATION

A. Introduction

1. **Probation** denotes the conditional release of the offender into the community under supervision. It imposes conditions and retains the authority of the sentencing court to modify the conditions of sentence or to re-sentence the offender. Conditions may include drug tests, curfews, and orders to stay away from certain people or parts of town.

2. Probation may be combined with other sanctions, such as fines, restitution, or community service.

3. The probationer who violates these terms or is arrested for another offense may have probation revoked by a judge and be sent to prison.

4. The number of probationers is at a record level and is still rising. Prison overcrowding forces judges to place more offenders convicted of serious crimes, especially drug crimes, on probation. This means that probation will be dealing with an increasing number of clients whose risk of recidivating is high.

5. The public frequently views probation as merely a "slap on the wrist."

6. Probation officers frequently have high case-loads that make it difficult to provide adequate supervision.

B. Origins and Evolution of Probation

1. **John Augustus,** a boot maker in Boston, has become known as the world's first probation officer. By persuading a judge in the Boston Police Court in 1841 to place a convicted offender in his custody for a brief period, Augustus was able to assist his probationer so that the man appeared to be rehabilitated when he returned for sentencing.

2. Massachusetts developed the first statewide probation system in 1880, and by 1920 twenty-one other states had followed suit. The federal courts were authorized to hire probation officers in 1925, and by the beginning of World War II forty-four states had implemented the concept.

3. Probation officers began with a casework model to be actively involved in the family, employment, free time, and religion of first-time and minor offenders.

4. With the rising influence of psychology in the 1920s, the probation officer continued as a caseworker, but the emphasis moved to therapeutic counseling in the office rather than on assistance in the field. This shift in emphasis brought a number of important changes.

   a. The officer was no longer primarily a community supervisor charged with enforcing a particular morality.

   b. The officer became more of a clinical social worker whose goal was to help the offender solve psychological and social problems.

   c. The offender was expected to become actively involved in the treatment program.

   d. In keeping with the goals of the Rehabilitation Model, the probation officer had extensive discretion to diagnose the problem and treat it.

5. During the 1960s, perhaps reflecting the emphasis of the war on poverty, a third shift occurred: rather than counseling offenders in their offices, probation officers provided

them with concrete social services, such as assistance with employment, housing, finances, and education.

    a.   Instead of being a counselor or therapist, the probation officer was to be an advocate, dealing with the private and public institutions on the offender's behalf.

6.   In the late 1970s the orientation of probation again changed. The goals of rehabilitation and reintegration gave way to an orientation widely referred to as risk control. This approach, dominant today, tries to minimize the probability that an offender will commit a new crime.

    a.   The amount and type of supervision provided are a function of estimates of risk that the probationer will return to criminal behavior.

C.   <u>Organization of Probation</u>

1.   As a form of corrections, probation falls under the executive branch and people usually see it as a concern of state government but in many states it is administered by the judiciary, usually with local control.

2.   Locally based probation accounts for about two thirds of all persons under probation supervision.

3.   Frequently the locally elected county judges are really in charge. However, judges usually know little about corrections and probation administration.

4.   Perhaps the strongest argument in favor of judicial control is that probation works best when there is a close relationship between the judge and the supervising officer.

5.   Some states have combined probation and parole in the same department, even though parolees are quite different than probationers. Parolees need greater supervision and have significant adjustment problems when they come out of prison.

D.   <u>Probation Services</u>

1.   Probation officers have come to be expected to act as both police personnel and social workers. They prepare presentence reports for the courts and they supervise clients in order to keep them out of trouble and to assist them in the community.

    a.   Individual officers may emphasize one role over the other, and the potential for conflict is great.

2.   The 50-unit caseload established in the 1930s by the National Probation Association was reduced to 35 by the President's Commission in 1967; yet the national average is currently about 150, and in extreme cases it reaches more than 300.

3.   However, recent evidence indicates that the size of the caseload is less significant than the quality of the services and supervision.

4.   During the past decade probation officials have developed methods of classifying clients according to their service needs, the element of risk that they pose to the community and the chance of recidivism.

    a.   Probationers may be granted less supervision as they continue to live without violation of the conditions of their sentence.

5.   In dangerous urban neighborhoods, direct supervision can be a dangerous task for the probation officer. In some urban areas, probationers are merely required to telephone or mail reports of their current residence and employment. It such cases, which justification for the criminal sanction--deserved punishment, rehabilitation, deterrence, or incapacitation-- is being realized? If none is being realized, the offender is getting off free.

E.   <u>Revocation and Termination of Probation</u>

1.   Probation ends by a person successfully completing probation or the probationary status is revoked because of misbehavior. In 2001, a national survey of probationers found that 60 percent of adults released from probation successfully completed their sentences, while only 13 percent had been reincarcerated. Revocation of parole can occur for either a technical violation (failure to abide by rules and conditions of probation) or a new arrest

2.   Probation officers and judges have widely varying notions of what constitutes grounds for revoking probation. Once the officer has decided to call a violation to the attention of the court, the probationer may be arrested or summoned for a revocation hearing.

3.   The current emphasis is on avoiding incarceration except for flagrant and continual violation of the conditions of probation, thus most revocations occur because of a new arrest or conviction

A QUESTION OF ETHICS: Should probation be revoked if a person is given an almost impossible assignment to complete as fulfillment of his/her probation?

4.   In **Mempa v. Rhay (1967)** and Gagnon v. Scarpelli (1973), the Supreme Court determined that a state probationer had the right to counsel at a revocation proceeding, but nowhere in the opinion did the Court refer to any requirement for a hearing. In the Supreme Court ruled that revocation of probation and parole requires a preliminary and a final hearing.

     a.   At these hearings the probationer has the right to cross-examine witnesses and to be given notice of the alleged violations and a written report of the proceedings.

     b.   The Supreme Court ruled that although there is no automatic right to counsel this decision is to be made on a case-by-case basis. It is then that the judge decides upon incarceration and its length. If the violation has been minor, the judge may simply continue probation, but with greater restrictions.

F.   Assessing Probation

1.   Critics argue that probation does nothing. Yet, the importance of probation for public safety has never been greater because it is critical for probationers to be tracked by their officers.

2.   Probation does produce less recidivism than incarceration, but researchers now wonder if this effect is a direct result of supervision or an indirect result of the maturation process.

     a.   Most offenders placed on probation do not become career criminals, their criminal activity is short-lived, and they become stable citizens as they get jobs and marry.

3.   What rallies support for probation is its relatively low cost: keeping an offender on probation rather than behind bars costs roughly $1,000 a year, resulting in a savings to the criminal justice system of more than $20,000 yearly.

4.   The new demands upon probation have given rise to calls for increased electronic monitoring and for risk management systems that will differentiate the levels of supervision required for different offenders.

IV.   INTERMEDIATE SANCTIONS IN THE COMMUNITY

A.   Introduction

1.   Intermediate sanctions may be viewed as a continuum--a range of punishments that vary in terms of level of intrusiveness and control.

     a.   Probation plus a fine or community service may be appropriate for minor offenses while six weeks of boot camp followed by intensive probation supervision may be the deserved punishment for someone who has been convicted of a more serious crime.

     b.   Each individual intermediate sanction may be imposed singly or in combination with others.

B.   Intermediate Sanctions Administered Primarily by the Judiciary

1.   All involve the transfer of money or property from the offender to the government, the judiciary is deemed as the proper branch to not only impose the sanction but also to collect that which is due.

2.   **Fines** are routinely imposed today for offenses ranging from traffic violations to felonies. Recent studies have shown that the fine is used very widely as a criminal sanction and that probably well over $1 billion in fines are collected annually by courts across the country.

3. Judges cite the difficulty of collecting and enforcing fines as the reason that they do not make greater use of this punishment. Judges report that fine enforcement, which is the judiciary's responsibility, receives a low priority.

4. Since offenders tend to be poor, the judges are concerned that fines would be paid from the proceeds of additional illegal acts.

    a. Reliance on fines as an alternative to incarceration might mean that the affluent would be able to "buy" their way out of jail and that the poor would have to serve time.

5. Fines are used extensively in Europe, and they are enforced. They are normally the sole sanction for a wide range of crimes. The amounts are geared to the severity of the offense and the resources of the offender.

    a. Sweden and West Germany have developed the "day fine:" fines levied are adjusted to take into account the differing economic circumstances of offenders who have committed the same crime.

    b. Experiments with the day fine concept are now taking place in several states.

6. **Restitution** is repayment to a victim who has suffered some form of financial loss as a result of the offender's crime.

    a. It is only since the late 1970s that it has been institutionalized in many areas. It is usually carried out as one of the conditions of probation.

7. Forfeiture: With passage of the Racketeer Influence and Corrupt Organizations Act (RICO) and the Continuing Criminal Enterprise Act (CCE) in 1970, Congress resurrected forfeiture, a criminal sanction that received little use since the American Revolution.

    a. Similar laws are now found in most states, particularly with respect to controlled substances and organized crime.

8. **Forfeiture** is seizure by the government of property derived from or used in criminal activity. Forfeiture proceedings can take both a civil and a criminal form. Using the civil law, property utilized in criminal activity (contraband, equipment to manufacture illegal drugs, automobiles) can be seized without a finding of guilt. Criminal forfeiture is a punishment imposed as a result of conviction at the time of sentencing. It requires that the offender relinquish various assets related to the crime.

    a. An estimated one billion dollar's worth of assets was confiscated from drug dealers by state and federal officials during 1990.

    b. In a 1993 opinion, the Supreme Court ruled that the Eighth Amendment's ban on excessive fines requires that there be a relationship between the seriousness of the offense and the property that is taken.

    c. Congress passed a law in 2000 that protected home owners' property from being seized if they could demonstrate their innocence by a preponderance of the evidence. This was necessary to protect a grandparent who might have a grandchild using the home for illegal activity such as drug trafficking.

WORK PERSPECTIVE: Carmell Dennis, Executive Director, STRIVE Program in Battle Creek, Michigan.

C. <u>Intermediate Sanctions Administered in the Community</u>

1. With electronic monitoring, **home confinement**, a sentence imposed by a court requiring convicted offenders to spend all or part of the time in their own residence, has gained new attention from criminal justice planners.

    a. Conditions are placed on permissible actions; some offenders are allowed to go to a place of employment, education, or treatment during the day, but must return to their residence by a specific hour.

    b. Can be used as a sole sanction or in combination with other penalties and can be imposed at almost any point in the criminal justice process: during the pretrial period, after a short term in jail or prison, or as a condition of probation or parole.

    c. There are estimates that 100,000 offenders are being monitored at any given time.

2. Two basic types of electronic devices are now in use.

a.　　A continuously signaling device has a transmitter that is attached to the probationer. A receiver-dialer is attached to the probationer's home telephone. It reports to a central computer at the monitoring agency when the signal stops, indicating that the offender is not in the house, alerting correctional officials of the unauthorized absence.

　　　b.　　A second device uses a computer programmed to telephone the probationer randomly or at specific times. The offender has a certain number of minutes to answer the phone and to verify that he or she is indeed the person under supervision.

3.　Problems:

　　　a.　　Some criminal justice scholars have questioned the constitutionality of the sanction, saying that it may violate the Fourth Amendment's protection against unreasonable searches and seizures.

　　　b.　　Technical problems with the monitoring devices have dogged many experiments.

　　　c.　　Failure rates among those under house arrest may prove to be high. Being one's own warden is a difficult task and visits by friends and enticements of the community may become too great for many offenders.

　　　d.　　Some observers believe that four months of full-time monitoring is about the limit before a violation will occur.

4.　**Community Service** is unpaid service to the public to overcome or compensate society for some of the harm caused by the crime; it may take a variety of forms, including work in a social service agency, cleaning parks, or assisting the poor.

　　　a.　　The sentence specifies the number of hours to be worked and usually requires supervision by a probation officer.

　　　b.　　Labor unions and workers criticize it, saying that offenders are taking jobs from crime-free citizens.

　　　c.　　Some experts believe that if community service is used as the sole sanction, the result will be that certain courts may allow affluent offenders to purchase relatively mild punishments.

5.　**Day reporting centers** incorporate a multitude of common correctional methods. For example, in some centers, offenders are required to be in the facility for eight hours, or to report into the center for urine checks before going to work. In others, the treatment regime is comparable to that of a halfway house—but without the offender living in a residential facility. Drug and alcohol treatment, literacy programs, and job searches may be carried out in the center.

　　　a.　　If only specially selected offenders are chosen for these centers, it is difficult to assess the centers' effectiveness.

6.　**Intensive probation supervision** is a way of using probation as an intermediate punishment. It is thought that daily contact between the probationer and officer may cut rearrests and may permit offenders who might otherwise go to prison to be released into the community.

　　　a.　　Probation diversion places offenders deemed too risky for routine supervision under intensive monitoring.

　　　b.　　Institutional diversion selects low-risk offenders sentenced to prison and provides supervision for them in the community.

　　　c.　　Each officer has only twenty clients, and frequent face-to-face contacts are required. Because the intention is to place high-risk offenders who would normally be incarcerated in the community instead, it is expected that resources will be saved.

　　　d.　　Judges and prosecutors may like ISP because it gives the appearance of being "tough" on offenders by setting many specific conditions.

　　　e.　　ISP programs have higher failure rates, in part because officers can detect more violations through close contact.

　　　f.　　In several states, offenders have expressed a preference for serving a prison term rather than being placed under the demanding conditions of ISP.

TECHNOLOGY ISSUES IN CRIMINAL JUSTICE: Stalker Trackers sounds an alarm and notifies authorities if an offender comes to close to a victim's home.

D.   Sanctions Administered in Institutions and Community
1.   **Boot camps** now operate in thirty-six states and the Federal Bureau of Prisons. They are all based on the belief that young offenders can be "shocked" out of their criminal ways if they undergo a physically rigorous, disciplined, and demanding regimen for a short period, usually three or four months, before being returned to the community for supervision. Programs sometimes referred to as **"shock incarceration."**
- a.   Like the Marine Corps, most programs emphasize a spit-and-polish environment and keep the offenders in a disciplined routine constantly to help build self-esteem.
- b.   On successful completion of the program, offenders are released to the community and remain under supervision. At this point probation officers take over, and the conditions of the sentence are imposed.
- c.   Critics believe that the emphasis on physical training does not get to the bottom of the real problems affecting young offenders.
- d.   Other critics note that shock incarceration builds esprit de corp and solidarity, characteristics that have the potential for improving the leadership qualities of the young offender and that when taken back to the streets may actually enhance a criminal career.
- e.   The director of Arizona's prisons asked for the elimination of boot camps because of the program's ineffectiveness.
2.   CLOSE-UP: After Boot Camp a Harder Discipline. **Nelson Colon's** four months in a New Jersey boot camp where he experienced the rigors of military life.

E.   Implementing Intermediate Sanctions
1.   In many states there is competition as to which agency will receive additional funding to run the intermediate sanctions programs. Probation organizations argue that they know the field, have the experienced staff, and --given the additional resources--could do an excellent job.
- a.   Critics of probation argue that the traditional agencies are hide-bound and not receptive to the innovations of intermediate sanctions.
2.   A second issue concerns the type of offender given an intermediate sanction. One school of thought emphasizes the seriousness of the offense, the other concentrates on the problems of the offender.
- a.   Some agencies want to accept into their intermediate sanctions program only those offenders who will succeed. The agencies are concerned about their success ratio, especially as this factor might jeopardize future funding.
- b.   Critics point out that this strategy leads to "creaming" (i.e., taking the cream of the crop), taking the most promising offenders and leaving those with problems to traditional sanctions.
3.   **"Net widening"** is the term used to describe a process in which the new sanction increases, rather than reduces the control over offender's lives. This can occur when a judge imposes a more intrusive sanction than usual, rather than the *less* intrusive option. For example, rather than merely giving an offender probation, the judge might also require that the offender perform community service.
4.   Critics of intermediate sanctions argue that they have created:
- a.   Wider nets: Reforms increase the proportion of individuals in society whose behavior is regulated or controlled by the state.
- b.   Stronger nets: Reforms augment the state's capacity to control individuals through intensification of the state's intervention powers.
- c.   Different nets: Reforms transfer or create jurisdictional authority from one agency or control system to another.

IV.   THE FUTURE OF COMMUNITY CORRECTIONS
        A.   Introduction
                1.   There were 1.4 million Americans under community supervision in 1980; by 1999 this
                        figure had grown to 3.9 million, an increase of more than 250 percent.
                2.   Yet, despite its wide usage, community corrections often lacks public support, in part
                        because it suffers from an image of being "soft on crime".
                3.   Offenders today require greater supervision based on their crimes, prior records, and drug
                        problems when compared to those placed on probation in previous eras.
                4.   Probation needs an infusion of resources to fulfill its responsibilities during an era of
                        prison overcrowding.
                5.   To garner support for community corrections, citizens must believe that these sanctions
                        are meaningful.

REVIEW OF KEY TERMS
Fill in the appropriate term from the list for each statement below
boot camp
shock incarceration
community service
day reporting centers
fines
forfeiture
home confinement
intensive supervision probation (ISP)
net widening
probation
recidivism
restitution
Mempa v. Rhay (1967)
technical violation
community corrections

1.   _____ is a sentence that requires the offender to remain inside his or her home during
specified periods.

2.   _____ is a punishment involving supervision and restrictions while living in the
community.

3.   _____ is repayment in the form of money or service by an offender to a victim who has
suffered loss.

4.   _____ is a sentence requiring the offender to perform a certain amount of unpaid labor in
the community.

5.   _____ is based upon the belief that young offenders, usually between 14 and 21 years of
age, can be shocked out of their criminal ways.

6.   _____ is a place that offenders may be ordered to report to every day to comply with
elements of a sentence.

7.   _____ is based on the goal of finding the least restrictive alternative-punishing the
offender only as severely as needed to protect the community and satisfy the public.

8.   _____ are sums of money to be paid to the state by a convicted person as a punishment for
an offense.

9. _____ is a short-term institutional sentence, usually followed by probation, that puts the offender through a physical regimen designed to develop discipline and respect for authority.

10. _____ is the seizure by the government of property and other assets derived from or used in criminal activity.

11. _____ was the decision granting a right to counsel at some probation revocation hearings.

12. _____ is the probationer's failure to abide by the rules and conditions of probation resulting in revocation of probation.

13. _____ is probation granted under conditions of strict reporting to a probation officer with a limited caseload.

14. _____ is the process in which new sentencing options increase, rather than reduce, control over offenders' lives.

15. _____ is a return to criminal behavior.

REVIEW OF KEY PEOPLE
Fill in the appropriate person from the list for each statement below
Nelson Colon
Joan Petersilia
Norval Morris and Michael Tonry
John Augustus
Winona Ryder
Michael Tonry and Mary Lynch

1. _____ was arrested for shoplifting in Saks Fifth Avenue and sentenced to three years probation and community service.

2. _____ was the originator of probation as a volunteer, community activist in nineteenth century Boston.

3. _____ and _____ have urged that punishments be created that are more restrictive than probation yet match the severity of the offense and the characteristics of the offender, and that can be carried out while still protecting the community.

4. _____ spent four months at a New Jersey boot camp and adapted to the rigors of military life with little difficulty.

5. In regard to intermediate sanction, _____ and _____ have written the discouraging news that "Few such programs have diverted large numbers of offenders from prison, saved public monies or prison beds, or reduced recidivism rates"

6. _____ argues that too many crime control policies focus solely on the short term.

SELF-TEST SECTION

Multiple Choice Questions

12.1. When was probation developed in the American criminal justice system?
a) 1790s
b) 1840s
c) 1870s
d) 1920s
e) 1980s

12.2. Which of the following factors is cited in support of community corrections?
a) Many offenders' criminal records are not serious enough to warrant incarceration
b) Community supervision is cheaper than incarceration
c) Rates of those returning to crime for those under community supervision are no higher than for those who go to prison
d) Ex-inmates require both support and supervision as they try to remake their lives in the community
e) all of the above

12.3. How many offenders are on probation in the American criminal justice system?
a) roughly 50,000
b) roughly 500,000
c) roughly 1.4 million
d) roughly 3.9 million
e) roughly 10.1 million

12.4. Which state developed the first statewide probation system in 1880?
a) Delaware
b) New Jersey
c) Pennsylvania
d) Massachusetts
e) New York

12.5. According to the Bureau of Justice Statistics for 2002, how many adults released from probation successfully completed their sentences?
a) 17 percent
b) 28 percent
c) 60 percent
d) 76 percent
e) 96 percent

12.6. According to the Bureau of Justice Statistics for 2002, how many adults released from probation had been reincarcerated?
a) 13 percent
b) 28 percent
c) 59 percent
d) 76 percent
e) 96 percent

12.7. Which of the following would most likely cause a revocation of parole?
a) credit problems
b) parking ticket
c) marital problems
d) failing a drug test
e) all of the above would cause a revocation of parole

12.8. Which of the following would least likely cause a revocation of parole?
a) violating curfew
b) failing a drug test
c) using alcohol
d) rearrest
e) credit problems

12.9. How much does it cost to keep an offender on parole?
a) $1,000 a year
b) $5,000 a year
c) $20,000 a year
d) $40,000 a year
e) there is no cost

12.10. How much money is saved by keeping an offender on parole instead of in prison?
a) $1,000 a year
b) $5,000 a year
c) $20,000 a year
d) $40,000 a year
e) there is no savings

12.11. Which of the following is TRUE about convicted felons?
a) convicted felons usually receive the severest penalties, but not the most lenient
b) convicted felons usually receive the most lenient penalties, but not the most severe
c) convicted felons usually receive either the severest penalties or the most lenient
d) convicted felons usually receive a moderate penalty
e) convicted felons usually receive no penalty

12.12. What sentence did Winona Ryder receive after a jury convicted her of second-degree burglary, grand theft, and possession of a controlled substance?
a) three years probation plus community service, counseling, and restitution   * (p. 276)
b) six months in prison and a $20,000 fine
c) two years in prison and a $50,000 fine
d) ten years in prison and a $100,000 fine
e) life in prison with the possibility of parole after fifteen years

12.13. How did probation begin in the late nineteenth century ?
a) probation began as a result of prison overcrowding
b) probation began as a humanitarian effort to allow first-time and minor offenders a second chance
c) probation began as a result of wealthy individuals buying their way out of prison
d) probation began because of a large increase in prison escapes
e) probation began because violent crimes decreased dramatically

12.14. What did the U. S. Supreme Court rule in *Austin v. United States (1993)*?
a) the Eighth Amendment's ban on excessive fines requires that the seriousness of the offense be related to property that is taken
b) the Fourth Amendment right against unreasonable search and seizure was violated by home confinement
c) the use of day reporting centers violated the right to travel in the privileges and immunities clause
d) the use of boot camps did NOT violate the cruel and unusual punishment clause
e) the use of intermediate sanctions did NOT violate the double jeopardy clause

12.15. Which constitutional right might be violated by electronic monitoring and home confinement?
a) double jeopardy clause
b) cruel and unusual punishment clause
c) quartering of troops clause
d) unreasonable search and seizure clause
e) reserved powers clause

12.16. During the 1960s, what shift occurred in probation?
a) offenders were given less probation
b) offenders began to refuse probation and select incarceration
c) offenders began to abuse probation
d) offenders were given assistance with employment, housing, finances, and education
e) offenders were given more counseling

12.17. In the late 1970s, how did the orientation of probation change?
a) emphasis was placed upon rehabilitation
b) efforts were made to minimize the probability that an offender would commit a new offense
c) emphasis was placed upon reintegration into society
d) efforts were made to eliminate probation
e) probation did not change during the late 1970s

12.18. Probation seems to work best when the...
a) judge and the victim of the offender have a close relationship
b) judge and the offender have a close relationship
c) judge and the supervising officer have a close relationship
d) judge and the community are in agreement on probation issues
e) judge and the defense attorney have a close relationship

12.19. Which of the following is an example of an intermediate sanction administered primarily by the judiciary?
a) home confinement
b) day reporting centers
c) forfeiture
d) all of the above
e) none of the above

12.20. Which of the following is an example of an intermediate sanction administered primarily inside institutions and followed by the community
supervision?
a) boot camp
b) day reporting centers
c) forfeiture
d) all of the above
e) none of the above

12.21. Which of the following is an example of an intermediate sanction administered primarily in the community with a supervision component?
a) home confinement   * (p. 284)
b) fines
c) forfeiture
d) all of the above
e) none of the above

12.22. Why don't American judges prefer to impose fines on offenders?
a) judges do not have time to factor fines into the budget of the court
b) money and justice should not become intertwined
c) fines are usually embezzled by court officials
d) fines are too light of a punishment for even minor offenses
e) fines are difficult to collect from offenders who are predominately poor

12.23. Which crime has the lowest percentage of offenders receiving probation in state court?
a) murder
b) weapons offenses
c) larceny
d) assault
e) drug trafficking

12.24. Which crime has the highest percentage of offenders receiving probation in state court?
a) murder
b) rape
c) larceny
d) robbery
e) all of the above have the same percentage receiving probation

12.25. What have Michael Tonry and Mary Lynch concluded about intermediate sanctions?
a) most programs have saved public monies
b) most programs have diverted large numbers of offenders from prison
c) most programs have reduced the number of criminals that return to criminal behavior
d) all of the above
e) none of the above

True and False Questions

_____12.1. The war on drugs increased the number of persons incarcerated as well as the number under probation supervision.

_____12.2. Before probation can be revoked, the offender is entitled to a preliminary hearing.

_____12.3. An offender is NOT entitled to counsel during a probation hearing.

_____12.4. Fines are used extensively in Europe as punishment.

_____12.5. In regard to forfeiture laws, owners' property cannot be seized if they can demonstrate their innocence by a preponderance of evidence.

_____12.6. Probation first developed in the U. S. when Joan Petersilia, an attorney, proposed the idea to the California state legislature.

_____12.7. Parole officers are given little power to restrict the parolee's life.

_____12.8. Parole officers are granted law enforcement powers.

_____12.9. The size of a probation officer's caseload is often less important for preventing recidivism than the quality of supervision and assistance provided to probationers.

_____12.10. Many judges do NOT order offenders to pay fines because most are poor and it is feared that fines will be paid from the proceeds of additional illegal acts.

_____12.11. There are few technical problems with electronic monitoring devices.

_____12.12. The legislative branch is largely responsible for administering intermediate sanctions.

_____12.13. Probation costs more than keeping an offender behind bars.

_____12.14. The Supreme Court ruled that frequent drug testing as a condition of probation violates the right to privacy.

_____12.15. Boot camps are similar to a military-type environment.

_____12.16. Community service imposes a high degree of control over the offender.

_____12.17. Probation diversion takes offenders who are thought to be too risky for routine supervision and places them under intensive surveillance. (p. 286)

_____12.18. Shock incarceration imposes a high degree of control over the offender.

_____12.19. The Arizona Department of Corrections cited an 85 percent failure rate in boot camps.

_____12.20. Winona Ryder is serving five years in prison for shoplifting.

WORKSHEET 12.1: PROBATION

If you were a judge, what kinds of offenders would you put on probation? What kinds of offenders would you *not* place on probation?

_____

_____

_____

_____

_____

_____

_____

_____

_____

If you were a probation officer, which aspect of your job would receive your strongest emphasis: surveillance/rule enforcement or social services/counseling to help reintegration? Why?

_____

_____

_____

_____

_____

_____

_____

If you were a judge, what conditions/restrictions would you impose on probationers? Why?

_____

_____

_____

_____

_____

_____

_____

WORKSHEET 12.2: INTERMEDIATE SANCTIONS

Take the following intermediate sanctions and list them in order of the sanctions that you believe are most effective (1 for most effective and 8 for least effective). For each one, describe its strengths and weaknesses with respect to the goals that should be accomplished: fines, restitution, boot camps, intensive probation supervision, forfeiture, day reporting centers, community service, home confinement.

1. _____ : _____

_____

_____

2. _____ : _____

_____

_____

3. _____ : _____

_____

_____

4. _____ : _____

_____

_____

5. _____ : _____

_____

_____

6. _____ : _____

_____

_____

7. _____ : _____

_____

_____

8. _____ : _____

_____

CHAPTER 13

INCARCERATION AND PRISON SOCIETY

LEARNING OBJECTIVES

After covering the material in this chapter, students should understand:

1.   the goals of incarceration, including the custodial model, rehabilitation model, and reintegration model;

2.   prison management and organization;

3.   the "defects of total power" and the co-optation of corrections officers;

4.   correctional officers' role;

5.   special populations, including the elderly, prisoners with HIV/AIDS, and long-term inmates;

6.   prison society, including adaptive roles, inmate code, and the prison economy;

7.   women in prison, including social relationships and differences between men's and women's prisons;

8.   prison classification and programs;

9.   violence in prison, including contributing causes, and the role of age, attitudes, race, and gangs.

CHAPTER SUMMARY
Since the 1940s, three models of incarceration have been prominent: 1) the custodial model which emphasizes the maintenance of security, 2) the rehabilitation model which views security and housekeeping activities as mainly a framework for treatment efforts, and 3) the reintegration model which recognizes that prisoners must be prepared for their return to society. Popular belief that the warden and officers have total power over the inmates is outdated. Good management through effective leadership can maintain the quality of prison life as measured by levels of order, amenities, and service. Because they are constantly in close contact with the prisoners, correctional officers are the real linchpins in the prison system. The effectiveness of the institution lies heavily on their shoulders. In the United States, state and federal prisoners do not serve their time in isolation but are members of a subculture with their own traditions, norms, and leadership structure. Inmates deal with the pain of incarceration by assuming an adaptive role and lifestyle. Today, major problems in prison society consist of AIDS, an increase in elderly and the mentally ill inmates and inmates serving long terms. The state provides housing, food, and clothes for all inmates. To meet the needs of prisoners for goods and services not provided by the state, an underground economy exists in the society of captives. Most prisoners are young men with little education and disproportionately from minority groups. Only a small portion of the inmate population is female. This is cited as the reason for the limited programs and services available to women prisoners. Social relationships among female inmates differ from those of their male counterparts. Women tend to form pseudo-families in prison. Many women experience the added stress of being responsible for their children on the outside. Educational, vocational, industrial, and treatment programs are available in prisons. Educational programs reduce the risk of an inmate committing a crime upon release from prison. Administrators also believe these programs are important for maintaining order. Prison violence is a major problem confronting administrators. The characteristics of the inmates and the rise of gangs contribute to this problem.

CHAPTER OUTLINE

I.   INTRODUCTION

Maximum security prison in Lucasville, Ohio erupted into a full-scale riot. Prisoners and correctional officers were killed in the process. This type of prison violence is infrequent but gains considerable attention from the public. It demonstrates the need to manage prisons effectively.

II.   THE MODERN PRISON: LEGACY OF THE PAST

A.   Overview

1.   Although "**big houses**" predominated in much of the country during the first half of this century, some prisons, especially in the South, did not conform to this model. There, racial segregation was maintained, prisoners were involved in farm labor, and the massive walled structures were not so dominant a form.

2.   The typical big house of the 1940s and 1950s was a walled prison made up of large, tiered cell blocks, a yard, shops, and industries. The prisoners, averaging about 2,500, came from both urban and rural areas, were poor, and, outside the South, were predominantly white.

3.   The prison society was essentially isolated; access to visitors, mail, and other kinds of communication was restricted. Prisoners' days were strictly structured, with rules enforced by the guards: custody was the primary goal.

4.   During the 1960s and early 1970s most penologists accepted the Rehabilitation Model of corrections. Many states built new facilities and converted others into "correctional institutions" that included treatment programs.

5.   During the past thirty years, as the population of the United States changed, so did that of the inmate population. The proportion of African-American and Hispanic inmates increased, and inmates from urban areas became more numerous, as did inmates convicted of drug-related and violent offenses. The average age decreased.

6.   Former street gangs regrouped inside prisons, disrupting the existing inmate society, raising the levels of violence in many institutions.

7.   A great increase in the number of persons being held in prisons made most overcrowded and under increased tension. Humane incarceration seems to have become the contemporary goal of correctional administrators.

III.   GOALS OF INCARCERATION

A.   Three Models

1.   The **custodial model** is based on the assumption that prisoners have been incarcerated for the protection of society and for the purpose of incapacitation, deterrence, or retribution.

       a.   Emphasis on maintenance of security and order through the subordination of the prisoner to the authority of the warden.

       b.   Discipline is strict, and most aspects of behavior are regulated. This model was prevalent within corrections prior to World War II, and it dominates most maximum security institutions today.

2.   The **rehabilitation model** of institutional organization developed in 1950s.

       a.   Security and housekeeping activities are viewed primarily as a framework for rehabilitative efforts.

       b.   Professional treatment specialists enjoy a higher status than that accorded other employees, in line with the idea that all aspects of the organization should be directed toward rehabilitation.

       c.   Since 1970s, the number of institutions geared toward this end has declined. Treatment programs still exist in most institutions, but very few prisons can be said to conform to this model.

3.   The **reintegration model** is linked to the structures and goals of community corrections.

       a.   Prisons that have adopted the reintegration model gradually give inmates greater freedom and responsibility during their confinement and move them to a halfway house, work release program, or community correctional center before their being released under supervision.

        b.   The reintegration model is based on the assumption that it is important for the offender to maintain or develop ties with the free community.

    4.   Most prisons for men fall much closer to the custodial than to the rehabilitation or reintegration models. Treatment programs do exist in prisons but they generally take second place to the requirements of custody. In many correctional systems, regardless of the basic model, inmates spend the last portion of their sentence in a prerelease facility.

    5.   Prisons are expected to pursue many different and often incompatible goals; hence as institutions they are almost doomed to failure.

        a.   **Charles Logan** believes that the mission of prisons should focus on confinement. He argues that the essential purpose of imprisonment is to punish offenders fairly and justly through lengths of confinement proportionate to the gravity of their crimes.

WHAT AMERICANS THINK: Most Americans think that the maintenance of security to keep prisoners from escaping is excellent or good. Fewer Americans think positively about how the prison system addresses the rehabilitation of inmates and the need for a safe environment for inmates.

IV.   PRISON ORGANIZATION

A.   Characteristics of Prison

    1.   Unlike in other governmental agencies, prison managers:

        a.   Cannot select their clients.

        b.   Have little or no control over the release of their clients.

        c.   Must deal with clients who are there against their will.

        d.   Rely on clients to do most of the work in the day-to-day operation of the institution and to do so by coercion and without fair compensation for their work.

        e.   Must depend on the maintenance of satisfactory relationships between clients and staff.

B.   Three Lines of Command

    1.   Because individual staff members are not equipped to perform all functions, there are separate organizational lines of command for the groups of employees that fulfill these different tasks of custody, prisoners' work assignments, and treatment.

    2.   The custodial employees are normally organized along military lines, from warden to captain to officer, with accompanying pay differentials and job titles that follow the chain of command.

    3.   The professional personnel associated with the using and serving functions, such as clinicians and teachers, are not part of the regular custodial organizational structure, and they have little in common with the others. All employees are responsible to the warden, but the treatment personnel and the civilian supervisors of the workshops have their own salary scales and titles.

    4.   As a result of multiple goals and separate employee lines of command, the administration of correctional institutions is often filled with conflict and ambiguity.

V.   GOVERNING A SOCIETY OF CAPTIVES

A.   Introduction

    1.   Much of the public believes that prisons are operated in an authoritarian manner. Corrections officers presumably possess the power to give orders and have those orders obeyed.

    2.   **John DiIulio** says that a good prison is one that "provides as much order, amenity, and service as possible given the human and financial resources."

<ol type="a" start="1">
<li>Order is the absence of individual or group misconduct that threatens the security of others with, for example, assaults and rape.</li>
<li>**Amenity** is anything that enhances the comfort of the inmates such as good food, clean cells, recreational opportunities and the like.</li>
<li>Service includes programs to improve the life prospects of inmates: vocational training, remedial education, and work opportunities.</li>
</ol>

3. Four factors that make the governing of prisons different from the administration of other public institutions:
   a. The defects of total power.
   b. The limited rewards and punishments that can be used by officials.
   c. The cooptation of correctional officers
   d. The strength of inmate leadership.

B.   The Defects of Total Power
Enforcing commands is an inefficient method of making them carry out complex tasks. Efficiency is further diminished by the realities of the usual 1:40 officer-to-inmate ratio and the potential danger of the situation. Thus correctional officers' ability to threaten the use of physical force is limited in practice.

C.   Rewards and Punishments: Since prisoners receive most privileges at the outset, there is little that can be offered for exceptional behavior.
1. Rewards may be in the form of privileges offered for obedience: *good time* allowances, choice job assignments, and favorable parole reports.
   a. Problems:
      i. Because prisoners are already deprived of many freedoms and valued goods--heterosexual relations, money, choice of clothing, and so on--there is little left to take away.
      ii. The system is often defective because the authorized privileges are given to the inmate at the start of the sentence and are taken away only if rules are broken.
      iii. Few additional authorized rewards can be granted for progress or exceptional behavior, although a desired work assignment or transfer to the honor cell block will induce some prisoners to maintain good behavior.

D.   Gaining Cooperation: Exchange Relationships
Correctional officers obtain inmates' cooperation through the types of exchange relationships described in earlier chapters.
1. The officers need the cooperation of the prisoners so that they will look good to their superiors, and the inmates depend on the guards to relax the rules or occasionally look the other way. Thus, guards exchange or "buy" compliance or obedience in some areas by tolerating violation of the rules elsewhere.
2. Secret relationships that turn into manipulation of the guards by the prisoners may result in the smuggling of contraband or other illegal acts.
3. Question of Ethics: Risk of officer being used by developing too much of a friendly relationship with a prisoner.

E.   Inmate Leadership
1. Inmate leaders enlisted by administrators to help maintain order.
2. Inmate leaders distribute benefits to other prisoners and thereby bolster their own influence within the prison. They are the essential communications link between staff and inmates.
3. However, today's prison population is divided along racial, ethnic, offense, and hometown lines so that there are multiple centers of power and no single set of leaders.

F.   The Challenge of Governing Prisons: Successful wardens have made their prisons "work" by the application of management principles within the context of a their own style of leadership.

A QUESTION OF ETHICS: Should correctional officers assist a prisoner who has become a friend with a gambling debt?

VI.   CORRECTIONAL OFFICERS: THE LINCHPIN OF MANAGEMENT

A.   The Officer's Role
    1.   The officer functions as a member of a complex bureaucratic organization and thus is expected to deal with clients impersonally and to follow formally prescribed procedures, yet must also face and cope with individual prisoners' personal problems. It is difficult to fulfill the varied and contradictory role expectations.
    2.   Contemporary officers are crucial to the management of prison since they are in closest contact with the prisoners and are expected to perform a variety of tasks, including counseling, supervising, protecting, and processing the inmates under their care.
    3.   Studies have shown that one of the primary incentives for becoming involved in correctional work is the security that civil service status provides.
    4.   In addition, prisons offer better employment options than most other jobs available in the rural areas where most correctional facilities are located. Because correctional officers are recruited locally, most of them are rural and white, in contrast to the majority of prisoners who come from urban areas and are either black or Hispanic.
    5.   Salaries have been increased so that now the yearly average entry level pay runs between $16,000 in some southern and rural states to $30,000 in places such as New Jersey and Massachusetts.
    6.   Special efforts have been made to recruit women and minorities. Women are no longer restricted to working with female offenders, and the number of correctional officers from minority groups has increased dramatically.
    7.   For most correctional workers a position as a custody officer is a dead-end job. Though officers who perform well may be promoted to higher ranks within the custodial staff, very few ever move into administrative positions.
        a.   Increasingly it is possible for college educated people to achieve administrative positions without having to advance up through the ranks of the custodial force.

WORK PERSPECTIVE: Robert Worley, Correctional Officer, Gorre Unit. Texas Department of Criminal Justice, Huntsville, Texas

B.   Use of Force
    1.   Corrections officers can use force in five specified situations:
        a.   Self-defense: if officers are threatened with physical attack
        b.   Defense of third persons: officer may use force to protect an inmate or another officer
        c.   Upholding prison rules: officers may use force if prisoners do not follow rule in order to ensure safety and security
        d.   Prevention of a crime: force may be used to stop a crime such as theft or destruction of property
        e.   Prevention of escape: officers may use force to prevent escape because escapes threaten the well-being of society

VII.   WHO IS IN PRISON?

A.   Inmate Characteristics
    1.   Prison inmates are primarily repeat offenders convicted of violent crimes. Most prisoners are in their late twenties to early thirties, have less than a high school education, and are disproportionately members of minority groups.

CLOSE-UP: One Man's Walk Through Atlanta's Jungle, by **Michael G. Santos**

B. Elderly Prisoners
  1. Longer sentences produce increasing numbers of elderly prisoners who have special security and medical needs.
  2. The average annual cost to the institution of caring for elderly prisoners is triple the cost for the average prisoner.
  3. Many elderly prisoners receive better medical care and nutrition than they would in the outside world because, if released, they would return to poor neighborhoods.

C. Prisoners with HIV/AIDS
  1. The rate of HIV/AIDS among prisoners is five times higher than the general U.S. population.
  2. Prisoners who test positive create many challenges for preventing transmission of disease, housing infected prisoners, and medical care.

D. Mentally Ill Prisoners
  Mass closings of mental hospitals has increased arrests and incarceration of mentally ill people. High percentages of inmates in some facilities are classified as mentally ill. Correctional facilities and workers are often poorly prepared to deal with mentally ill prisoners.

E. Long-Term Inmates
  1. More prisoners serve long sentences in the U.S. than in any other Western country.
  2. The average first-time offender serves about twenty-two months, but an estimated eleven to fifteen percent of all prisoners will serve more than seven years--this amounts to more than 100,000 people.
  3. Long-term prisoners are less likely to cause disciplinary infractions, but they present administrators with challenges for maintaining livable conditions.
  4. Timothy Flanagan says administrators adhere to three principles for long-term inmates:
     a. Maximize opportunities for choice in living arrangements.
     b. Create opportunities for meaningful living.
     c. Help inmates maintain contact with the outside world.

VIII. THE CONVICT WORLD

A. Introduction
  1. Inmates in today's prisons do not serve their terms in internal isolation. They form a society with traditions, norms, and a leadership structure.
  2. Membership in a group affords mutual protection from theft and physical assault, serves as the basis of wheeling and dealing activities, and provides a source of cultural identity.
  3. The **Inmate Code**: the values and norms that emerge within the prison social system and help to define the inmate's image of the model prisoner. The code also helps to emphasize the solidarity of all inmates against the staff.
     a. For example: never rat on a con, be nosy, have a loose lip, or put another con on the spot.
     b. Guards are "hacks or screws", and the officials are wrong and the prisoners are right.
  4. Some sociologists believe that the code emerges from within the institution as a way to lessen the pain of imprisonment.
  5. Others believe that it is part of the criminal culture that prisoners bring with them.
  6. Inmates who violate the code will probably spend their prison life at the bottom of the convict social structure, alienated from the rest of the population and preyed upon by other inmates.
  7. A single overriding inmate code may not exist in some institutions. Instead, race has become a key variable dividing convict society.

8.   In the absence of a single code accepted by the entire population, administrators find their task more difficult.
      a.   They must be aware of the variations that exist among the groups, recognize the norms and rules that members hold, and deal with the leaders of many cliques rather than with a few inmates who have risen to top positions in the inmate society.

B.   Adaptive Roles
1.   Newcomers entering prison must decide how to serve their time: isolate themselves from others or become full participants in the convict social system.
      a.   This choice of identity is influenced by prisoners' values. Are they interested primarily in achieving prestige according to the norms of the prison culture, or do they try to maintain or realize the values of the free world?
2.   Four categories have been used to describe the lifestyles of male inmates as they adapt to prison:
      a.   **"Doing time"** is the choice of those who try to maintain their links with and the perspective of the free world. They avoid trouble and form friendships with small groups of inmates.
      b.   **"Gleaning"** is taking advantage of prison programs. Usually inmates not committed to a life of crime.
      c.   **"Jailing"** is the style used by those who cut themselves off from the outside and try to construct a life within the prison.   Often "state-raised youth" who grew up in foster homes and juvenile detention centers.
      d.   The **"disorganized criminal"** includes those who are unable to develop role orientations to prison life; often afflicted with low intelligence or psychological problems.
3.   Prisoners are not members of an undifferentiated mass; individual members choose to play specific roles in the convict society.

C.   The Prison Economy
1.   In prison, as in the outside world, individuals desire goods and services that are not freely provided.
2.   Although in some institutions inmates may own television sets, civilian clothing, hot plates, etc., the prison community generally has been deliberately designated as an island of poverty in the midst of a society of relative abundance.
      a.   Prisoners are limited as to what they may have in their cells, restrictions are placed on what gifts may come into the institution, and money may not be in the inmate's possession.
3.   Officials have created a formal economic system in the form of a commissary or **"store"** in which inmates may, on a scheduled basis, purchase a limited number of items--toilet articles, tobacco, snacks, and other food items--in exchange for credits drawn upon their "bank accounts" -- composed of money deposited on the inmate's entrance, gifts sent by relatives, and amounts earned in the low-paying prison industries.
4.   An informal, underground economy exists as a major element in the society of captives. Many items taken for granted on the outside are inordinately valued on the inside.
      a.   For example, talcum power and deodorant take on added importance because of the limited bathing facilities.
5.   Mark Fleisher has documented the prison economy at the U. S. Penitentiary at Lompoc, California. He learned that a complete market economy provided the goods and services not available to prisoners through legitimate sources.
      a.   This informal economy reinforces the norms and roles of the social system, influences the nature of interpersonal relationships, and is thus one of the principal features of the culture.
      b.   The extent of the economy and its ability to produce desired goods and services -- food, drugs, alcohol, sex, preferred living conditions--vary according to the

extent of official surveillance, the demands of the consumers, and the opportunities for entrepreneurship.

6.   The standard medium of exchange in the prison economy is cigarettes. Because possession of coins or currency is prohibited and a barter system is somewhat restrictive, "cigarette money" is a useful substitute. Prison currency may change in the future as more prisons consider banning smoking.

7.   Almost every job offers possibilities for stealing from the state: e.g., kitchen workers steal food for trading.

8.   Economic transactions may lead to violence when goods are stolen, debts are not paid, or agreements are violated.

IX. WOMEN IN PRISON

A.   <u>Introduction</u>

1.   Women constitute only 6.6 percent (about 92,000) of the entire U.S. prison population. But the rate of growth of incarcerated women has been greater than that of men since 1981, primarily due to drug offenses. Since 1990, the number of men behind bars rose 77 percent; the number of women 108 percent.

2.   Women's prisons are smaller; security is less tight; the relationships between inmates and staff are less structured; physical aggression seems less common; the underground economy is less well developed; and female prisoners appear to be even less committed to the convict code than men now are. Women serve shorter sentences, and there is perhaps more fluidity in the prison society as new members join and others leave.

3.   Problems of remoteness and heterogeneity: Because few states operate more than one prison for women and some operate none, inmates are generally far removed from their families, friends, and attorneys. In addition, because the number of inmates is small, there is less pressure to design programs to meet an individual offender's security and treatment needs. Dangerous inmates are not segregated from those who have committed minor offenses.

4.   Women prisoners are typically like male prisoners, disadvantaged losers in a complex and competitive society. Men are sentenced more often for violent offenses but men are less often sentenced for drug-related offenses as opposed to women. Women receive shorter maximum sentences than men.

B.   <u>The Subculture of Women's Prisons</u>

1. Female inmates tend to form pseudofamilies in which they adopt various roles--father, mother, daughter, sister--and interact as a unit.

     a.   **Esther Hefferman** views these "play" families as a "direct, conscious substitution for the family relationships broken by imprisonment, or . . . the development of roles that perhaps were not fulfilled in the actual home environment."

     b.   **Kimberly Greer** found that prisons for women are less violent, with less gang activity and far less racial tension than men's prisons.

     c.   **Barbara Owen** found that inmates at the Central California Women's Facility developed various styles of doing time. Most wanted to avoid **"the mix"**-behavior that can bring trouble and conflict with staff and other prisoners. A primary feature of the mix is anything for which one can lose good time or can result in being sent to administrative segregation.

C.   <u>Male versus Female Subcultures Compared</u>

1.   A principal difference between male and female prison subcultures is in interpersonal relations.

a.   Male prisoners act as individuals and their behavior is evaluated by the yardstick of the prison culture; autonomy, self-sufficiency, and the ability to cope with one's problems.

b.   In prisons for women, close ties seem to exist among small groups of inmates. These extended families may essentially provide emotional support and emphasize the sharing of resources.

c.   There are debates among researchers about whether these differences reflect distinctive female qualities (e.g., nurturing, etc.).

D.   <u>Issues in the Incarceration of Women</u> Under pressures for equal opportunity, states seem to believe that they should run women's prisons as they do prisons for men, with the same policies And procedures. Joycelyn Pollock believes that when prisons emphasize parity, then use a male standard, women lose.

1.   <u>Sexual Misconduct:</u> As the number of women prisoners has increased, cases of sexual misconduct by male correctional officers have escalated.

2.   <u>Educational and Vocational Training Programs</u>
   a.   Major criticisms:
      i.   Women's prisons do not have the variety of vocational and educational programs available in male institutions.
      ii.   Existing programs for women tend to conform to sexual stereotypes of "feminine" occupational roles: cosmetology, food service, housekeeping, sewing.
   b.   Vocational and educational opportunities during incarceration are crucial; both for speeding time in prison and improving life after prison. Upon release most women have to support themselves, and many are financially responsible for children as well; education and training are vital.
   c.   By the 1980s, increases had occurred in the availability of programs for women, including vocational programs such as business, computers, auto repair, etc.
   d.   Women's prisons also suffer from a relative lack of medical, nutritional, and recreational services.

3.   <u>Medical services</u>
   a.   Women often have special or more serious medical problems. Pregnancies raise important issues because surveys show about 25 percent of incarcerated women were pregnant upon admission to prison or had given birth within the prior year.
   b.   Leslie Acoca argues that the failure to provide basic preventive and medical treatments such as immunization, breast cancer screenings, and management of chronic diseases is resulting in the development of more serious health problems that are exponentially more expensive to treat.

4.   <u>Mothers and Children</u>
   a.   The greatest concern to incarcerated women is the fate of their children. About 65 percent of women inmates are mothers and on average they have two dependent children; estimated total of 167,000 children in the United States--two-thirds of whom are under ten years of age--have mothers who are in jail or prison.
   b.   One recent study found that roughly half of these children do not see their mothers while they are in prison. Children were most often taken care of by their maternal grandmothers.
   c.   When an inmate had no relative who would care for the children, they were often put up for adoption or placed in state-funded foster care.
   d.   Enforced separation from children is bad for the children and bad for the mothers; source of significant stress and anxiety.

<blockquote>

i.   Mothers have difficulty maintaining contact: distance from prison, restrictive visiting hours, may be restrictions against physical contact during visits, etc.

ii.   Increasingly, programs are being developed to deal with the problems of mothers and their children (e.g. nurseries, playrooms, transportation arranged, etc.).

iii.   Some states permit overnight visits; may include husband in mobile home on prison grounds.
</blockquote>

e.   In most states a baby born in prison must be placed with a family member or social agency within three weeks, to the detriment of the early mother-child bonding thought to be important for the development of a baby. Some innovative programs make longer periods possible.

X.   PRISON PROGRAMS

A.   <u>Introduction</u>

1.   Because the public has called for harsher treatment of criminals, legislators have reduced education and other programs in many states.

2.   Administrators must use institutional programs to manage the problem of time. They know that the more programs they are able to offer, the less likely it is that inmates' idleness and boredom will turn to hostility. Activity is the administrator's tool for controlling and stabilizing prison operations.

3.   Contemporary programs include educational, vocational, and treatment.

4.   WHAT AMERICANS THINK: A majority of Americans responded that prisons do a poor or very poor job of rehabilitating prisoners.

B.   <u>Classification of Prisoners</u>

1.   Determining the appropriate program for an individual prisoner is usually made through a **classification** process.

2.   Most states now have diagnostic and reception centers that are physically separated from the main prison facility.

3.   A classification committee usually consists of the heads of security, treatment, education, and industry departments evaluates the inmates.

4.   Unfortunately, classification decisions are often made on the basis of administrative needs rather than inmate needs. Prison housekeeping, for example, requires inmate labor to cook and mop floors.

a.   Inmates from the city may be assigned to farm work because that is where they are needed.

b.   What is most upsetting to some prisoners is that release on parole often depends on a good record of participation in treatment or educational programs, some of which may have been unavailable.

C.   <u>Educational Programs</u>

1.   Education programs are the most popular programs in prison. In many prisons, inmates who have not completed eighth grade are assigned full-time to a prison school. Many programs permit inmates to earn a high school equivalency diploma (GED).

2.   In some facilities, college-level courses are offered through an association with a local community college. Federal law and the laws of many states are increasingly banning any educational programs beyond high school.

3.   Studies have shown that inmates who were assigned to the prison school are good candidates to achieve a conviction-free record after release. Evidence has also suggested, however, that this outcome may be due largely to the type of inmate selected for schooling rather than the schooling itself.

D.   Vocational Education
    1.   Programs in modern facilities are designed to teach a variety of skills: plumbing, automobile mechanics, printing, computer programming. Unfortunately, most such programs are unable to keep abreast of technological advances and needs of the free market.
    2.   Too many programs are designed to train inmates for trades that already have an adequate labor supply or in which new methods have made the skills taught obsolete.
    3.   Some vocational programs are even designed to prepare inmates for careers on the outside that are closed to former felons. The restaurant industry, for example, would seem to be a place where former felons might find employment, yet in many states they are prohibited from working where alcohol is sold.

E.   Prison Industries
    1.   Some scholars now point to the early industries established at Auburn as a reflection of the industrialization of the United States and the need for prison to instill good work habits and discipline in potential members of the labor force.
    2.   Traditionally, prisoners have been required to work at tasks that are necessary to maintain and run their own and other state facilities: food service, laundry, and building maintenance jobs. Also prison farms produce food for the institution in some states.
    3.   Industry shops make furniture, repair office equipment, and fabricate items. Prisoners receive a nominal fee (perhaps 50 cents an hour) for such work.
    4.   During the nineteenth century, factories were set up inside many prisons and inmates manufactured items that were sold on the open market. With the rise of the labor movement, however, state legislatures and Congress passed laws restricting the sale of prison-made goods so that they would not compete with those made by free workers.
    5.   The 1980s saw initiatives promoted by the federal government efforts to encourage private-sector companies to set up "factories within fences" so as to use prison labor effectively.
    6.   A survey showed that the number of inmates employed within prisons ranges from more than 20 percent in states such as Utah and North Carolina to less than 5 percent in most states.
    7.   Prison industries are often inefficient due to turnover of prisoners, low education levels, and poor work habits. Also need good security to keep materials from being stolen by prisoners.

F.   Rehabilitative Programs
    1.   There is much dispute about the degree of emphasis that should be given to these programs and the types that should be offered.
    2.   Reports in the mid-1970s cast doubt on the ability of treatment programs to stem recidivism and raised questions about the ethics of requiring inmates to participate in such programs in exchange for the promise of parole.
    3.   In most correctional systems a range of psychological, behavioral, and social services is available to inmates. Nationally very little money is spent for treatment services and these programs reach only 5 percent of the inmate population.

G.   Medical Services
    1.   Most prisons offer medical services through a full-time staff of nurses, augmented by part-time physicians under contract to the correctional system.

XI.   VIOLENCE IN PRISON

A.   Introduction
    1.   Crowded conditions; an angry, frustrated population, many with psychological problems and histories of violence; also ethnic conflict, etc.

2. Many well-known violent riots produced in such conditions: Attica (1971), Santa Fe, New Mexico (1980), Atlanta (1987), etc.

3. About 150 prisoners commit suicide each year. About 90 are killed by others and 400 die of undetermined causes, which likely includes some homicides. Annually, about 27,000 assaults by other inmates and 15,000 assaults against staff take place.

4. Great numbers of prisoners live in a state of constant uneasiness, always on the lookout for persons who might subject them to homosexual demands, steal their few possessions, or make their time more painful.

B. Assaultive Behavior and Inmate Characteristics

1. *Age*: Studies have shown that young people, both inside and outside prison, are more prone to violence than their elders. Not only do young prisoners have greater physical strength, they lack those commitments to career and family that are thought to restrict antisocial behavior.

   a. Many young men have difficulty defining their position in society; thus many of their interactions with others are interpreted as challenges to their status. **Machismo**-to be macho is, for one thing, to have a reputation for physically retaliating against those who make slurs on one's honor.

2. *Attitudes*: One of the sociological theories advanced to explain crime is that there is a subculture of violence among certain economic, racial, and ethnic groups. Arguments are settled and decisions made by the fist rather than by verbal persuasion. These attitudes are brought into the prison as part of an inmate's heritage.

3. *Race*: Race has become the major factor that divides the contemporary prison population, reflecting tensions in the larger society. Racist attitudes seem to be acceptable in most institutions and have become part of the **convict code**. Violence against members of another race may be the way that some inmates deal with the frustrations of their lives both inside and outside of prison. Also prison gangs often organized along racial lines and this contributes to violence in prison.

C. Prisoner-Prisoner Violence-Most of the violence in prison is inmate to inmate. Leads many prisoners to avoid contact with other prisoners, request isolation, etc.

1. *Prison Gangs:* racial or ethnic gangs are linked to acts of violence in many prison systems. In essence the gang wars of the streets are often continued in prison. Many facilities segregate rival gangs by housing them in separate units of the prison.

2. *Protective Custody:* For many victims of prison violence, protective custody offers the only escape. About 5,000 state prisoners are in protective custody in state prisons. Life is not pleasant because they only are let out of their cells briefly to shower and exercise.

D. Prisoner-Officer Violence

1. Annually, more than 14,000 prison staff members were injured by inmate assaults.

2. Violence against officers is situational and individual. Correctional officers do not carry weapons within the walls of the institution because a prisoner may seize them. Prisoners do manage to obtain lethal weapons and can use the element of surprise to inflict injury on an officer.

3. In the course of a workday an officer may encounter situations that require the use of physical force against an inmate--for instance, breaking up a fight or moving a prisoner to segregation. Officers know that such situations are especially dangerous and may enlist the assistance of others to minimize the risk of violence.

E. Officer-Prisoner Violence

1. Unauthorized physical violence against inmates by officers to enforce rules, uphold the officer-prisoner relationship, and maintain order is a fact of life in many institutions.

   a. In some institutions, authorized "goon squads" made up of physically powerful correctional officers use their muscle to maintain order and the status quo.

2.   Prisoner complaints about officer brutality are often given little credence until an individual officer gains a reputation for harshness. Wardens may feel that they must uphold the actions of their officers if they are going to maintain their support.

F.   Decreasing Prison Violence
    1.   **Lee Bowker** lists five factors contributing to prison violence:
        a.   inadequate supervision by staff members;
        b.   architectural design that promotes rather than inhibits victimization;
        c.   the easy availability of deadly weapons;
        d.   the housing of violence-prone prisoners near relatively defenseless prisoners;
        e.   a general high level of tension produced by close quarters.
    2.   The Effect of Size: The social and physical environment of the institution also plays a part. Such variables as the physical size and condition of the prison, and the relations between inmates and staff all have a bearing on violence.
        a.   The massive scale of some institutions provides opportunities for aggressive inmates to hide weapons, carry out private justice, and engage in other illicit activities free from supervision.
        b.   As the prison population rises and the personal space of each inmate is decreased, we may expect an increase in antisocial behavior.
    3.   The Role of Management: The degree to which inmate leaders are allowed to take matters into their own hands may have an impact on the amount of violence among inmates. Effective prison management that provides few opportunities for attacks may decrease the level of assaultive behavior. Administrators need to run a tight ship and to prevent sexual assaults, the making of "shivs" and "shanks" (knives) and open conflict among inmate groups.

TECHNOLOGY ISSUES IN CRIMINAL JUSTICE: Scanning for Drugs. Prison officials are using devices that look like handheld vacuum cleaners to scan prisoners for drugs. The scanners detect traces of drugs more effectively than drug-sniffing dogs.

REVIEW OF KEY TERMS
Fill in the appropriate term from the list for each statement below
custodial model
rehabilitation model
reintegration model
big house
amenities
inmate code
doing time
gleaning
convict code
machismo
jailing
disorganized criminal
fish
store
the mix
classification

1.   Prisoners have a _____ from which they may purchase a limited number of items such as toilet articles, tobacco, snacks, and other food products.

2.   _____ is behavior that can bring trouble and conflict with staff and other prisoners.

211

3. _____ is the process of assigning an inmate to a category specifying his or her needs for security, treatment, education, work assignment, and readiness for release.

4. _____ is the norms and values that develop within the prison social system and help to define the inmate's idea of the model prisoner.

5. _____ is a prisoner's view that his or her prison term is a brief, inevitable break in a criminal career.

6. _____ is taking advantage of prison programs.

7. _____ is the style used by those who cut themselves off from the outside and try to construct a life within the prison.

8. The _____ includes those who are unable to develop role orientations to prison life and find functioning in prison very difficult.

9. _____ is the model of correctional institutions that emphasizes maintenance of the offender's ties to family and the community as a method of reform.

10. _____ represents the stereotypical picture of the prison as a walled fortress with tiered cell blocks.

11. _____ is the model of corrections that emphasizes security, discipline, and order.

12. _____ is the model of corrections that emphasizes a treatment program designed to reform the offender.

13. _____ include anything that enhances the comfort of the inmates, such as good food, clean cells, and recreational opportunities.

14. A(n) _____ is a newcomer to prison who must decide how to do his or her time.

15. _____ is the concept of male honor, and the sacredness of one's reputation as a man.

16. The _____ is the implicit rules of life in prison.

REVIEW OF KEY PEOPLE
Fill in the appropriate person from the list for each statement below
John DiIulio
Lee Bowker
Esther Hefferman
Kimberly Greer
Barbara Owen
Charles Logan
Michael Santos

1. _____ found support for the idea that prisons for women are less violent, involved less gang activity, and had far less racial tension than did men's prisons.

2. _____ found that the inmates at a women's prison developed various styles of doing time.

3. _____ was a 24-year old first time who served time in the U. S. Penitentiary in Atlanta.

212

4. _____ argues that the mission of prisons is confinement.

5. _____ stated that a good prison is one that "provides as much order, amenity, and service as possible given the human and financial resources."

6.   In women's prisons, _____ found that women develop "play" families as a "direct, conscious substitution for the family relationships broken by imprisonment .

7. _____ lists five factors that contribute to prison violence: 1) inadequate supervision, 2) architectural design that promotes victimization, 3) availability of deadly weapons, 4) housing of violence-prone prisoners, and 5) high level of tension produced by close quarters.

SELF-TEST SECTION

Multiple Choice Questions

13.1. Prison organizations are expected to fulfill goals related to…
a) incarcerating inmates
b) maintaining the inmates' ties to family
c) treating inmates
d) all of the above
e) none of the above

13.2. Which model of incarceration prevailed before World War II and dominates maximum-security institutions today?
a) organizational model
b) amenities model
c) rehabilitation model
d) reintegration model
e) custodial model

13.3. Who is listed at the top of the formal organization of a prison?
a) warden
b) deputy warden
c) counselors
d) physicians
e) accountants

13.4. Who are the most numerous employees in prison?
a) warden
b) deputy wardens
c) custodial
d) teachers
e) clinicians

13.5. Which of the following is TRUE about prisons?
a) prisons have multiple goals and separate lines of command
b) prison goals are characterized by simplicity and consensus
c) individual staff members are equipped to perform all functions
d) all of the above are TRUE
e) all of the above are FALSE

13.6. Which of the following is a situation when a correctional officer CANNOT use force?
a) self-defense
b) to defend a third person
c) when he/she has a right to be angry at an inmate
d) to prevent a crime
e) to prevent an escape

13.7. Which of the following describes most correctional officers?
a) Hispanic and rural
b) white and rural
c) white and urban
d) African-American and rural
e) African-American and urban

13.8. Who was a 24-year old who spent time in a U. S. Penitentiary in Atlanta?
a) Charles Logan
b) Lee Bowker
c) John DiIulio
d) Robert Worley
e) Michael Santos

13.9. Who found an inmate running a "store" in most every cell block in the U.S. Penitentiary at Lompoc, California?
a) Timothy Flanagan
b) Esther Hefferman
c) Joseph Fishman
d) David Kalinich
e) Mark Fleischer

13.10. What fraction of inmates were serving a sentence for a violent crime or had previously been convicted of a violent crime?
a) one-half
b) one-third
c) one-fourth
d) two-thirds
e) three-fifths

13.11. Which of the following is a factor in prison violence?
a) age
b) race
c) attitudes
d) all of the above
e) none of the above

13.12. What percent of inmates have been either incarcerated or on probation three times or more times?
a) 60%
b) 45%
c) 30%
d) 20%
e) 10%

13.13. What percent of inmates have been either incarcerated or on probation six or more times?
a) 70%
b) 55%
c) 40%
d) 20%
e) 5%

13.14. Which of the following is TRUE about prison gangs?
a) they exist in most state and federal prisons
b) they are loosely organized
c) they assist wardens in maintaining control
d) they are NOT a source of inmate-inmate violence
e) none of the above are TRUE

13.15. What percent of inmates have been either incarcerated or on probation at least twice?
a) 60%
b) 35%
c) 20%
d) 10%
e) 4%

13.16. How many state prisoners are in protective custody?
a) 1000
b) 5000
c) 10,000
d) 20,000
e) 50,000

13.17. Which of the following does NOT contribute to prison violence?
a) prison gangs
b) boredom among prisoners
c) availability of deadly weapons
d) architectural design that promotes victimization
e) housing of violence-prone prisoners

13.18. The Bureau of Justice statistics reports that most prisoners are…
a) 40 years or older
b) college graduates
c) females
d) recidivist offenders
e) none of the above

13.19. Which of the following factors affect correctional operations?
a) the increased number of elderly prisoners
b) the many prisoners with HIV/AIDS
c) the thousands of prisoners who are mentally ill
d) the increase in long-term prisoners.
e) all of the above

13.20. What is the rate of AIDS cases in U. S. prisons compared to the U. S. general population?
a) about the same
b) twice as high
c) three times as high
d) five times as high
e) ten times as high

13.21. When did mass closings of public hospitals for the mentally ill begin in the United States?
a) 1920s
b) 1940s
c) 1960s
d) 1990s
e) 2000s

13.22. The average first-time offender in the U. S. serves…
a) six months
b) nine months
c) thirteen months
d) twenty two months
e) forty months

13.23. Which of the following is NOT provided by the state prison system?
a) housing
b) food
c) clothing
d) cigarettes
e) all of the above are provided by the state

13.24. What is another name for a newcomer in prison society?
a) dog
b) fish
c) gleaner
d) jailer
e) woman

13.25. Which of the following best describes the outward appearance of a women's prison?
a) upper-class country club
b) military institution
c) college campus
d) homeless shelter
e) third world country

True and False Questions

_____13.1. The custodial model emphasizes security and order.

_____13.2. During the 1960s and 1970s, the custodial model prevailed in the operation of prisons.

_____13.3. Prison managers must rely on clients to do most of the work in the daily operation of the institution.

_____13.4. The most numerous employees in prisons are the custodial workers.

_____13.5. The goals and lines of command often bring about clarity and consensus in the administration of prisons.

_____13.6. The use of force by correctional officers is a controversial issue.

_____13.7. The state provides housing, food, and clothing for all prisoners.

_____13.8. Most prisoners are in their late forties and have attended college, but few have college degrees.

_____13.9. Prison management CANNOT decrease the level of assaultive behavior because some groups are unmanageable.

_____13.10. Prisoners can be legally isolated from one another.

_____13.11. Over the last two decades, the number of persons in U. S. prison have decreased significantly.

_____13.12. Correctional officers are constantly in close contact with prisoners.

_____13.13. Correctional officers who are women are restricted to working with female offenders.

_____13.14. Elderly prisoners cost the same as the average prisoner.

_____13.15. A correctional officer may use force to protect an inmate or another officer.

_____13.16. The inmate code emphasizes that all inmates should unite against the staff.

_____13.17. Violent behavior in prisons is related to the age of the inmates.

_____13.18. Race has become a major divisive factor in today's prisons.

_____13.19. More prisoners in the U. S. serve shorter sentences than do prisoners in other Western nations.

_____13.20. There are more of the mentally ill in U. S. jails and prisons than in state hospitals.

WORKSHEET 13.1   PRISONS AND THEIR PURPOSES

If you were in charge of a state corrections department, how would you design your prisons? For each question, assume that the prisons have one primary purpose (listed below) and describe the physical design, policies, and programs that you would implement to help the institution advance the overriding goal.

1. CUSTODIAL MODEL_____

_____

_____

_____

_____

_____

_____

2. REHABILITATION MODEL_____

_____

_____

_____

_____

_____

_____

3. REINTEGRATION MODEL_____

_____

_____

_____

_____

_____

_____

_____

WORKSHEET 13.2   PRISON PROGRAMS

You are in charge of developing programs at a new prison. For each category of possible programs discuss whether you will recommend such programs for your prison. Why? If so, describe the goals and details of those programs.

EDUCATIONAL PROGRAMS_____

_____

_____

_____

_____

_____

VOCATIONAL PROGRAMS_____

_____

_____

_____

_____

_____

PRISON INDUSTRIES_____

_____

_____

_____

_____

_____

_____

REHABILITATIVE PROGRAMS_____

_____

_____

_____

_____

WORKSHEET 13.3   PRISON PROBLEMS

If you were a prison warden, name three things that you would do to address each of the following issues. How effective do you think your strategies would be?

1. Racial tensions between groups of inmates _____

_____

_____

_____

_____

_____

_____

2. Prison gangs controlling the internal economy _____

_____

_____

_____

_____

_____

_____

3. Mothers of small children serving long sentences in an isolated institution

_____

_____

_____

_____

_____

_____

_____

CHAPTER 14

REENTRY INTO THE COMMUNITY

LEARNING OBJECTIVES

After covering the material in this chapter, students should understand:

1.   origins and development of parole in the United States

2.   release mechanisms and their impact

3.   problems facing parolees;

4.   community programs following release;

5.   the role of the parole officer;

6.   problems facing parolees;

7.   revocation of parole;

8.   the future of prisoner reentry.

CHAPTER SUMMARY

The origin of parole in the U. S. began in the late nineteenth century during the prison reform movement with influence from England, Australia, and Ireland. Parole in the U. S. developed with a nationwide sentencing and release policy focusing on indeterminate sentences. In the 1970s, a move toward determinate sentences occurred because the public viewed the system as "soft" on criminals. The four basic mechanisms for release are: 1) discretionary release,
2) mandatory release, 3) other conditional release, and 4) expiration release. Parolees are released from prison on the condition that they abide by laws and follow rules, known as conditions of release. Community programs reduce the risk of an inmate committing a crime upon release from prison. Most inmates will receive parole, but they face a multitude of problems such as finding employment and avoiding a return to the criminal life. Parole officers are assigned to assist ex-inmates make the transition to society, and to ensure that they follow the conditions of their release. The problem of reentry has become a major policy issue because it plays such an important role in the criminal justice system.

CHAPTER OUTLINE
I.   INTRODUCTION

The murder of **Megan Kanka** by a paroled sex offender demonstrates the problems associated with releasing an offender into the community but it also illustrates how the public's assumptions about ex-offenders is shaped by news reports of brutal crimes committed by parolees. As a result of Megan Kanka's murder, sex offender notification laws have been enacted which require the public to be notified of the whereabouts of "potentially dangerous" sex offenders. With the great expansion of incarceration during the past two decades, the number of offenders now returning to the community has decreased dramatically.

II.   PRISONER REENTRY

    A.   Prison reentry is an important public issue because there is a sudden flood o offenders leaving prison coupled with the fact that almost one-half will return to prison because of a new crime or parole violation

    B.   Travis and Petersilia point to several factors that contribute to the reentry problem:

1. More inmates are automatically leaving prison whether they are ready or not, because they simply meet the requirements of their sentence.
2. the curtailment of prison education, job training, and other rehabilitative programs
3. Longer sentences keep inmates away from family and friends for longer periods of time which means weaker links to the community when they return

III. RELEASE AND SUPERVISION

A. Introduction

Parole is the conditional release of an offender from incarceration but not from the legal custody of the state. Parole rests on three concepts:
1. **Grace** of privilege: The prisoner could be kept incarcerated but government extends the privilege of release.
2. **Contract** of consent: The government enters into an agreement with the prisoner whereby the prisoner promises to abide by certain conditions in exchange for being released.
3. **Custody**: Even though the offender is released from prison, he or she is still a responsibility of the government. Parole is an extension of correctional programs into the community.

B. The Origins of Parole
1. Parole in the United States evolved during the nineteenth century as a result of the English, Australian, and Irish practices of conditional pardon, apprenticeship by indenture, transportation of criminals from one country to another, and the issuance of **"tickets-of-leave"** or licenses.
    a. In most cases, such problems as overcrowding, unemployment, and the cost of incarceration appear to have motivated the practice of releasing prisoners rather than any rationale linked to a goal of the criminal sanction.
2. British Captain **Alexander Maconochie** criticized definite prison terms and devised a system of reward for good conduct, labor, and study. He developed a classification procedure by which prisoners could pass through five stages of increasing responsibility and freedom:
    a. strict imprisonment;
    b. labor on government chain gangs;
    c. freedom within a limited area;
    d. a ticket-of-leave or parole resulting in a conditional pardon;
    e. full restoration of liberty.
3. In Ireland, **Sir Walter Crofton** built on Maconochie's idea that an offender's progress in prison and a ticket-of-leave were linked.
    a. Prisoners who graduated through Crofton's three successive levels of treatment were released on parole with a series of conditions.
    b. Parolees were required to submit monthly reports to the police. In Dublin a special civilian inspector helped releasees find jobs, visited them periodically, and supervised their activities.

C. The Development of Parole in the United States
1. In the United States, parole developed during the prison reform movement of the nineteenth century.
    a. Relying on the ideas of Maconochie and Crofton, **Zebulon Brockway** started to release prisoners on parole. Under the new sentencing law, prisoners could be released when their conduct during incarceration showed that they were ready to return to society.
    b. The parole system in New York as originally implemented did not require supervision by the police, as in Ireland; rather, responsibility for assisting the parolees was assumed by private reform groups.

        c.   With increased use of parole, states replaced the volunteer supervisors with correctional employees who were charged with helping and observing the parolees.

     2.   By 1900, twenty states had parole systems; by 1932, forty-four states and the federal government had adopted this method. Today all jurisdictions have some mechanism for the release of offenders into the community before the end of their sentences.

     3.   Parole is still controversial. The general public seems to believe that paroled felons serve much less time than the interests of crime control and justice dictate. These contemporary criticisms have led about half the states and the federal government to restructure their sentencing laws and release mechanisms.

IV. RELEASE MECHANISMS: There are four basic mechanisms for persons to be released from prison:

    A.   Discretionary Release
       1.   In states retaining indeterminate sentences, **discretionary release** by the parole board is the manner by which most felons leave prison. In the context of discretionary release it is underscored that the offender's past, the nature of the offense committed, the inmate's behavior and participation in rehabilitative programs, and the prognosis for a crime-free future should guide the decision.

    B.   Mandatory Release
       1.   The use of determinate sentences and parole guidelines to fix the end of a prisoner's incarceration is referred to as **mandatory release**, because the correctional authority has little leeway in considering whether the offender is ready to return to society. Many states have devised ways to get around the rigidity of mandatory release through the use of furlough, home supervision, halfway houses, emergency release, and other programs.

A QUESTION OF ETHICS: Are the results of a behavior-modification program for sex offenders relevant to the parole board's decision?

    C.   Other Conditional Release
       1.   Because of the growth of prison populations, many states have devised ways to get around the rigidity of mandatory release by placing inmates in the community through furloughs, home supervision, halfway houses, emergency release, and other programs. These **other conditional releases** also avoid the appearance of the politically sensitive label, discretionary parole.

    D.   Expiration Release
       1.   An increasing percentage of prisoners receive an **expiration release**. These inmates are released from any further correctional supervision and cannot be returned to prison for their current offense. Such offenders have served the maximum court sentence, minus good time--they have "maxed out."

CLOSE-UP : A Roomful of Strangers: Armed Robber, Ben Brooks, goes before a parole review board.

    E.   The Impact of Release Mechanisms
       1.   There is considerable variation among the states but, on a national basis it is estimated that felony inmates serve on the average less than two years before release -- based on good time, credit for time served in jail, and parole release.

       2.   Supporters of discretion for the paroling authority argue that the courts do not adequately dispense justice and that the possibility of parole has invaluable benefits for the system.

       3.   Discretionary release mitigates the harshness of the penal code, it equalizes disparities inevitable in sentencing behavior, and it is necessary to assist prison administrators in maintaining order.

       4.   Supporters also contend that the postponement of sentence determination to the parole stage offers the opportunity for a more detached evaluation than is possible in the

atmosphere of a trial and that early release is economically sensible because the cost of incarceration is considerable.

5.   A major criticism of the effect of parole is that it has shifted responsibility for many of the primary decisions of criminal justice from a judge, who holds legal procedures uppermost, to an administrative board, where discretion rules.

6.   In most states that allow discretion, states' parole decisions are made in secret hearings, with only the board members, the inmate, and correctional officers present. Often there are no published criteria to guide decisions, and the prisoners are given no reason for either the denial or granting of their release.

V.   PAROLE SUPERVISION IN THE COMMUNITY

A.   <u>Introduction</u>

1.   Parolees are released from prison on condition that they do not further violate the law and that they live according to rules designed both to help them readjust to society and to control their movements.

    a.   These rules may require them to abstain from alcoholic beverages, to keep away from bad associates, to maintain good work habits, and not to leave the state without permission.

    b.   Question: Should parolees be subject to restrictions that are not placed on law-abiding citizens?

2.   When they first come out of prison, parolees lack jobs, money, clothes, etc. In most states they are given only clothes, a token amount of money, the list of rules governing their conditional release, and the name and address of the parole supervisor to whom they must report within twenty-four hours.

3.   Parolees often lack job skills, cannot move to areas where jobs may be located, and face discrimination because of their criminal record -- are even barred from some jobs by state laws against employing "ex-cons" in certain positions.

    a.   Many parolees just do not have the social, psychological, and material resources to adequately cope with the temptations and complications of modern life.

    b.   Many face difficulties in leaving the highly structured environment of prison.

4.   CLOSE-UP: Returning to America. Prisoner's description of being free in New York City after sixteen years in a maximum-security prison.

5.   TECHNOLOGY ISSUES IN CRIMINAL JUSTICE: Drug Testing has been ineffective because parolees will dilute their urine by drinking jugs of water before a drug test. A new drug patch has been developed to increase the effectiveness of drug testing.

B.   <u>Community Programs Following Release</u>

1.   Some programs provide employment and housing assistance in the community following release. Other programs are designed to prepare the prisoner prior to release for life in the community through evaluation and testing so that the individual can steadily move toward reintegration into the community.

2.   In pursuit of pre-release assistance, programs of partial confinement are used to test the readiness of the offender for full release.

3.   **Work and Educational Release**: By 1972 most states and the federal government had release programs that allowed inmates to go into the community to work or to attend school during the day and return at night to an institution.

    a.   Although most of the programs are justifiable in terms of rehabilitation, many correctional administrators and legislators like them because they cost little.

    b.   In some states, a portion of the inmate's employment earnings may even be deducted for room and board.

    c.   One of the problems of administering the programs is that the person on release is often viewed by other inmates as being privileged, and such perceptions can lead to social troubles within the prison.

d. Another problem is that in some states organized labor complains that jobs are being taken from free citizens.

4. **Furloughs**: Consistent with the focus of community corrections, brief home furloughs have come into increasing use in the United States. In some states an effort is made to ensure that all eligible inmates are able to use the furlough privilege on Thanksgiving and Christmas.

   a. In other states, however, the program has been much more restrictive, and often only those about to be released are given furloughs.

   b. Furloughs are thought to offer an excellent means of testing an inmate's ability to cope with the larger society. Through home visits, family ties can be renewed, the tensions of confinement lessened, and prisoners' morale lifted.

   c. There are serious risks involved because of the inevitable public outrage if a prisoner on furlough commits a crime or disappears.

5. **Halfway Houses**: A correctional facility housing convicted felons who spend a portion of their day at work in the community but reside in the halfway house during nonworking hours.

   a. Often these facilities are established in former private homes or small hotels, which permit a less institutional atmosphere. Individual rooms, group dining rooms, and other homelike features are maintained whenever possible.

   b. "Halfway houses" range from secure institutions in the community with programs designed to assist inmates preparing for release on parole to shelters where parolees, probationers, or persons diverted from the system are able to live with minimal supervision and direction.

      i. Some halfway houses are organized to deliver special treatment services, such as programs designed to deal with alcohol, drug, or mental problems.

   c. Problems of Residential Programs: Resistance from neighborhoods can produce major political issue.

   d. It is difficult and expensive to provide high-quality, effective programs and services. Thus far the data on recidivism have been discouraging.

C. Parole Officer: Cop or Social Worker?

   1. Parole officers are asked to play two different roles: cop and social worker.

      a. As police officers, they are given the power to restrict many aspects of the parolee's life, to enforce the **conditions of release,** and to initiate revocation proceedings if violations occur.

      b. Like other officials in the criminal justice system, the parole officer has extensive discretion in low-visibility situations.

      c. The parole officer's broad authority can produce a sense of insecurity in the ex-offender and hamper the development of mutual trust, which is important to the parole officer's other roles in assisting the parolee's readjustment to the community.

      d. Parole officers must act as social workers by helping the parolee to find a job and restore family ties.

      e. Parole officers must be prepared to serve as agent-mediators between parolees and the organizations with which they deal and to channel them to social agencies, such as psychiatric clinics.

      f. Some researchers have suggested that parole officers' conflicting responsibilities of cop and social worker should be separated.

D. The Parole Bureaucracy: Parole officers work in a bureaucratic environment. Due to limitations on resources and expertise, officers often spend more time with the recently released offenders and check only periodically on parolees who have proven themselves to be reliable.

WORK PERSPECTIVE: Lara Pellegrini, Parole Officer, Austin, Texas.
    E.   Adjustment to Life Outside Prison
        1.   With little preparation, the ex-offender moves from the highly structured, authoritarian life of the institution into a world that is filled with temptations, that presents complicated problems requiring immediate solution, and that expects him to assume responsibilities to which he has long been unaccustomed.
        2.   Due to extensive news coverage of crimes committed by parolees, there has been public hostility and even
            physical attacks on parolees, especially released sex offenders. Many states have enacted notification statutes which require sex offenders to register their addresses on lists with the police that are made available to the public.
    F.   **Revocation of Parole**
        1.   Parole may be revoked for either committing a new crime or for violating the conditions of parole.
        2.   WHAT AMERICANS THINK: There is strong support among the American public for sending parolees who fail a drug test back to prison.
        3.   If the parole officer alleges that a technical (noncriminal) violation of the parole contract has occurred, a revocation proceeding will be held.
            a.   The U.S. Supreme Court, in the case of **Morrissey v. Brewer (1972),** distinguished the requirements of such a proceeding from the normal requirements of the criminal trial but held that many of the due process rights must be accorded the parolee.
            b.   The Court has required a two-step hearing process whereby the parole board determines whether the contract has been violated. Parolees have the right to be notified of the charges against them, to know the evidence against them, to be heard, to present witnesses, and to confront the witnesses against them.
        4.   Over the past 20 years, parole violators represent an increasing portion of people committed to prison.
        5.   There are differences among states in the percentage of parolees returned to prison for violations.

    VI.   THE FUTURE OF PRISONER REENTRY
        1.   Parole has been under attack since the 1970s because it is viewed as a symbol of leniency. The media reports of gruesome crimes committed by parolees adds to the public outrage.
        2.   Correctional experts argue that parole plays an important role in the criminal justice system, given that early release from prison must be earned.
        3.   As prison populations rise, demands that felons be allowed to serve part of their time in the community will undoubtedly mount. These demands will come from legislators and corrections officers rather than from the public.
        4.   Research has shown that most prisoners receive little or no assistance for their transition from incarceration to life on the streets.
        5.   Because of high recidivism rates, various innovations are being tested such as **"reentry courts"** where judges oversee a prisoner's return to society.
VII. PRISON: INSIDE THE CRIMINAL JUSTICE SYSTEM AND BEYOND: ONE MAN'S JOURNEY written by Chuck Terry

REVIEW OF KEY TERMS
Fill in the appropriate term from the list for each statement below
parole
grace
contract
custody
ticket of leave
reentry court
discretionary release

expiration release
mandatory release
other conditional release
conditions of release
work and educational release
furlough
halfway house
Morrissey v. Brewer (1972)
revocation of parole

1. _____ is when the prisoner could be kept incarcerated but the government extends the privilege of release.

2. _____ is the release of an inmate from incarceration without any further correctional supervision.

3. _____ is the release of an inmate from prison to conditional supervision at the discretion of the parole board within the boundaries set by the sentence and the penal law.

4. _____ is a system of conditional release from prison, devised by Captain Alexander Maconochie and first developed in Ireland by Sir Walter Crofton. It was an early form of parole.

5. _____ provides for release according to a time frame stipulated by a determinate sentence and/or parole guidelines.

6. _____ a term used in some states to avoid the rigidity of mandatory release by placing convicts under supervision in various community settings.

7. Parolees are released from prison on condition that they abide by laws and follow rules, known as _____.

8. _____ is the conditional release of an offender from incarceration but not from the legal custody of the state.

9. _____ means that even though the offender is released from prison, he or she is still a responsibility of the government.

10. _____ provides for release during the day in order for prisoners to work or attend school.

11. The U.S. Supreme Court ruled in _____ that if the parole officer alleges a technical violation, a two-step revocation proceeding is required.

12. _____ provides a mechanism for temporary release for a few days in order to visit family.

13. _____ is a correctional facility housing convicted felons who spend a portion of their day at work in the community but reside in the halfway house during nonworking hours.

14. _____ can be the result of violations of parole conditions.

15. _____ when the government enters into an agreement with the prisoner whereby the prisoner promises to abide by certain conditions in exchange for being released.

16. _____ is an innovative idea being tested whereby a judge oversees a prisoner's return to society.

REVIEW OF KEY PEOPLE
Fill in the appropriate person from the list for each statement below
Megan Kanka
Alexander Maconochie
Zebulon Brockway
Sir Walter Crofton

1. _____ was a key figure who developed the concept of parole in the nineteenth century.

2. _____ was murdered and her death resulted in 30 states enacting sexual offender notification laws.

3. _____developed the ticket of leave, an early form of parole, in Ireland.

4. _____ experimented with parole in New York at the Elmira State Reformatory.

SELF-TEST SECTION

Multiple Choice Questions
14.1. When was parole developed in the American criminal justice system?
a) 1770s
b) 1790s
c) 1870s
d) 1920s
e) 1980s

14.2. What actions were taken by state legislators after the murders of 12-year old Polly Klaus and seven-year old Megan Kanka?
a) state legislators passed laws allowing life sentence without parole for sex offenders
b) state legislators passed laws punishing parents for being absent in the lives of their children
c) state legislators passed laws to castrate sexual offenders
d) state legislators passed laws to enact sexual offender notification laws
e) state legislators passed laws to allow for the death penalty for sex offenders

14.3. Which of the following factors contributes to the reentry problem of inmates into society?
a) too much prerelease planning
b) decrease in prison education programs
c) shorter prison terms
d) all of the above
e) none of the above

14.4. Which of the following is part of Alexander Maconochie's system of rewards for good conduct, labor, and study?
a) freedom in an unlimited area
b) partial restoration of liberty
c) undisciplined imprisonment
d) all of the above
e) none of the above

14.5. What is a major criticism of discretionary release?
a) responsibility is shifted from the parole board to the parolee
b) responsibility is shifted from the parole board to a judge
c) responsibility is shifted from a judge to the parole board
d) responsibility is shifted from the parolee to the parolee's family
e) there are no major criticisms of discretionary release

14.6. Which of the following is a disadvantage for parolees upon reentering society?
a) former convict status
b) transition from highly structured life in prison to open society
c) lack of money
d) all of the above
e) none of the above

14.7. Who murdered Megan Kanka?
a) Alexander Maconochie
b) Jesse Timmendequas
c) Zebulon Brockway
d) Walter Crofton
e) Robert Blake

14.8. According to Cole and Smith, what is the status of prison reentry as a public issue?
a) not important
b) slightly important
c) important
d) non-existent
e) the most important issue in the criminal justice system

14.9. Which of the following influenced parole in the U. S.?
a) English
b) Australian
c) Irish
d) all of the above
e) none of the above

14.10. How many states have some procedure for release of offenders before the end of their sentences?
a) ten
b) twenty
c) thirty
d) forty
e) all fifty states

14.11. How much money is given to parolees when they exit prison?
a) none
b) $10-$20
c) $50-$100
d) $100 per year spent in prison
e) $1000 per year spent in prison

14.12. Reentry programs are available in all states. How many prisoners have access to them?
a) no prisoners because it applies only to those being held in jails
b) relatively few
c) the majority of prisoners
d) all of the prisoners
e) only those prisoners in the Northeast region of the U. S.

14.13. What percentage of inmates are served by residential programs known as halfway houses?
a) less than 1%
b) 10%
c) 25%
d) 47%
e) 85%

14.14. Which of the following is TRUE about parole?
a) parole was originally designed to help offenders make the transition from prison to the community
b) safety and security have become less important in recent years
c) a parolee's principal contact with the criminal justice system is the judge
d) all of the above are true
e) none of the above are true

14.15. Which of the following is TRUE about parole officers?
a) the parole officers' responsibilities of cop and social worker are separate
b) parole officers are NOT permitted to visit the home of the parolee
c) parole officers are NOT permitted to visit the place of employment of the parolee
d) all of the above are true
e) none of the above are true

14.16. Which of the following is TRUE about parolees today?
a) parolees today face fewer obstacles in living a crime-free life than those released prior to 1990
b) parolees today face the same obstacles in living a crime-free life as those released prior to 1990
c) parolees today face greater obstacles in living a crime-free life than those released prior to 1990
d) parolees today face no obstacles at all and those prior to 1990 also faced no obstacles
e) there have been no comparison studies done of parolees today and those prior to 1990

14.17. What do Americans think about parolees who fail a drug test?
a) a majority of Americans strongly disagree or somewhat disagree that the parolee should be sent back to prison
b) a majority of Americans strongly agree or somewhat agree that the parolee should be sent back to prison
c) a majority of Americans strongly don't know if the parolee should be sent back to prison
d) Americans almost unanimously think the parolee should be sent back to prison
e) Americans almost unanimously do NOT think the parolee should be sent back to prison

14.18. What do Americans think about the government making the records available of a person convicted of a crime?
a) a majority of Americans think the government should NOT make records available to employers if a person serves his or her sentence and does not violate the law for five years
b) a majority of Americans do NOT know whether the government should make records available to employers if a person serves his or her sentence and does not violate the law for five years
c) a majority of Americans think the government should make records available to employers, even if a person serves his or her sentence and does not violate the law for five years
d) Americans almost unanimously Americans think the government should NOT make records available to employers if a person serves his or her sentence and does not violate the law for five years
e) Americans almost unanimously Americans think the government should make records available to employers if a person serves his or her sentence and does not violate the law for five years

14.19. What is the term used to describe persons who have served prison terms for prior offenses and are being let out again?
a) churners
b) halfways
c) maxers
d) NIMBY's
e) all of the above

14.20. Which of the following is TRUE about the public and ex-offenders?
a) news reports of brutal crimes committed by parolee shape the public's assumptions
b) public attention is focused intensely on all adult felons that leave state prisons
c) public attention is focused intensely on all adult felons that leave federal prisons
d) all of the above are true
e) none of the above are true

14.21. Which of the following was a method of moving prisoners out of prison that influenced parole in the U. S.?
a) apprenticeship by indenture
b) ticket of leave
c) transporting of criminal from one country to another
d) all of the above
e) none of the above

14.22. Which of the following is TRUE about parole?
a) If a parolee breaks a rule, parole is always revoked
b) only felons are released on parole
c) adults who commit misdemeanors are usually released immediately after they have finished serving their sentences
d) all of the above are true
e) b and c are true

14.23. In what country did Maconochie's idea of requiring prisoners to earn their early release catch on first?
a) Australia
b) Canada
c) United States
d) France
e) Ireland

14.24. Which of the following is TRUE about the parole system of New York in the late nineteenth century?
a) the parole system required supervision by the police
b) the parole system was organized in New York by Sir Walter Crofton of the Elmira State Reformatory
c) the parole system relied on volunteers from citizen reform groups to assist with the parolee's reintegration into society
d) all of the above are true
e) none of the above are true

14.25. Who are considered the "baddest of the bad"?
a) parolees who are returned to prison more than once
b) parole officers who neglect their duties
c) those offenders who serve mandatory sentences for violent crimes who are ineligible for early release
d) those offenders who serve indeterminate sentences for multiple drug offenses
e) news reporters who sensationalize the crimes of a small percentage of parolees

True and False Questions

_____14.1. Before parole is revoked, the offender is NOT entitled to a preliminary hearing.

_____14.2. Most work and educational release programs cost relatively little.

_____14.3. The French had the most influence on the U. S. in terms of the development of parole.

_____14.4. When adults who commit misdemeanors are released from prison, it is usually with parole.

_____14.5. Parole release mechanisms simply determine the date at which a prisoner will be sent back into the community.

_____14.6. After the murder of Megan Kanka, most states enacted sexual offender notification laws.

_____14.7. A sexual offender notification law only notifies the police of the whereabouts of "potentially dangerous" sex offenders.

_____14.8. Parolees usually are given no money upon their release from prison.

_____14.9. Parolees are handicapped by their status as former convicts.

_____14.10. There are few programs to assist parolees.

_____14.11. Safety and security have become major issues in parole services.

_____14.12. Parole agencies have plenty of resources and a great deal of expertise.

_____14.13. Local police are in charge of checking for parole violations.

_____14.14. Parolees face few temptations upon release from prison.

_____14.15. Congress and state legislatures have imposed a restriction upon ex-felons by prohibiting them from obtaining welfare benefits.

_____14.16. Community corrections assumes that reentry should be a gradual process where parolees receive help.

_____14.17. Parole boards have considerable discretion.

_____14.18. Parole rests on the concepts of grace, custody, and contract.

_____14.19. It is popular for politicians to call for the abolition of parole.

_____14.20. As prison populations increase, the demand for felons to serve part of their sentences in the community decreases.

WORKSHEET 14.1: PAROLE

If you were sitting on a parole board, how would you react to the violations listed below? Write a brief statement explaining why you would or would NOT revoke parole.

Failure to report for drug treatment : _____

_____

_____

_____

serious credit problems: _____

_____

_____

_____

Left state without permission: _____

_____

_____

_____

possession of drugs: _____

_____

_____

_____

fired from job: _____

_____

_____

Maintained contact with known offenders _____

_____

_____

Caught stealing food from a grocery store _____

_____

_____

CHAPTER 15

JUVENILE JUSTICE

LEARNING OBJECTIVES

After covering the material in this chapter, students should understand:

1.   the nature and extent of youth crime;

2.   the history of juvenile justice, including the five eras: Puritan, Refuge; Juvenile Court; Juvenile Rights; Crime Control;

3.   the importance of age and jurisdiction in the juvenile system;

4.   the role of police, intake screening, pretrial procedures and transfer to adult court;

5.   adjudication and disposition in the juvenile system;

6.   juvenile corrections, including probation, custodial care, institutional programs, and aftercare.

CHAPTER SUMMARY

This chapter explores the extent and nature of juvenile crime by listing a variety of statistics regarding juvenile crime. It also traces the history of the juvenile justice system from the colonial era to the modern era using five distinct periods: 1) the Puritan period, 2) the Reform period, 3) the Juvenile Court period, 4) the Juvenile Rights period and 5) the Crime Control period. The chapter examines the development of juvenile courts in the United States, the specific rulings by the U. S. Supreme Court that established constitutional protections for juveniles in the 1960s, and the movement to get tough on juveniles that has developed since the 1980s. Finally, the problems that are faced today within the juvenile justice system are presented such as whether juveniles should be tried as adults in specific circumstances.

CHAPTER OUTLINE

I.   INTRODUCTION

A.   17-year old **John Lee Malvo** was arrested on October 23, 2002 along with 41-year old John A. Muhammad in the D. C. sniper shootings which resulted in the deaths of ten people and the wounding of three. As society confronts the reality that young offenders can commit terrible acts, no consensus exists about how to solve the problem of juvenile criminality. The juvenile justice system is separate but interrelated part of the broader criminal justice system. Because juveniles commit a significant portion of criminal offenses, serious attention must be given to the juvenile justice system.

II. YOUTH CRIME IN THE UNITED STATES

A.   Introduction
  1.   In all, about 2.4 million juveniles under 18 years are arrested each year; 99,000 for violent crimes. Only 28 percent of arrestees under 18 years of age were females. Youths commit violent crimes out of proportion with their numbers.
  2.   Some researchers have estimated that one boy in three will be arrested by the police at some point before his eighteenth birthday.

3.   Gang violence from youth gangs has exacerbated many problems. Gangs such as CRIPS (Common Revolution in Progress) have increased their numbers and moved into suburban and rural areas.

4.   Adding to the problem is the role that technology may be playing in promoting violence. There is a growing debate concerning the effect of the entertainment industry's influence on juveniles

TECHNOLOGY ISSUES IN CRIMINAL JUSTICE: The Impact of Entertainment Technology on Behavior. Do video games and other technology-based forms of entertainment teach young people inappropriate values or otherwise encourage crimes and violence?

III.   THE DEVELOPMENT OF JUVENILE JUSTICE

A.   Introduction
1.   The English common law had long declared that children under seven years of age were incapable of felonious intent and were therefore not criminally responsible. Children aged seven to fourteen could be held accountable only if it could be shown that they understood the consequences of their actions.

2.   Under the doctrine of **parens patriae**, which held the king to be the father of the realm, the chancery courts exercised protective jurisdiction over all children, particularly those involved in questions of dependency, neglect, and property.
     a.   These courts, however, had civil jurisdiction, and juvenile offenders were dealt with by the criminal courts.

3.   The concept of parens patriae was important for the development of juvenile justice, for it legitimized the intervention of the state on behalf of the child.

B.   **The Puritan Period** (1646-1824)
1.   The earliest attempt by a colony to deal with problem children was passage of the Massachusetts Stubborn Child Law in 1646. With this law, the Puritans of the Massachusetts Bay Colony imposed the view that the child was evil and emphasized the need for the family to discipline and raise youths.

C.   **The Refuge Period** (1824-1899)
1.   As the population of American cities began to grow in the half century following independence, the problem of youth crime and neglect was a concern for reformers.

2.   These reformers focused their efforts primarily on the urban immigrant poor, and sought to have parents declared "unfit" if their children roamed the streets and were apparently "out of control."

3.   The state's power was used to create institutions for these children where they could learn good work and study habits, live in a disciplined and healthy environment, and develop "character."

4.   The first of these institutions was The House of Refuge of New York, which opened in 1825. It was followed by similar facilities in Boston, Philadelphia, and Baltimore. Children were placed in these homes by court order usually because of neglect or vagrancy. They often stayed there until they reached the age of majority.

5.   Some states created "reform schools" to provide the discipline and education needed by wayward youth in a "homelike" atmosphere, usually in rural areas. The first, the Lyman School for Boys, was opened in Westboro, Massachusetts, in 1848. A similar school for girls was opened in Lancaster, Massachusetts, in 1855. Ohio created the State Reform Farm in 1857, and the states of Maine, Rhode Island, New York, and Michigan soon followed suit.

D.   **The Juvenile Court Period** (1899-1960)
1.   Focus on juvenile criminality.
2.   Members of the **Progressive** Movement sought to use the power of the state to provide individualized care and treatment of deviants of all kinds--adult criminals, the mentally ill, juvenile delinquents. They pushed for adoption of probation, treatment, indeterminate sentences, and parole for adult offenders and were successful in establishing similar programs for juveniles.

3.   Referred to as the **"child savers,"** these upper-middle class reformers sought to use the power of the state to "save" children from a life of crime.

4.   They were stimulated by: concern over the influence of environmental factors on behavior; the rise of the social sciences, which claimed they could treat the problems underlying deviance; and a belief that state action could be benevolent in serving to rectify social problems.

5.   It was argued that a separate juvenile court system was needed so that the problems of the individual youth could be treated in an atmosphere in which flexible procedures would rid them of thoughts of crime.

6.   **The Juvenile Court Act by Illinois in 1899** was first comprehensive system of juvenile justice. By 1917, all but three states provided for a juvenile court.

7.   The philosophy of the juvenile court was the idea that the state should deal with a child who broke the law much as a wise parent would deal with a wayward child. The doctrine of *parens patriae* again helped legitimize the system. Procedures were to be informal and private, records were to be confidential, children were to be detained apart from adults, and probation and social worker staffs were to be appointed.

8.   The term criminal behavior was replaced by **delinquent behavior** as it pertained to the acts of children. This shift in terminology serves to underscore the view that these children were wayward; but they could be returned to society as law-abiding citizens. But it also underscores the fact that the juvenile court could deal with behaviors that were not criminal if committed by adults such as smoking cigarettes, consensual sexual activity, truancy, or living a "wayward, idle, and dissolute life": **status offenses.**

9.   Rejection of due process protections. Because procedures were not to be adversarial, lawyers were unnecessary; psychologists and social workers, who could determine the juvenile's underlying behavior problem, were the main professionals attached to the system.

E.   **The Juvenile Rights Period** (1960-1980)
   1.   During the 1960s period of the "due process revolution" regarding the rights of adult defendants, lawyers and scholars began to criticize the extensive discretion exercised by juvenile justice officials.

   2.   In *Kent v. United States* (1966), the Supreme Court extended due process rights to children. In this case a sixteen year old boy was remanded from the juvenile to the adult court without his lawyer present. The Court ruled that juveniles had the right to counsel at a waiver hearing.

   3.   *In re Gault* (1967) extended due process rights to juvenile court. **Gerald Gault,** a juvenile, sentenced for making prank phone calls. The U.S. Supreme Court said juveniles should have procedural rights, including notice of charges, right to counsel, right to confront and cross-examine witnesses, and privilege against compelled self-incrimination.

   4.   In the case of **In re Winship (1970)** the Court held that proof must be established "beyond a reasonable doubt" before a juvenile may be classified as a delinquent for committing an act that would be a crime if it were committed by an adult.

   5.   The Supreme Court held in McKeiver v. Pennsylvania (1971) that "trial by jury in the juvenile court's adjudicative stage is not a constitutional requirement."

   6.   In Breed v. Jones (1975*)* the Court extended the protection against double jeopardy to juveniles by requiring that before a case is adjudicated in juvenile court, a hearing must be held to determine if it should be transferred to the adult court.

   7.   Although the court decisions would seem to have placed the rights of juveniles on a par with those of adults, critics have charged that the states have not fully implemented these rights.

   8.   Many states closed juvenile institutions and instead placed children in group homes and community treatment centers. Other states decreased the number of children held in institutions.

   9.   In 1974, Congress passed the Juvenile Justice and Delinquency Prevention Act which included provisions for the deinstitutionalization of status offenders (truants, runaways, etc.).
      a.   Since then efforts have been made to divert such children out of the system, to reduce the possibility of incarceration, and to rewrite the laws with regard to status offenses.

236

F.   The Crime Control Period (1980-Present)
      1.   With the public demanding that there be a "crackdown on crime," legislators have responded with changes in the juvenile system.
      2.   In Schall v. Martin (1984), the Supreme Court significantly departed from the trend toward increased juvenile rights. The Court confirmed the general notion of parens patriae as a primary basis for the juvenile court, equal in importance to the Court's desire to protect the community from crime. Thus, juveniles may be detained before trial if they are found to be a "risk" to the community, even though this rationale is not applicable to adult pretrial detention.
      3.   Just as legislators have upped the penalties for adult offenders, juveniles convicted of serious crimes are now spending much longer terms either in youth facilities or adult prisons. The present crime control policy has resulted in many more juveniles being tried in adult courts, including juveniles facing less serious charges such as alcohol possession.
      4.   Public support for a get-tough stance toward older juveniles seems to be growing.

IV.   THE JUVENILE JUSTICE SYSTEM

A.   Introduction
      1.   Juvenile justice operates through a variety of procedures in different states. Because the offenses committed by juveniles are mostly violations of state law, there is little federal involvement in the juvenile justice system.
      2.   Two basic factors characterize the juvenile justice system. These factors are: (1) ages of the clients, and (2) jurisdiction of the system.

B.   Age of Clients
      1.   The upper age limit for a juvenile varies from sixteen to eighteen: in thirty-eight states and the District of Columbia it is the eighteenth birthday; in eight states, the seventeenth; and in the remainder, the sixteenth.
      2.   In forty-nine states, judges have the discretion to transfer juveniles to adult courts through a waiver hearing as discussed above. Some state laws permit waiver for children as young as ten years of age.

C.   Categories of Cases
      1.   Four types of cases enter the juvenile justice system: delinquency, status offenses, neglect, and dependency.
            a.   Delinquent children have committed acts that if committed by an adult would be criminal--for example, auto theft, robbery, and assault.
            b.   Acts that are illegal only if they are committed by juveniles are known as status offenses.
                  i.   Rather than having committed a violation of the penal code, status offenders have been designated as ungovernable or incorrigible: as runaways, truants, or **persons in need of supervision (PINS).**
            c.   Some states do not distinguish between delinquent offenders and status offenders, and label both as juvenile delinquents.
            d.   Beginning in the early 1960s, many state legislatures attempted to distinguish status offenders and to exempt them from a criminal record. As previously noted, in 1974 Congress required states to remove noncriminal offenders from secure detention and correctional facilities.
            e.   Juvenile justice also deals with problems of neglect and dependency--situations in which children are viewed as being hurt through no fault of their own, because their parents have failed to provide a proper environment for them.
                  i.   Illinois, for example, defines a **neglected child** as one who is neglected as to proper or necessary support, education as required by law, or as to medical or other remedial care recognized under state law or other care necessary for his well being, or who is abandoned by his parents, guardians or custodians, or whose environment is injurious to his welfare or whose behavior is injurious to his own welfare or that of others.

        ii.   A **dependent child** is either without a parent or guardian or is not receiving proper care because of the physical or mental disability of that person.

2.   Nationally about 75 percent of the cases referred to the juvenile courts are delinquency cases, of which 20 percent are concerned with status offenses; about 20 percent are dependency and neglect cases; and about 5 percent involve special proceedings, such as adoption.

V.   JUVENILE JUSTICE PROCESS

A.   <u>Introduction</u>
1.   Prevention of delinquency is the system's justification for intervening in the lives of juveniles who are involved in either status or criminal offenses.
2.   It is still assumed that the juvenile proceedings are to be conducted in a nonadversarial environment, and that the court should be a place where the judge, social workers, clinicians, and probation officers work together to diagnose the child's problem and select a rehabilitative program to attack this problem.
3.   More discretion is exercised in the juvenile than in the adult justice system.
4.   Juvenile justice is a particular type of bureaucracy that is based on an ideology of social work and is staffed primarily by persons who think of themselves as members of the helping professions.
5.   Exchange relations: The juvenile court must deal not only with children and their parents but also with patrol officers, probation officers, welfare officials, social workers, psychologists, and the heads of treatment institutions. These others all have their own goals, their own perceptions of delinquency, and their own concepts of treatment.

B.   <u>Police Interface</u>
1.   Many police departments have special units to deal with youth matters.
2.   Most complaints against juveniles are brought by the police, although they may be initiated by an injured party, school officials, or even the parents.
3.   The police must make three major decisions with regard to the processing of juveniles:
    a.   Whether to take the child into custody;
    b.   Whether to request that the child be detained following apprehension;
    c.   Whether to refer the child to court.
4.   The police exercise enormous discretion with regard to these decisions.
5.   A number of factors play a role in the way that the police dispose of a case of juvenile delinquency. These factors include:
    a.   predominant attitude of the community;
    b.   the officer's attitude toward the juvenile;
    c.   the juvenile's family;
    d.   the offense and the court;
    e.   officer's conception of his or her role.
6.   The disposition of juvenile cases at the arrest stage also relies on the seriousness of the offense, the child's prior record, and his or her demeanor.

C.   <u>Intake Screening at the Court</u>: Juvenile process begins with a referral in the form of a petition, not an arrest warrant as in the adult system. When a petition is filed, an intake hearing is held presided over by a hearing officer.
1.   During this intake stage, a review of the case is made by an hearing officer to determine whether the alleged facts are sufficient to cause the juvenile court to take jurisdiction or whether some other action would be in the child's interest.
2.   **Diversion** is the process of screening children out of the system without a decision by the court

D.   <u>Pretrial Procedures</u>: At the initial hearing, a juveniles are informed of their rights and told that any plea must be voluntary. If a juvenile is to be detained pending trial, then a detention hearing is held. Detention Hearing: a hearing by the juvenile court to determine if a juvenile is to be detained or released prior to adjudication.

1.   Children are held in detention for a number of reasons:
   a.   The possibility that they will commit other crimes while awaiting trial;
   b.   The possibility of harm from gang members or parents if they are released;
   c.   The possibility that they may not appear in court as required;

E.   Transfer to the Adult Court: Transfer is accomplished by a judge **waives** jurisdiction.
   1.   In the past during a waiver hearing the state had to make a case that the youth was not amenable to rehabilitation in the juvenile system before a transfer to the adult court. Now many states place the burden on the youth to show amenability to treatment.

THE POLICY DEBATE: Should juveniles be tried as adults? Supporters of trying juveniles as adults point to the continuing high levels of violence and the heinous nature of some crimes committed by youths. Opponents of trying juveniles as adults point out that treating adolescents as adults ignores the fact that they are at a different stage of social and emotional development.

F.   Adjudication
   1.   The changes in criminal proceedings mandated by the due process decisions of the Supreme Court following *Gault* have brought about shifts in the philosophy and actions of the juvenile court.
      a.   Copies of formal petitions with specific charges must be given to the parents and child, counsel may be present and free counsel appointed if the juvenile is indigent, witnesses may be cross-examined, and a transcript of the proceedings must be kept
   2.   As with other Supreme Court decisions, the reality of local practice may differ sharply from the stipulations in the opinion.
      a.   Juveniles and their parents often waive their rights in response to suggestions made by the judge or probation officer.
      b.   The lower social status of the offender's parents, the intimidating atmosphere of the court, and judicial hints that the outcome will be more favorable if a lawyer is not present are reasons the procedures outlined in *Gault* are not demanded.
      c.   The litany of "treatment," "doing what's right for the child," and "working out a just solution" may sound enticing, especially to people who are unfamiliar with the intricacies of formal legal procedures.
   3.   With the increased concern about crime, prosecuting attorneys are taking a more prominent part in the system.
   4.   Juvenile court records and proceedings have traditionally been closed to the public. Judges in adult courts do not necessarily have access to juvenile records and thus cannot tell if adult first offenders actually have a prior juvenile crime record.

G.   Disposition: If the court makes a finding of delinquency, a dispositional hearing is required. This hearing may be held immediately following the entry of a plea or at a later date.
   1.   Typically, the judge receives a social history or predispositional report before passing sentence. Few juveniles are found by the court to be not delinquent at trial, since the intake and pretrial processes normally filter out cases in which a law violation cannot be proved.
   2.   In addition to dismissal of a petition, four other choices are available:
      a.   probation;
      b.   alternative dispositions;
      c.   custodial care;
      d.   community treatment.
   3.   Throughout most of this century judges have sentenced juveniles to indeterminate sentences so that correctional administrators would have the discretion to determine when release was appropriate under a rehabilitation model.

WHAT AMERICANS THINK?: Most Americans (65%) think juveniles between the ages of 14 and 17 who commit violent crimes should be treated the same as adults.

H. Corrections
1. Both adult and juvenile systems mix rehabilitative and retributive sanctions.
2. Differences between adult and juvenile systems flow from the *parens patriae* concept and the youthful, seemingly innocent persons with whom the system deals.
3. One predominant aim of juvenile corrections is to avoid unnecessary incarceration.
    a. Placing children in institutions has labeling effects; the children begin to perceive themselves as "bad," because they have received punitive treatment, and children who see themselves as bad are likely to behave that way.
    b. Treatment is believed to be more effective when the child is living in a normal, supportive home environment.
4. *Probation*: In 54 percent of cases, the juvenile offenders is placed on probation and released to the custody of a parent or guardian. Juvenile probation can be very different from adult probation in two respects:
    a. Traditionally, juvenile probation has been more satisfactorily funded, and hence caseloads of officers are much lower in number.
    b. Second, juvenile probation itself is often infused with the sense that the offender can change, that the job is enjoyable, and that the clients are worthwhile. Such attitudes make for greater creativity than is possible with adult probation.
        i. One of the most common probation strategies is to pair the juvenile with a "big brother" or "big sister," who spends time with the offender, providing a positive adult role model.
5. *Alternative Dispositions*: Although probation and commitment to an institution are the major dispositional alternatives, judges have wide discretion to warn, to fine, to arrange for restitution, to refer a juvenile for treatment at either a public or a private community agency, or to withhold judgment. Judges sometimes suspend judgment, or continue cases without a finding, when they wish to put a youth under supervision but are reluctant to apply the label "delinquent." Judgment may be suspended for a definite or indefinite period of time. The court thus holds a definitive judgment in abeyance for possible use should a youth misbehave while under the informal supervision of a probation officer or parents.
6. *Custodial Care:* 29 percent of juvenile delinquents are placed in public or private residential facilities. The national incarceration rate per 100,000 juveniles aged ten to eighteen is 368. Nationally, 74 percent of incarcerated juveniles are held in public facilities, the remainder in private facilities.
    a. There is an overrepresentation of African-Americans in juvenile facilities.
    b. Boot camps for juvenile offenders grew rapidly in the 1990s

WORK PERSPECTIVE: Kia N. Harris, Juvenile Probation Officer, Lansing, Michigan.

7. *Institutional Programs*: Because of the emphasis on rehabilitation that has dominated juvenile justice for much of the past fifty years, a wide variety of treatment programs has been used: counseling, education, vocational training, and an assortment of psychotherapy methods have been incorporated into the juvenile correctional programs of most states.
    Unfortunately for many offenders, incarceration in a juvenile training institution appears to be mainly preparation for entry into adult corrections.
8. *Aftercare*: The juvenile equivalent of parole supervision is known as **aftercare**. Upon release, a parole officer supervises the offender who gets assistance with educational, counseling, and treatment services.
9. *Community Treatment*: Treatment in community-based facilities has become much more common during the past decade.
    a. Today, there are a number of private, nonprofit agencies that contract with the states to perform services for troubled youths.
    b. Foster homes are one type of community-based option where juvenile offenders live with families for a short period. Group homes are another option which are privately run facilities for groups of 12-20 juvenile offenders.

A QUESTION OF ETHICS: a group home that places the emphasis on order rather than treatment and uses older boys to intimidate younger or smaller boys into good behavior. Does this situation raise ethical questions?

CLOSEUP: Fernando, 16, Finds a Sanctuary in Crime. Youthful drug dealer, **Fernando Morales,** living as if he has no future; difficult childhood in poverty and parental neglect; gang membership.

VI.   PROBLEMS AND PERSPECTIVES

A.   Introduction
        1.   Much of the criticism of juvenile justice has emphasized the disparity between the treatment ideal and the institutionalized practices of an ongoing bureaucratic system.
        2.   In many states the same judges, probation officers, and social workers are asked to deal with neglected children as well as with young criminals. Although departments of social services may deal primarily with neglect cases, the distinction is often not maintained.
        3.   We must acknowledge that our understanding of the causes of delinquency and its prevention or treatment is extremely limited. The array of theories has occasioned an array of proposed—and often contradictory--treatments.
        4.   The conservative crime control policies that have hit the adult criminal justice system--with their emphasis on deterrence, retribution, and getting tough--have influenced juvenile justice by way of overcrowding in juvenile institutions, increased litigation challenging the abuse of children in training schools and detention centers, and higher rates of minority youth incarceration. All of these problems have emerged during a period of declining youth populations and fewer arrests of juveniles. With the demographic trend now reversing and the increased concern about drugs, one can see a surge of adolescents going through their criminally high-risk years in a system and community unable to cope with them.

REVIEW OF KEY TERMS
Fill in the appropriate term from the list for each statement below
Puritan
status offense
 parens patriae
waive
aftercare
delinquent
neglected child
dependent child
In re Winship (1970)
detention
"child savers"
Progressive reformers
Juvenile Court
Crime Control
Refuge Period
Juvenile Rights
foster home
PINS
Juvenile Court Act of Illinois (1899)
diversion

1.   _____ pushed for the state to provide individualized care and treatment to deviants of all kinds, including juveniles, in the early twentieth century.

2.   The _____ period is when retributive and deterrent elements became more influential upon juvenile justice.

3.   A _____ hearing determines whether a juvenile is to be detained or released prior to adjudication.

4.   _____ is the juvenile justice equivalent of parole.

5.   _____ established the first comprehensive system of juvenile justice.

6.   _____ is the concept of the state as the guardian and protector of juveniles and other citizens who cannot protect themselves.

7.   The _____ period is when constitutional law concerning juvenile justice developed.

8.   _____ is a child who has committed a criminal or status offense.

9.   _____ is the process of discretionary decisions that move children away from the system's most punitive consequences.

10.   _____ is a type of nonsecure placement for a significant number of nonoffenders, youths referred for abuse, neglect or emotional disturbance.

11.   The _____ period is when comprehensive juvenile justice institutions developed.

12.   _____ is any act committed by a juvenile that would not be a crime if it were committed by an adult but that is considered unacceptable for a juvenile.

13.   _____ is the nickname given to Progressive era reformers who sought to reshape the juvenile system.

14.   _____ stands for "person in need of supervision."

15.   In the case of _____, the Supreme Court ruled that proof must be established "beyond a reasonable doubt" before a juvenile may be classified as a delinquent.

16.   The procedure by which the juvenile court transfer a case to the adult criminal court is called a _____.

17.   _____ is a child whose parents are unable to give proper care.

18.   _____ is the period in which juvenile policy focused on urban, immigrant, poor children and the alleged inadequacies of their parents.

19.   The passage of the Massachusetts Stubborn Child Law in 1646 occurred during the _____ period.

20.   _____ is a child who is not receiving proper care because of parental inaction.

REVIEW OF KEY PEOPLE

Fill in the appropriate person(s) from the list for each statement below

Gerald Gault
John Lee Malvo
Jane Addams
Fernando Morales
Henry Thurston
Julia Lathrop
Abe Fortas

1. _____ was a social educator who successfully promoted the juvenile court concept.

2. _____ wrote the Court's majority opinion in the case of In re Gault where he outlined the due process rights of juveniles.

3. _____ was the boy whose case elicited an important decision from the Supreme Court.

4. Activists such as _____ and _____, both of the settlement house movement, also promoted the juvenile court concept, so that by 1904 ten states had implemented procedures similar to those of Illinois.

5. _____ was a sixteen year-old who found a sanctuary in crime as a youthful drug dealer.

6. _____ was arrested in October 2002 for murdering ten persons in the D. C. sniper shootings.

SELF-TEST SECTION

Multiple Choice Questions

15.1. Who was the seventeen year-old arrested in the D. C. sniper shootings?
a) John Lee Malvo
b) John Muhammad
c) Fernando Morales
d) Derek King
e) no juvenile was arrested in the D. C. sniper shooting

15.2. What did the Supreme Court decide in *McKevier v. Pennsylvania (1971)?*
a) the Court declared that juveniles have the right to counsel
b) the Court declared that there is no constitutional right for a jury trial for juveniles
c) the Court declared that school officials may search a student based on reasonable suspicion
d) the Court declared that the standard of "proof beyond a reasonable doubt" applies to juvenile proceedings
e) the Court declared that juveniles cannot be found delinquent in juvenile court and then waived to adult court without violating double jeopardy

15.3. Which of the following is a status offense?
a) living a wayward life
b) skipping school
c) running away from home
d) all of the above
e) none of the above

15.4. What did the Supreme Court decide in the case of *In re Winship (1970)?*
a) the Court declared that juveniles have the right to counsel
b) the Court declared that there is no constitutional right for a jury trial for juveniles
c) the Court declared that school officials may search a student based on reasonable suspicion
d) the Court declared that the standard of "proof beyond a reasonable doubt" applies to juvenile proceedings
e) the Court declared that juveniles cannot be found delinquent in juvenile court and then waived to adult court without violating double jeopardy

15.5. What did the Supreme Court decide in *Breed v. Jones (1975)?*
a) the Court declared that juveniles have the right to counsel
b) the Court declared that there is no constitutional right for a jury trial for juveniles
c) the Court declared that school officials may search a student based on reasonable suspicion
d) the Court declared that the standard of "proof beyond a reasonable doubt" applies to juvenile proceedings
e) the Court declared that juveniles cannot be found delinquent in juvenile court and then waived to adult court without violating double jeopardy

15.6. What did the Supreme Court decide in *Schall v. Martin (1984)?*
a) the Court declared that juveniles have the right to cross-examination
b) the Court declared that there is a constitutional right for a jury trial for juveniles
c) the Court declared that preventive pretrial detention of juveniles is allowable at times
d) the Court declared that the standard of "proof beyond a reasonable doubt" applies to juvenile proceedings
e) the Court declared that juveniles cannot be found delinquent in juvenile court and then waived to adult court without violating double jeopardy

15.7. What coincided with an epidemic of violent youth crime in the early 1990s?
a) increase in gun purchases by juveniles
b) increase in drug arrests
c) increase in the sale of video games
d) decrease in high school graduation rates
e) all of the above

15.8. According to the *Uniform Crime Reports*, how many people taken into custody each year are under 18 years of age?
a) one out of every two
b) one out of every five
c) one out of every ten
d) one out of every twenty
e) one out of every hundred

15.9. According to most Americans, what are the two most important problems facing children?
a) internet and media
b) education and teen pregnancy
c) depression and suicide
d) drugs and crime
e) parental neglect and loneliness

15.10. What legislation was the earliest attempt by a colony to deal with problem children?
a) Georgia Juvenile Delinquent Act of 1678
b) Massachusetts Stubborn Child Law in 1646
c) New York Troubled Child Act of 1702
d) Illinois Juvenile Court Act
e) Virginia Child Protection Act of 1656

15.11. During what period did New York open a school house for orphaned and destitute children as well as those convicted of crime?
a) The Juvenile Court Period
b) The Juvenile Rights Period
c) The Crime Control Period
d) The Puritan Period
e) The Refuge Period

15.12. Which of the following best describes the House of Refuge?
a) one half prison and one half nursery home
b) one half school house and one house nursery home
c) one half prison and one-half school house
d) school house
e) prison

15.13. During what period did the first reform school, the Lyman School for Boys, open in Westboro, Massachusetts?
a) The Juvenile Court Period
b) The Juvenile Rights Period
c) The Crime Control Period
d) The Puritan Period
e) The Refuge Period

15.14. During what period did Illinois pass the Juvenile Court Act by Illinois?
a) The Juvenile Court Period
b) The Juvenile Rights Period
c) The Crime Control Period
d) The Puritan Period
e) The Refuge Period

15.15. During what period brings the development of upper-middle- class reformers who sought to use the power of the state to "save" children from a life of crime?
a) The Juvenile Court Period
b) The Juvenile Rights Period
c) The Crime Control Period
d) The Puritan Period
e) The Refuge Period

15.16. During what period did Activists such as Jane Addams and Julia Lathrop, successfully promote the juvenile court concept?
a) The Juvenile Court Period
b) The Juvenile Rights Period
c) The Crime Control Period
d) The Puritan Period
e) The Refuge Period

15.17. During what period was the passage of the Massachusetts Stubborn Child Law?
a) The Juvenile Court Period
b) The Juvenile Rights Period
c) The Crime Control Period
d) The Puritan Period
e) The Refuge Period

15.18. During what period did the U.S. Supreme Court expand the rights of juveniles?
a) The Juvenile Court Period
b) The Juvenile Rights Period
c) The Crime Control Period
d) The Puritan Period
e) The Liberties and Freedoms for Juveniles Period

15.19. During what period did the U. S. Supreme Court depart from the trend toward increased juvenile rights?
a) The Juvenile Court Period
b) The Juvenile Rights Period
c) The Crime Control Period
d) The Puritan Period
e) The Refuge Period

15.20. During what period did the doctrine of *parens patriae* develop and legitimize the U. S. juvenile justice system?
a) The Juvenile Court Period
b) The Juvenile Rights Period
c) The Crime Control Period
d) The Puritan Period
e) The Refuge Period

15.21. What did the Supreme Court decide in *Kent v. U. S. (1966)?*
a) the Court declared that juveniles have the right to cross-examination
b) the Court declared that there is a constitutional right for a jury trial for juveniles
c) the Court declared that preventive pretrial detention of juveniles is allowable at times
d) the Court ruled that juveniles had the right to counsel at a hearing at which a juvenile judge may waive jurisdiction and pass the case to the adult court
e) the Court declared that the minimum age for the death penalty is sixteen.

15.22. Which of the following included provisions for taking status offenders out of corrections institutions?
a) Juvenile and Status Act
b) Massachusetts Stubborn Child Law
c) Delaware Troubled Child Act
d) Illinois Juvenile Court Act
e) Juvenile Justice and Delinquency Prevention Act

15.23. Which of the following is NOT emphasized with conservative crime control policies?
a) deterrence
b) retribution
c) getting tough
d) rehabilitation
e) all of the above are emphasized

15.24. For which of the following crimes is the percentage of juveniles arrested in lesser proportion than their percentage of the general population?
a) fraud
b) vandalism
c) motor vehicle theft
d) burglary
e) arson

15.25. For which of the following crimes is the percentage of juveniles arrested in greater proportion than their percentage of the general population?
a) arson
b) vandalism
c) motor vehicle theft
d) burglary
e) all of the above

True and False Questions

_____15.1. Youth gangs are NOT a problem in most American cities.

_____15.2. Most juvenile crimes are committed by females.

_____15.3. A separate juvenile justice system has not yet developed in the U. S.

_____15.4. England had great influence over the U. S. in the area of juvenile justice.

_____15.5. For the crime of arson, juveniles are arrested in greater proportion than their percentage of the general population.

_____15.6. For the crime of vandalism, juveniles are arrested in lesser proportions than their percentage of the general population.

_____15.7. For the crime of burglary, juveniles are arrested in greater proportions than their percentage of the general population.

_____15.8. For the crime of prostitution, juveniles are arrested in lesser proportions than their percentage of the general population.

_____15.9. For the crime of motor vehicle theft, juveniles are arrested in lesser proportions than their percentage of the general population.

_____15.10. Few states provided services to neglected youth at the end of the nineteenth century.

_____15.11. "Child savers" were lower-class reformers who fought to "save" children from the state.

_____15.12. Illinois established the first comprehensive system of juvenile justice in the United States.

_____15.13. Aftercare is equivalent to parole.

_____15.14. The number of incarcerated African–American juveniles is NOT a problem facing policy makers.

_____15.15. The U. S. Supreme Court began to afford constitutional protections to juveniles in the 1960s.

_____15.16. Skipping school is a status offense for a juvenile.

_____15.17. Murder is a status offense for a juvenile.

_____15.18. Running away from home is a status offense for a juvenile.

_____15.19. Since the 1980s, the juvenile justice system has emphasized less crime control.

_____15.20. Recently, the public has expressed support for a get-tough stance toward older juveniles.

WORKSHEET 15.1 HISTORY OF JUVENILE JUSTICE
For each era listed below, assume the role of the listed person. Describe how much discretionary authority you have
to determine which children will be drawn into the system and what will be done with them. Briefly describe what
you would decide to do with such children during that era.

THE PURITAN PERIOD (1646-1824). The Father: _____

_____

_____

_____

THE REFUGE PERIOD (1824-1899). Police officer:_____

_____

_____

_____

_____

JUVENILE COURT PERIOD (1899-1960). Juvenile Court Judge: _____

_____

_____

_____

_____

JUVENILE RIGHTS PERIOD (1960-1980). Social Worker: _____

_____

_____

_____

_____

_____

CRIME CONTROL PERIOD (1980-Present). Prosecutor: _____

_____

_____

_____

_____

WORKSHEET 15.2 TREATMENT OF DELINQUENTS

Assume each of the following occupational roles. In each role, formulate a recommendation for what should happen to a fourteen-year-old boy whose seventeen-year-old companion killed a man while the two of them attempted to steal a bicycle.

Social Worker:_____

_____

_____

_____

_____

_____

State Legislator:_____

_____

_____

_____

_____

_____

Director of Group Home for Delinquents:_____

_____

_____

_____

_____

_____

Juvenile Court Judge:_____

_____

_____

_____

_____

_____

ANSWER KEY

ANSWERS-CHAPTER ONE

Key Terms
1. discretion (p. 9)
2. doing justice (p. 2)
3. bench (p. 15)
4. information (p. 15)
5. resource dependence (p. 9)
6. dual court system (p. 11)
7. bail (p. 14)
8. arrest (p. 14)
9. U. S. President's Commission on Law Enforcement and Administration of Justice (1967) (p. 2)
10. system (p. 7)
11. decentralization (p. 4)
12. sequential tasks (p. 9)
13. Department of Homeland Security (p. 6)
14. filtering process (p. 9)
15. controlling crime (p. 3)
16. arraignment (p. 15)
17. Congress (p. 4)
18. booking (p. 14)
19. jury (p. 15)
20. "wedding cake" (p. 16)
21. warrant (p. 14)
22. preliminary hearing (p. 15)
23. due process model (p. 21)
24. preventing crime (p. 3)
25. U.S. Constitution (p. 4)
26. grand jury (p. 15)
27. Backscatter X-Ray (p. 4)
28. felonies (p. 20)
29. adjudication (p. 12)
30. exchange (p. 7)
31. indictment (p. 15)
32. plea bargain (p. 7)
33. misdemeanors (p. 21)
34. crime control model (p. 22)

Key People
1. Michael Kennedy (p. 12)
2. Lee Harvey Oswald (p. 5)
3. Christopher Jones (p. 18)
4. Herbert Packer (p. 21)
5. Robert Chambers (p. 1)

Multiple Choice
1.1. c (p. 4)
1.2. d (p. 4)
1.3. d (p. 9)
1.4. a (p. 10)
1.5. c (p. 3)
1.6. d (p. 5)
1.7. d (p. 11)
1.8. e (p. 11)
1.9. a (p. 11)
1.10. e (p. 12)
1.11. c (p. 12)
1.12. c (p. 12)
1.13. b (p. 12)
1.14. e (p. 12)
1.15. e (p. 12)
1.16. c (p. 16)
1.17. b (p. 16)
1.18. a (p. 16)
1.19. a (p. 18)
1.20. b (p. 18)
1.21. d (p. 18)
1.22. e (p. 18)
1.23. b (p. 15)
1.24. d (p. 25)
1.25. d (p. 25)

True and False
1.1. F (p. 4)
1.2. F (p. 4)
1.3. T (p. 5)
1.4. F (p. 5)
1.5. T (p. 15)
1.6. T (p. 16)
1.7. F (p. 9)
1.8. T (p. 8)
1.9. F (p. 16)
1.10. F (p. 24)
1.11. F (p. 11)
1.12. F (p. 12)
1.13. F (p. 12)
1.14. T (p. 17)
1.15. F (p. 19)
1.16. F (p. 18)
1.17. T (p. 12)
1.18. T (p. 27)
1.19. T (p. 27)
1.20. F (p. 25)

ANSWERS-CHAPTER TWO

<u>Key Terms</u>
1. social process theories (p. 50)
2. classical criminology (p. 46)
3. labeling theories (p. 50)
4. social conflict theories (p. 51)
5. anomie (p. 49)
6. learning theories (p. 50)
7. biological explanations (p. 47)
8. social structure theories (p. 49)
9. control theories (p. 50)
10. victimology (p. 40)
11. positivist criminology (p. 47)
12. criminogenic factors (p. 47)
13. psychological explanations (p. 48)
14. differential association theories (p. 50)
15. sociological explanations (p. 49)
16. dark figure of crime (p. 36)
17. Uniform Crime Reports (p. 36)
18. visible (p. 31)
19. crimes without victims (p. 32)
20. mala in se (p. 30)
21. National Crime Victimization Survey (p. 37)
22. National Incident-Based Reporting System (p. 37)
23. occupational crimes (p. 31)
24. political crimes (p. 33)
25. mala prohibita (p. 30)
26. organized crime (p. 31)
27. money laundering (p. 31)
28. Carnivore (p. 34)
29. negligence (p. 45)
30. precipitation (p. 45)
31. cybercrime (p. 34)
32. hate crime (p. 35)

<u>Key People</u>
1. Cesare Lombroso (p. 47)
2. James Q. Wilson & Richard Hernnstein (p. 47)
3. Robert Merton (p. 49)
4. Sigmund Freud (p. 48)
5. Edwin Sutherland (p. 50)
6. Cesare Beccaria (p. 46)
7. Laci Peterson (p. 29)

<u>Multiple Choice Questions</u>
2.1. b (p. 29)
2.2. c (p. 32)
2.3. d (p. 30)
2.4. e (p. 30)
2.5. e (p. 52)
2.6. a (p. 30)
2.7. d (p. 34)
2.8. b (p. 33)
2.9. e (p. 33)
2.10. c (p. 31)
2.11. a (p. 31)
2.12. c (p. 35)
2.13. b (p. 44)
2.14. e (p. 36)
2.15. b (p. 30)
2.16. d (p. 34)
2.17. c (p. 37)
2.18. d (p. 44)
2.19. c (p. 43)
2.20. d (p. 47)
2.21. c (p. 48)
2.22. c (p. 50)
2.23. d (p. 49)
2.24. d (p. 51)
2.25. a (p. 51)

<u>True and False Questions</u>
2.1. F (pp. 29-30)
2.2. T (p. 30)
2.3. T (p. 30)
2.4. F (p. 36)
2.5. T (p. 31)
2.6. T (p. 33)
2.7. F (p. 38)
2.8. T (p. 32)
2.9. F (p. 34)
2.10. T (p. 39)
2.11. F (p. 46)
2.12. F (p. 50)
2.13. F (p. 44)
2.14. T (p. 51)
2.15. T (p. 47)
2.16. F (p. 51)
2.17. T (p. 51)
2.18. T (p. 37)
2.19. F (p. 40)
2.20. T (p. 40)

ANSWERS-CHAPTER THREE

<u>Key Terms</u>
1. substantive criminal law (p. 57)
2. New York v. Quarles (p. 72)
3. self-defense (p. 62)
4. fundamental fairness (p. 68)
5. Fourteenth Amendment (p. 67)
6. malice aforethought (p. 60)
7. insanity defense (p. 63)
8. civil law (p. 57)
9. right to counsel (p. 73)
10. incorporation (p. 68)
11. necessity (p. 62)
12. intoxication (p. 63)
13. Eighth Amendment (p. 74)
14. mens rea (p. 59)
15. ex post facto (p. 58)
16. actus reus (p. 58)
17. Irresistible Impulse Test (p. 64)
18. duress (p. 62)
19. Fifth Amendment (p. 71)
20. causation (p. 58)
21. self-incrimination (p. 71)
22. Fourth Amendment (p. 68)
23. procedural due process (p. 58)
24. capital punishment (p. 75)
25. entrapment (p. 61)
26. M'Naghten Rule (pp. 63-64)
27. exclusionary rule (p. 65)
28. Sixth Amendment (p. 73)
29. Bill of Rights (p. 67)
30. immaturity (p. 63)
31. Eighth Amendment (p. 74)
32. Durham Rule (pp. 63-64)
33. double jeopardy (p. 72)
34. inchoate offenses (p. 59)
35. Escobedo v. Illinois (p. 71)
36. Gideon v. Wainwright (p. 73)
37. Mapp v. Ohio (p. 65)
38. United States v. Leon (p. 69)
39. Miranda v. Arizona (p. 71)
40. Austin v. United States (p. 74)
41. The Queen v. Dudley & Stephens (p. 62)
42. Barron v. Baltimore (p. 67)
43. Dickerson v. United States (p. 72)
44. United States v. Salerno and Cafaro (p. 74)
45. Weeks v. United States (p. 69)
46. Wyoming v. Houghton (p. 70)
47. Trop v. Dulles (p. 75)

<u>Key People</u>
1. William Rehnquist (p. 69)
2. Earl Warren (p. 68)

3. King John of England (p. 67)
4. Timothy McVeigh (p. 56)
5. John Hinckley (p. 65)

<u>Multiple Choice</u>
3.1. b (p. 56)
3.2. a (p. 57)
3.3. e (p. 57)
3.4. d (p. 57)
3.5. c (p. 58)
3.6. b (p. 58)
3.7. e (p. 60)
3.8. d (p. 61)
3.9. e (p. 64)
3.10. e (p. 58)
3.11. b (p. 63)
3.12. a (p. 69)
3.13. b (p. 72)
3.14. e (p. 70)
3.15. b (p. 62)
3.16. c (p. 68)
3.17. a (p. 72)
3.18. c (p. 67)
3.19. a (p. 71)
3.20. d (p. 67)
3.21. d (p. 68)
3.22. d (p. 69)
3.23. c (p. 77)
3.24. b (p. 68)
3.25. b (p. 68)

<u>True and False</u>
3.1. T (p. 57)
3.2. F (p. 57)
3.3. T (p. 57)
3.4. F (p. 60)
3.5. F (p. 57)
3.6. T (p. 63)
3.7. F (p. 64)
3.8. T (p. 58)
3.9. T (p. 66)
3.10. F (p. 68)
3.11. F (p. 68)
3.12. T (p. 62)
3.13. T (p. 68)
3.14. F (p. 56)
3.15. F (p. 67)
3.16. T (p. 75)
3.17. T (p. 67)
3.18. F (p. 68)
3.19. T (p. 67)
3.20. F (p. 77)

ANSWERS-CHAPTER FOUR

Key Terms
1. federal agencies (or FBI) (p. 88)
2. legalistic style (p. 95)
3. Community policing era (p. 86)
4. watchman style (p. 95)
5. state police (p. 90)
6. Bow Street Runners (p. 82)
7. community crime prevention (p. 100)
8. special (p. 99)
9. "broken windows theory" (p. 86)
10. Federal Bureau of Investigation (p. 88)
11. Professional policing era (p. 84)
12. discretion (p. 97)
13. law enforcement function (p. 92)
14. "posse comitatus" (p. 84)
15. service style (p. 93)
16. frankpledge (p. 81)
17. order maintenance function (p. 92)
18. Political policing era (p. 83)
19. Secret Service (p. 88)
20. sheriff (p. 90)
21. domestic violence (p. 97)
22. service function (p. 93)
23. bobbies (p. 82)
24. Statute of Winchester (p. 82)

Key People
1. J. Edgar Hoover (p. 88)
2. James Q. Wilson & George Kelling (p. 86)
3. Henry Fielding (p. 82)
4. August Vollmer (p. 84)
5. Sir Robert Peel (p. 82)
6. O.W. Wilson (p. 85)

Multiple Choice
4.1. e (p. 81)
4.2. e (p. 80)
4.3. b (p. 88)
4.4. a (p. 88)
4.5. e (pp. 88-89)
4.6. c (p. 90)
4.7. a (p. 93)
4.8. a (p. 95)
4.9. b (p. 95)
4.10. c (p. 95)
4.11. c (p. 95)
4.12. a (p. 95)
4.13. b (p. 95)
4.14. e (p. 84)
4.15. d (p. 91)
4.16. a (pp. 83-86)
4.17. d (p. 85)
4.18. d (p. 86)
4.19. c (p. 85)
4.20. b (p. 85)
4.21. d (p. 84)
4.22. b (p. 84)
4.23. c (p. 86)
4.24. b (p. 85)
4.25. a (p. 83)

True and False
4.1. T (p. 81)
4.2. F (p. 89)
4.3. F (p. 82)
4.4. T (p. 85)
4.5. F (p. 85)
4.6. T (p. 86)
4.7. T (p. 85)
4.8. T (p. 93)
4.9. F (p. 95)
4.10. F (p. 84)
4.11. F (p. 100)
4.12. F (p. 83)
4.13. T (p. 97)
4.14. F (p. 86)
4.15. F (p. 81)
4.16. T (p. 85)
4.17. T (p. 88)
4.18. T (p. 95)
4.19. F (p. 95)
4.20. T (p. 96)

ANSWERS-CHAPTER FIVE

<u>Key Terms</u>
1. patrol (p. 117)
2. line functions (p. 117)
3. productivity (p. 116)
4. reactive patrol (p. 114)
5. Equal Employment Opportunity Act of 1972
6. incident-driven policing (p. 115)
7. free patrol (p. 118)
8. subculture (p. 108)
9. sworn officers (p. 118)
10. S.W.A.T. (p. 122)
11. forensic techniques (p. 120)
12. proactive patrol (p. 118)
13. clearance rate (p. 124)
14. differential response (p. 115)
15. vice (p. 123)
16. traffic (p. 122)
17. CSI (p. 120)
18. staff functions (p. 117)
19. preventive patrol (p. 118)
20. working personality (p. 109)
21. socialization (p. 108)
22. external stress (p. 111)
23. operational stress (p. 112)
24. CODIS (p. 122)
25. personal stress (p. 112)
26. organizational stress (p. 111)
27. DNA "fingerprinting" (p. 122)

<u>Key People</u>
1. Steve Herbert (p. 110)
2. Jeff Postell (p. 104)
3. Eric Rudolph (p. 104)
4. Lola Baldwin (p. 106)

<u>Multiple Choice</u>
5.1. a (p. 106)
5.2. e (p. 117)
5.3. e (p. 117)
5.4. b (p. 104)
5.5. a (p. 111)

5.6. b (p. 111)
5.7. c (p. 112)
5.8. d (p. 118)
5.9. c (p. 106)
5.10. c (p. 122)
5.11. c (p. 117)
5.12. b (p. 104)
5.13. e (p. 120)
5.14. d (p. 124)
5.15. c (p. 112)
5.16. c (p. 113)
5.17. b (p. 114)
5.18. c (p. 114)
5.19. c (p. 112)
5.20. d (pp. 106-107)
5.21. a (p. 111)
5.22. c (p. 112)
5.23. b (p. 111)
5.24. a (p. 111)
5.25. d (p. 112)

<u>True and False</u>
5.1. F (p. 106)
5.2. F (p. 119)
5.3. T (p. 106)
5.4. F (p. 105)
5.5. F (p. 123)
5.6. T (p. 106)
5.7. T (p. 122)
5.8. F (p. 118)
5.9. T (p. 117)
5.10. T (p. 108)
5.11. T (p. 112)
5.12. F (p. 114)
5.13. T (p. 115)
5.14. F (p. 114)
5.15. F (p. 114)
5.16. F (p. 121)
5.17. T (p. 117)
5.18. T (p. 117)
5.19. F (p. 122)
5.20. F (p. 123)

ANSWERS-CHAPTER SIX

<u>Key terms</u>
1. stop (p. 128)
2. Terry v. Ohio (p. 133)
3. United States v. Leon (p. 142)
4. New York v. Class (p. 137)
5. Chimel v. California (p. 134)
6. Miranda v. Arizona (p. 138)
7. Mapp v. Ohio (p. 141)
8. Wolf v. Colorado (p. 141)
9. Nix v. Williams (p. 143)
10. automobile search (p. 136)
11. exclusionary rule (p. 141)
12. search by consent (p. 135)
13. good faith exception (p. 142)
14. public safety exception (p. 140)
15. search incident to a lawful arrest (p. 134)
16. inevitable discovery rule (p. 142)
17. search warrant (p. 129)
18. right to counsel (p. 138)
19. plain view (p. 130)
20. Fourth Amendment (p. 127)
21. search (p. 127)
22. probable cause (p. 129)
23. reasonable suspicion (p. 128)
24. totality of circumstances (p. 130)
25. arrest (p. 128)
26. stop and frisk exception (p. 133)
27. Miranda warnings (p. 138)
28. exigent circumstances (p. 135)

<u>Key Persons</u>
1. O. J. Simpson
2. Steven Hatfill (p. 127)
3. Nicodemo Sarfo Jr.
4. Tom Clark
5. Earl Warren
6. Warren Burger

<u>Multiple Choice</u>
6.1. b (p. 127)
6.2. b (p. 136)
6.3. d (p. 128)
6.4. c (p. 127)
6.5. e (p. 130)
6.6. d (p. 130)
6.7. e (p. 132)
6.8. d (pp. 127-129)
6.9. a (p. 131)
6.10. d (p. 133)
6.11. d (p. 140)
6.12. b (p. 134)
6.13. b (p. 136)
6.14. a (p. 136)
6.15. a (p. 138)
6.16. c (p. 138)
6.17. e (p. 133)
6.18. b (p. 140)
6.19. a (p. 138)
6.20. d (p. 142)
6.21. c (p. 142)
6.22. d (p. 137)
6.23. e (p. 141)
6.24. a (p. 141)
6.25. d (p. 142)

<u>True and False</u>
6.1. F (p. 140)
6.2. F (p. 128)
6.3. T (p. 130)
6.4. F (p. 132)
6.5. T (p. 141)
6.6. F (p. 135)
6.7. T (p. 141)
6.8. T (p. 141)
6.9. T (p. 142)
6.10. F (p. 129)
6.11. F (p. 127)
6.12. T (p. 138)
6.13. F (p. 138)
6.14. T (p. 142)
6.15. T (p. 135)
6.16. F (p. 139)
6.17. F (p. 137)
6.18. F (p. 142)
6.19. F (p. 139)
6.20. T (pp. 130-131)

ANSWERS-CHAPTER SEVEN

Key Terms
1. motorized (p. 149)
2. aggressive patrol (p. 150)
3. preventive patrol (p. 147)
4. Kansas City Preventive Patrol Experiment (p. 147)
5. private policing (p. 161)
6. problem-oriented policing (p. 152)
7. Monell v. Dept. of Social Services (1978) (p. 161)
8. legitimate force (p. 156)
9. civic accountability (p. 159)
10. moonlighting (p. 164)
11. broken windows theory (p. 150)
12. internal affairs units (p. 159)
13. Tennessee v. Garner (p. 157)
14. community policing (p. 151)
15. civil liability suits (p. 161)
16. civilian review board (p. 160)
17. public order crimes (p. 151)
18. nonlethal weapons (p. 155)
19. hot spots (p. 148)
20. accreditation (p. 160)
21. "meat eaters" (p. 158)
22. police corruption (p. 157)
23. Graham v. Connor (1989) (p. 157)
24. foot (p. 149)
25. directed patrol (p. 148)
26. "grass eaters" (p. 158)
27. police brutality (p. 156)
28. excessive force (p. 156)

Key People
1. William Spelman and Dale Brown (p. 148)
2. Abner Louima (p. 146)
3. Justin Volpe (p. 146)
4. Ellywn Stoddard (p. 158)
5. Amadou Diallo (p. 156)

Multiple Choice
7.1. b (p. 146)
7.2. d (p. 147)
7.3. b (p. 148)
7.4. e (p. 150)
7.5. a (p. 148)
7.6. a (p. 148)
7.7. a (p. 150)
7.8. c (p. 151)
7.9. b (p. 151)
7.10. c (p. 156)
7.11. c (p. 153)
7.12. b (p. 154)
7.13. b (p. 158)
7.14. e (p. 156)
7.15. d (p. 155)
7.16. a (p. 165)
7.17. c (p. 164)
7.18. c (p. 164)
7.19. d (p. 155)
7.20. e (p. 159)
7.21. c (p. 164)
7.22. e (p. 154)
7.23. b (p. 149)
7.24. d (p. 150)
7.25. a (p. 153)

True and False
7.1. T (p. 155)
7.2. T (p. 160)
7.3. F (p. 150)
7.4. T (p. 150)
7.5. F (p. 149)
7.6. T (p. 150)
7.7. T (p. 151)
7.8. F (p. 148)
7.9. T (p. 153)
7.10. F (p. 154)
7.11. F (p. 155)
7.12. T (p. 155)
7.13. T (p. 156)
7.14. F (p. 155)
7.15. F (p. 153)
7.16. F (p. 146)
7.17. T (p. 147)
7.18. F (p. 151)
7.19. T (p. 158)
7.20. F (p. 159)

ANSWERS-CHAPTER EIGHT

<u>Key Terms</u>
1. continuance (p. 191)
2. workgroup (p. 192)
3. local legal culture (p 191)
4. public defender (p. 189)
5. defense attorney (p. 184)
6. assigned counsel (p. 188)
7. contract counsel (p. 188)
8. United States Attorney (p. 179)
9. accusatory process (p. 183)
10. count (p. 181)
11. nolle prosequi (p. 181)
12. state attorney general (p. 179)
13. discovery (p. 181)
14. prosecution complex (p. 179)
15. prosecuting attorney (p. 179)
16. partisan election (p. 176)
17. trial courts of limited jurisdiction (p. 172)
18. jurisdiction (p. 171)
19. merit selection (p. 177)
20. appellate court (p. 172)
21. going rate (p. 191)
22. trial courts of general jurisdiction (p. 172)
23. nonpartisan election (p. 176)
24. community prosecution (p. 183)

<u>Key People</u>
1. Johnnie Cochran and O. J. Simpson (p. 184)
2. Madelyne Gorman Toogood (p. 179)
3. Clara Harris (p. 170)
4. Ally McBeal (p. 184)

<u>Multiple Choice</u>
8.1. d (p. 171)
8.2. d (p. 174)
8.3. b (p. 175)
8.4. d (p. 176)
8.5. a (p. 176)
8.6. d (p. 178)
8.7. e (p. 178)

8.8. a (p. 179)
8.9. d (p. 182)
8.10. a (p. 186)
8.11. c (p. 186)
8.12. e (p. 187)
8.13. a (p. 187)
8.14. d (p. 172)
8.15. e (p. 172)
8.16. a (p. 174)
8.17. c (p. 176)
8.18. e (p. 178)
8.19. b (p. 171)
8.20. c (p. 182)
8.21. d (p. 183)
8.22. e (p. 184)
8.23. a (p. 191)
8.24. d (p. 192)
8.25. d (p. 179)

<u>True and False</u>
8.1. T (p. 171)
8.2. T (p. 171)
8.3. F (p. 172)
8.4. T (p. 172)
8.5. T (p. 174)
8.6. F (p. 178)
8.7. T (p. 180)
8.8. F (p. 181)
8.9. F (p. 183)
8.10. F (p. 186)
8.11. F (p. 187)
8.12. T (p. 188)
8.13. F (p. 172)
8.14. F (p. 174)
8.15. T (p. 175)
8.16. F (p. 176)
8.17. F (p. 191)
8.18. F (p. 191)
8.19. F (p. 184)
8.20. T (p. 192)

ANSWERS-CHAPTER NINE

Key Terms
1. Santobello v. New York (1971) (p. 204)
2. peremptory challenge (p. 211)
3. circumstantial evidence (p. 212)
4. plea bargaining (p. 204)
5. demonstrative evidence (p. 212)
6. appeals (p. 216)
7. bench trials (p. 209)
8. North Carolina v. Alford (1970) (p. 207)
9. voir dire (p. 211)
10. habeas corpus (p. 217)
11. Bordenkircher v. Hayes (1978) (p. 208)
12. challenge for cause (p. 211)
13. jury (p. 209)
14. reasonable doubt (p. 214)
15. Williams v. Florida (1970) (p. 211)
16. real evidence (p. 212)
17. Boykin v. Alabama (1969) (p. 207)
18. direct evidence (p. 212)
19. jury (p. 209)
20. arraignment (p. 197)
21. motion (p. 198)
22. bail (p. 199)
23. citation (p. 201)
24. percentage bail (p. 201)
25. release on own recognizance (ROR) (p. 201)
26. preventive detention (p. 202)
27. United States v. Salerno and Cafero (1987) (p. 202)

Key persons
1. John Walker Lindh (p. 204)
2. Potter Stewart (p. 204)
3. Robert Blake (p. 195)
4. Ricardo Armstrong (p. 203)
5. Hernando Williams (p. 203)

Multiple Choice
9.1. c (p. 199)
9.2. a (p. 198)
9.3. b (p. 195)
9.4. d (p. 197)
9.5. c (p. 199)
9.6. d (p. 199)
9.7 .b (p. 199)
9.8. c (p. 199)
9.9. d (p. 199)
9.10. a (p. 199)
9.11. e (pp. 198-199)
9.12. d (p. 199)
9.13. b (p. 199)
9.14. a (p. 199)
9.15. c (p. 200)
9.16. a (p. 200)
9.17. d (p. 210)
9.18. e (p. 211)
9.19. c (p. 211)
9.20. d (p. 211)
9.21. c (p. 214)
9.22. c (p. 212)
9.23. d (p. 212)
9.24. a (p. 212)
9.25. b (p. 216)

True and False
9.1. F (p. 199)
9.2. F (p. 197)
9.3. F (p. 202)
9.4. T (p. 199)
9.5. F (p. 199)
9.6. F (p. 200)
9.7. F (p. 210)
9.8. T (p. 210)
9.9. F (p. 211)
9.10. F (p. 211)
9.11. T (p. 212)
9.12. F (p. 216)
9.13. T (p. 204)
9.14. T (p. 200)
9.15. F (p. 195)
9.16. F (p. 202)
9.17. T (p. 203)
9.18. F (p. 204)
9.19. F (p. 207)
9.20. T (p. 21)

ANSWERS–CHAPTER TEN

<u>Key Terms</u>
1. selective incapacitation (p. 224)
2. indeterminate sentence (p. 227)
3. specific deterrence (p. 223)
4. shock probation (p. 231)
5. restorative justice (p. 225)
6. presumptive sentence (p. 228)
7. mandatory sentence (p. 228)
8. Gregg v. Georgia (1976) (p. 233)
9. truth-in-sentencing (p. 229)
10. intermediate sanctions (p. 229)
11. probation (p. 229)
12. retribution (p. 222)
13. Stanford v. Kentucky
14. incapacitation (p. 224)
15. McCleskey v. Kemp (1987) (p. 233)
16. determinate sentence (p. 227)
17. sentencing guidelines (p. 241)
18. rehabilitation (p. 225)
19. good time (p. 228)
20. Furman v. Georgia (1972) (p. 232)
21. general deterrence (p. 223)
22. presentence report (p. 241)
23. Atkins v. Virginia (2002) (p. 233)
24. wrongful conviction (p. 243)
25. Witherspoon v. Illinois (1968) (p. 235)

<u>Key People</u>
1. Norval Morris and Michael Tonry (p. 229)
2. George Ryan (p. 236, p. 238)
3. Thurgood Marshall (p. 234)
4. Jeremy Bentham (p. 223)
5. Napoleon Beasley (p. 234)
6. Marjorie Knoller (p. 221)

<u>Multiple Choice Questions</u>
10.1. e (p. 233)
10.2. c (p. 236)
10.3. e (p. 229)
10.4. a (p. 229)
10.5. a (p. 233)

10.6. b (p. 233)
10.7. d (p. 234)
10.8. e (p. 234)
10.9. b (p. 221)
10.10. d (p. 237)
10.11. b (p. 231)
10.12. a (p. 232)
10.13. e (p. 235)
10.14. a (p. 235)
10.15. c (p. 235)
10.16. c (p. 236)
10.17. c (p. 223)
10.18. b (p. 237)
10.19. a (p. 239)
10.20. c (p. 225)
10.21. d (p. 240)
10.22. b (p. 227)
10.23. c (p. 228)
10.24. e (p. 228)
10.25. e (p. 222)

<u>True and False Questions</u>
10.1. T (p. 228)
10.2. F (p. 233)
10.3. F (p. 228)
10.4. F (p. 227)
10.5. T (p. 229)
10.6. T (p. 229)
10.7. T (p. 223)
10.8. F (p. 224)
10.9. F (p. 227)
10.10. F (p. 225)
10.11. T (p. 242)
10.12. T (p. 232)
10.13. T (p. 229)
10.14. F (p. 231)
10.15. F (p. 234)
10.16. T (p. 228)
10.17. F (p. 239)
10.18. F (p. 240)
10.19. F (p. 241)
10.20. T (p. 242)

ANSWERS-CHAPTER ELEVEN

<u>Key Terms</u>
1. corrections (p. 249)
2. lease system (p. 252)
3. reformatory (p. 253)
4. Cincinnati Declaration of Principles (p. 253)
5. the Enlightenment (p. 249)
6. medical model (p. 255)
7. crime control model of corrections (p. 256)
8. supermax prisons (p. 257)
9. congregate system (p. 252)
10. penitentiary (p. 250)
11. separate confinement (p. 251)
12. community corrections (p. 255)
13. rehabilitation model (p. 255)
14. hands off policy (p. 262)
15. Hudson v. Palmer(1984) (p. 263)
16. Cooper v. Pate (1964) (p. 262)
17. Wolff v. McDonnell(1974) (p. 264)
18. The Fourteenth Amendment (p. 264)
19. Fourth Amendment (p. 263)
20. First Amendment (p. 263)
21. Eighth Amendment (p. 263)

<u>Key People</u>
1. Charles Williams (p. 251)
2. Elam Llynds (p. 252)
3. Elizabeth Fry (p. 254)
4. John Howard (p. 249)
5. Zebulon Brockway (p. 253)
6. Mary Belle Harris (p. 254)

<u>Multiple Choice</u>
11.1. c (p. 248)
11.2. c (p. 248)
11.3. e (p. 248)
11.4. d (p. 248)
11.5. c (p. 248)
11.6. e (p. 256)
11.7. a (p. 249)
11.8. a (p. 249)
11.9. a (p. 251)
11.10. d (p. 251)
11.11. e (p. 252)
11.12. c (p. 252)
11.13. b (p. 253)
11.14. b (p. 253)
11.15. d (p. 253)
11.16. b (p. 255)
11.17. b (p. 254)
11.18. c (pp. 254)
11.19. d (p. 253-54)
11.20. c (p. 254)
11.21. a (p. 254)
11.22. a (p. 263)
11.23. d (p. 264)
11.24. c (p. 264)
11.25. c (p. 272)

<u>True and False</u>
11.1. F (p. 48)
11.2. T (p. 52)
11.3. T (pp. 53-54)
11.4. T (p. 55)
11.5. F (p. 49)
11.6. T (pp. 50-51)
11.7. T (p. 48)
11.8. F (p. 49)
11.9. T (p. 56)
11.10. F (p. 56)
11.11. T (p. 55)
11.12. T (p. 63)
11.13. F (p. 58)
11.14. F (pp. 58-59)
11.15. F (p. 59)
11.16. F (p. 56)
11.17. F (p. 60)
11.18. F (pp. 63-64)
11.19. T (p. 61)
11.20. T (p. 60)

ANSWERS-CHAPER TWELVE

Key Terms
1. home confinement (p. 284)
2. probation (p. 277)
3. restitution (p. 283)
4. community service (p. 285)
5. shock incarceration (p. 287)
6. day reporting centers (p. 286)
7. community corrections (p. 277)
8. fines (p. 282)
9. boot camp (p. 287)
10. forfeiture (p. 283)
11. Mempa v. Rhay (1967) (p. 280)
12. technical violation (p. 280)
13. intensive supervision probation (ISP) (p. 286)
14. net widening (p. 289)
15. recidivism (p. 277)

Key People
1. Winona Ryder (p. 276)
2. John Augustus (p. 278)
3. Norval Morris and Michael Tonry (p. 281)
4. Nelson Colon (p. 288)
5. Michael Tonry and Mary Lynch (p. 289)
6. Joan Petersilia (p. 290)

Multiple Choice
12.1. b (p. 278)
12.2. e (p. 277)
12.3. d (p. 278)
12.4. d (p. 278)
12.5. c (p. 280)
12.6. a (p. 280)
12.7. d (p. 280)
12.8. e (p. 280)
12.9. a (p. 281)
12.10. c (p. 281)

12.11. c (p. 281)
12.12. a (p. 276)
12.13. b (p. 278)
12.14. a (p. 284)
12.15. d (p. 285)
12.16. d (p. 279)
12.17. b (p. 279)
12.18. c (p. 279)
12.19. c (p. 282)
12.20. a (p. 287)
12.21. a (p. 284)
12.22. e (p. 283)
12.23. a (p. 278)
12.24. c (p. 278)
12.25. e (p. 289)

True and False
12.1. T (pp. 276-277)
12.2. T (p. 280)
12.3. F (p. 280)
12.4. T (p. 283)
12.5. T (p. 284)
12.6. F (p. 278)
12.7. F (p. 279)
12.8. T (p. 279)
12.9. T (p. 280)
12.10. T (p. 283)
12.11. F (p. 285)
12.12. F (p. 282)
12.13. F (p. 281)
12.14. F (p. 280)
12.15. T (p. 287)
12.16. F (p. 282)
12.17. T (p. 286)
12.18. T (p. 282)
12.19. T (p. 288)
12.20. F (p. 276)

ANSWERS-CHAPTER THIRTEEN

<u>Key Terms</u>
1. store (p. 306)
2. the mix (p. 309)
3. classification (p. 312)
4. inmate code (p. 304)
5. doing time (p. 305)
6. gleaning (p. 305)
7. jailing (p. 305)
8. disorganized criminal (p. 305)
9. Reintegration Model (p. 294)
10. "big house" (p. 293)
11. Custodial Model (p. 294)
12. Rehabilitation Model (p. 294)
13. amenities (p. 296)
14. fish (p. 305)
15. machismo (p. 315)
16. convict code (p. 304)

<u>Key People</u>
1. Kimberly Greer (p. 309)
2. Barbara Owen (p. 309)
3. Michael Santos (p. 300)
4. Charles Logan (p. 294)
5. John DiIulio (p; 296)
6. Esther Hefferman (p. 308)
7. Lee Bowker (p. 316)

<u>Multiple Choice</u>
13.1. d (p. 295)
13.2. e (p. 294)
13.3. a (p. 295)
13.4. c (p. 295)
13.5. a (p. 295)
13.6. c (p. 300)
13.7. b (p. 298)
13.8. e (p. 301)
13.9. e (p. 306)
13.10. d (p. 300)
13.11. e (pp. 314-315)
13.12. b (p. 300)
13.13. d (p. 300)
13.14. a (p. 315)
13.15. a (p. 300)
13.16. b (p. 315)
13.17. b (p. 316)
13.18. d (p. 300)
13.19. e (pp. 302-303)
13.20. d (p. 303)
13.21. c (p. 303)
13.22. d (p. 303)
13.23. d (pp. 305-306)
13.24. b (p. 305)
13.25. c (p. 307)

<u>True and False</u>
13.1. T (p. 294)
13.2. F (p. 293)
13.3. T (p. 295)
13.4. T (p. 295)
13.5. F (p. 295)
13.6. T (p. 299)
13.7. T (p. 305)
13.8. F (p. 300)
13.9. F (p. 317)
13.10. T (p. 296)
13.11. F (p. 293)
13.12. T (p. 298)
13.13. F (p. 299)
13.14. F (p. 302)
13.15. T (p. 300)
13.16. T (p. 304)
13.17. T (p. 314)
13.18. T (p. 315)
13.19. F (p. 303)
13.20. T (p. 303)

ANSWERS-CHAPTER FOURTEEN

Key Terms
1. grace (p. 322)
2. expiration release (p. 324)
3. discretionary release (p. 323)
4. ticket of leave (p. 322)
5. mandatory release (p. 323)
6. other conditional release (p. 324)
7. conditions of release (p. 326)
8. parole (p. 322)
9. custody (p. 322)
10. work and educational release (p. 328)
11. Morrissey v. Brewer (1972) (p. 332)
12. furlough (p. 329)
13. halfway house (p. 329)
14. revocation of parole (p. 332)
15. contract (p. 322)
16. reentry court (p. 333)

Key People
1. Alexander Maconochie (p. 322)
2. Megan Kanka (p. 320)
3. Sir Walter Crofton (p. 322)
4. Zebulon Brockway (p. 322)

Multiple Choice
14.1. c (p. 323)
14.2. d (p. 320)
14.3. b (p. 321)
14.4. e (p. 322)
14.5. c (p. 325)
14.6. d (p. 327)
14.7. b (p. 320)
14.8. c (p. 321)
14.9. d (p. 322)
14.10. e (p. 323)
14.11. c (p. 327)
14.12. b (p. 327)
14.13. a (p. 329)
14.14. a (p. 329)
14.15. e (p. 330)
14.16. c (p. 331)
14.17. b (p. 333)
14.18. c (p. 332)
14.19. a (p. 321)
14.20. a (p. 320)
14.21. d (p. 322)
14.22. e (p. 322)
14.23. e (p. 322)
14.24. c (p. 323)
14.25. c (p. 326)

True and False
14.1. F (p. 332)
14.2. T (p. 328)
14.3. F (p. 322)
14.4. F (p. 322)
14.5. F (p. 324)
14.6. T (p. 320)
14.7. F (p. 320)
14.8. F (p. 327)
14.9. T (p. 327)
14.10. F (p. 327)
14.11. T (p. 329)
14.12. F (p. 330)
14.13. F (p. 330)
14.14. F (p. 331)
14.15. T (p. 331)
14.16. T (p. 327)
14.17. T (p. 325)
14.18. T (p. 322)
14.19. T (p. 333)
14.20. F (p. 333)

ANSWERS-CHAPTER FIFTEEN

Key Terms
1. Progressive reformers (p. 343)
2. Crime Control (p. 345)
3. detention (p. 350)
4. aftercare (p. 355)
5. Juvenile Court Act of Illinois (1899)
6. parens patriae (p. 340)
7. Juvenile Rights (p. 343)
8. delinquent (p. 346)
9. diversion (p. 349)
10. foster home (p. 354)
11. Juvenile Court (p. 343)
12. status offense (p. 345)
13. "child savers" (p. 343)
14. PINS (p. 347)
15. In re Winship (1970) (p. 344)
16. waive (p. 350)
17. dependent child (p. 347)
18. Refuge (p. 341)
19. Puritan (p. 341)
20. neglected child (p. 347)

Key People
1. Henry Thurston (p. 343)
2. Abe Fortas (p. 344)
3. Gerald Gault (p. 344)
4. Jane Addams and Julia Lathrop (p. 343)
5. Fernando Morales (p. 356)
6. John Lee Malvo (p. 338)

Multiple Choice Questions
15.1. a (p. 338)
15.2. b (p. 344)
15.3. d (p. 345)
15.4. d (p. 344)
15.5. e (p. 344)
15.6. c (p. 344)
15.7. b (p. 339)
15.8. d (p. 339)
15.9. d (p. 339)
15.10. b (p. 341)
15.11. e (p. 342)
15.12. c (p. 342)
15.13. e (p. 342)
15.14. a (p. 343)
15.15. a (p. 343)
15.16. a (p. 343)
15.17. d (p. 341)
15.18. b (p. 344)
15.19. c (p. 345)
15.20. a (p. 343)
15.21. d (p. 344)
15.22. e (p. 345)
15.23. d (p. 357)
15.24. a (p. 340)
15.25. e (p. 340)

True and False Questions
15.1. F (p. 339)
15.2. F (p. 339)
15.3. F (p. 340)
15.4. T (p. 340)
15.5. T (p. 340)
15.6. F (p. 340)
15.7. T (p. 340)
15.8. T (p. 340)
15.9. F (p. 340)
15.10. F (p. 343)
15.11. F (p. 343)
15.12. T (p. 343)
15.13. T (p. 355)
15.14. F (p. 354)
15.15. T (p. 344)
15.16. T (p. 345)
15.17. F (p. 345)
15.18. T (p. 345)
15.19. F (p. 345)
15.20. T (p. 345)